The Evolution of Household Technology and Consumer Behavior, 1800–2000

The increasing division and specialization of labor between the market and the nonmarket sector is a central stylized fact of long-run economic development. Over time, a large share of activities which had formerly been carried out by the private household itself has become replaced by market alternatives, raising at the same time the demand for consumer goods.

The neoclassical economic framework of household production theory relates the increasing demand for household technology to rising wages and opportunity costs of time: the higher the wage rate, the more costly it is to spend time in unpaid housework activities. Consumer products are thus purchased to make household production processes more efficient and to substitute capital goods for the household's time (time substitution hypothesis). Although this hypothesis sounds plausible at first sight, it cannot capture the essential phenomena underlying the complex process of the mechanization of the home over the past 200 years. Its major weakness lies in the treatment of consumer preferences, whose explanatory potential is explicitly factored out.

Using the washing of clothes as a microcosm of household economics, this book examines long-term changes in cleanliness consumption patterns from the perspective of an evolutionary economic, psychologically informed consumer theory. Woersdorfer shows how the historical evolution of cleanliness consumption over the past 200 years is the result of the interplay of supply and demand side factors, namely, technical change in washing technology on one side and motivational driving forces and consumer learning capabilities on the other. Hence, not changing relative prices but innate consumer needs and consumer learning processes, leading to a growing understanding of how to satisfy those needs, are the essential driving forces behind the rising technological endowment of the home and the corresponding demand for household appliances.

The Evolution of Household Technology and Consumer Behavior, 1800–2000 will be of interest to researchers in the field of evolutionary economics, history of technology, economic history, innovation economics and sociology.

Julia Sophie Woersdorfer received her Ph.D. in Economics from the University of Jena, Germany in 2010. Afterward, she took a position as a research associate at the National Academy of Science and Engineering (acatech) before joining the Federal Competition Authority (Bundeskartellamt), Germany, as a civil servant.

Modern Heterodox Economics
Edited by Carol M. Connell
Brooklyn College, City University of New York

For a full list of titles in this series, please visit www.routledge.com/Modern-Heterodox-Economics/book-series/MHEE

The Evolution of Household Technology and Consumer Behavior, 1800–2000

Julia Sophie Woersdorfer

Routledge
Taylor & Francis Group

LONDON AND NEW YORK

First published 2017 by Routledge

2 Park Square, Milton Park, Abingdon, Oxfordshire OX14 4RN

52 Vanderbilt Avenue, New York, NY 10017

Routledge is an imprint of the Taylor & Francis Group, an informa business

First issued in paperback 2020

British Library Cataloguing in Publication Data
A catalogue record for this book is available from the British Library

Library of Congress Cataloging in Publication Data
A catalog record for this book has been requested.

ISBN: 978-1-8489-3595-2 (hbk)
ISBN: 978-0-367-59529-6 (pbk)

Typeset in Bembo
by Deanta Global Publishing Services, Chennai, India

Contents

Figures

Tables

Preface

It is widely recognized now that consumer behavior participates in essential ways in the innovative change in the economy. However, the explanation of innovative consumer behavior is still a much-neglected topic in economics. Consumers buy newly introduced products, it is often argued, because they are cheaper and/or of better quality than existing products. But this is hardly more than a truism. In order to offer more profound explanations of innovative consumer behavior, one has to dig deeper. What are the circumstances under which consumers do, or do not, consider purchases of things they have not previously known? Does it make a difference how consumers learn about them? How do they come to appreciate new goods and services? What motives induce consumers to adopt them, if they do? Exploring questions like these requires acknowledging and theorizing about a huge number of context-dependent influences on consumer liking, learning and problem solving.

Certainly, income and innovation-induced changes in relative prices do play a role in understanding consumer behavior, as do income and substitution effects. But they are far from telling the whole story. The complexity of innovative consumer behavior cannot fully be captured at the level of abstraction of the utility maximization framework – not even when skillfully paired with opportunity cost hypotheses as in Gary Becker's household production theory, with its opportunity costs of time as a one-fits-all explanatory variable. This is one of the main theoretical insights offered by this splendid, insightful book. It is substantiated by a careful discussion of the multi-level learning processes by which consumers form opinions about, and preferences over, consumer innovations and what they are supposed to be good for. In her case study of the sequence of innovations in a commonplace household production activity – the laundering of clothes – Julia Sophie Woersdorfer persuasively concludes that a huge number of factors and historical contingencies need to be considered to eventually be able to offer a satisfactory explanation of innovative consumer behavior.

The massive technological upgrading with household appliances of U.S. homes over the past 150 years has been described by several authors. This process made the rise of an entirely new manufacturing sector, the household appliances industry, possible. Yet, describing what happened is one thing and giving reasons for why it happened is another. In the case of the washing machines explored in this book in an exemplary fashion, it turns out – as would be expected in view of the preceding theoretical reflections about consumer learning – that the reasons require a complex argument. The adoption of ever new vintages of washing machines was not just consumption for the sake of enjoying something new. Nor was it only a reaction to the slowly declining relative price of every vintage of washing machines. Has one reason been the homemakers' intention to save time in an unpaid domestic activity that made households interested in new technologies promising to save their time as household production theory would claim? Yes, but as this book convincingly demonstrates, it played a role only in explaining the adoption of rather late vintages of washing machines. Indeed, understanding why every vintage of innovative machines appealed differently to fundamental consumer needs is the key, Julia Sophie Woersdorfer convincingly argues, to a complete explanation of the historical process.

In this vein, the case study shows, for instance, that in the beginning, there was, on the one hand, a change in the homemakers' attitude towards caring for the family's health. It induced rising cleanliness aspirations. On the other hand, there were the physically extremely strenuous laundry practices culminating in the drudgery of the weekly washing day. A conflict built up here. The emerging industry tried to offer solutions of mechanical devices that helped ease the hard work. With the diffusion of the first vintage of washers, the challenge could by-and-by be mastered. The intriguing reconstruction of the further development of the laundry technology shows that whenever such point of mastery of a homemaker's major problem was reached, the industry focused on innovations that offered solutions to new problems. These problems emerged, or started to be taken seriously, once the previous ones tended to be solved. A vital part of the industry's innovative activity therefore consisted in arousing an interest and awareness among homemakers of the problems the new vintage of washing machines was designed to take care of.

Insightful as Julia Sophie Woersdorfer's book is at the theoretical and historical level, it also breaks new ground by developing a congenial method for empirically proving the suggested hypotheses. Woersdorfer reconstructs the problems that motivate households to purchase new vintages of washing machine by thoroughly analyzing the content of washing machine advertisements in the *Ladies' Home Journal*. This unique source is available over the period 1888–1989, i.e. almost the entire period of the diffusion of washing machines since they appeared on the market. The changing content of the advertisements reflects why, in the perception of the advertising industry, consumers may value the new technological features of the next vintage of washers. Mirrored by the changing content of the advertisements, Woersdorfer finds that the innovative transformation of the laundering technology does not only focus on ever more improved solutions to one and the same problem, the economizing on the opportunity costs of time, say. It rather appears as a sequence of innovations offering solutions to one problem of the homemaker after the other. In the case study center stage in this book, innovative consumer behavior thus turns out to be a double learning process. Households learn to solve problems they face by means of purchasing innovative products. But they also learn to identify or to take seriously new problems once their purchases have succeeded in solving the previously recognized problems.

With her book, Julia Sophie Woersdorfer introduces, in an exemplary fashion, an empirical theory of innovative consumer behavior that leaves the textbook consumer theory in economics behind. She portrays the consumer as a learning individual or household – learning about new opportunities for solving existing problems *and* learning about new problems to be solved. Her fascinating case study demonstrates the potential of the theory. As important as innovative consumer behavior is for understanding the innovative transformations of the industries and the role of innovations in explaining economic growth, it has so far been neglected in the literature. This book is a path-breaking contribution that changes our knowledge about consumer innovations. It deserves a broad readership and may inspire other scholars anxious to try out new paths in microeconomic thinking.

Ulrich Witt
Professor of Economics and Director Emeritus
Evolutionary Economics Group
Max Planck Institute of Economics, Jena, Germany

Acknowledgments

I would like to express my gratitude foremost to my supervisor Prof. Dr. Ulrich Witt, who invited me to pursue my dissertation at the former Max Planck Institute of Economics in Jena, Germany and encouraged me to step into this scientifically challenging territory. The conversations with Ulrich Witt have strongly shaped my ideas on the subject and helped me to develop the major thread of my argument. I have benefitted greatly, both scientifically and personally, from writing this dissertation in the stimulating research environment of the Max Planck Institute of Economics.

My thanks also go to the referees, who have commented on an earlier version of the manuscript, for broadening my perspective on the subject.

I would like to thank the University of Mainz (USA Library) and the John F. Kennedy Institute (JFKI) at Freie Universität Berlin for providing the microfilms of *Ladies' Home Journal*, on which the advertisement analysis has been based. Many thanks go to several people who have made an effort to get hold of these microfilms, particularly Hella Bruns and Katja Müller from the former Max Planck Institute of Economics, Karin Julich from the Thuringian University and Federal State Library in Jena and Ursula Seipel from the University of Mainz (USA Library).

Additional thanks go to John Wiley & Sons, Inc. for the permission to reuse my article formerly published in 2009 in *Metroeconomica* 'When do social norms replace status-seeking consumption? An application to the consumption of cleanliness'.

Finally, I would like to thank my husband Steffen and my daughter Brigitta Elisabeth for their support, confidence and patience.

1 Beyond Time Substitution

An Evolutionary Economic Analysis into the Patterns of Cleanliness Consumption

1.1 Patterns of Cleanliness Consumption

In our everyday lives, we are surrounded by a multitude of electrical devices, which we are used to employing without much careful thought. We switch on the electric light when getting up, then start the coffee machine and listen to the news on the radio. Coming home from work, dinner will be prepared at the range or in the microwave and dishes put in the dishwasher before finding recreation in front of the television while the washing machine is running in the background. The existence of these devices has become so much taken for granted that the majority of U.S. consumers views these items as 'necessities', i.e. things that 'cannot be lived without' (Taylor *et al.*, 2009).[1] In fact, nine out of ten consumers rate washing machines as an item of 'necessity'; similarly, seven out of ten consumers assess home air conditioning and microwaves as truly necessary products.

The taken-for-granted technological endowment of modern homes has developed only gradually during the twentieth century and has been accompanied by a substantial increase in consumer spending. Particularly remarkable is the trend in the United States, where consumer expenditure on household appliances has grown by more than 2,000 per cent from 1900 to 1990 (Lebergott, 1993, p. 76). To give an example, today, nearly every U.S. household is equipped with a refrigerator, every second household owns a dishwasher and about four out of five U.S. households are owners of an automatic, electric washing machine (EIA, 2011). In contrast to that, around 1920, only about 8 per cent of U.S. families possessed a washing machine, while the conventional scrub board represented the prevailing equipment (Lebergott, 1993, p. 113).

The mechanization of the home is embedded into the larger historical context of industrial development during the past 200 years, being characterized by an increasing division and specialization of labor, the outsourcing of home production activities to the market and the substantial growth of personal income – the *condition sine qua non* for this growth in consumer expenditures to occur (cf. Cowan, 1983; Matthews, 1987; Strasser, 2000 [1982]; Mokyr, 2002; de Vries, 2008). Over the course of time, a large share of activities which had been carried out by the private household itself have become replaced by market alternatives. The production of foodstuff and the manufacture of pieces of clothing are a case in point. At the same time, many housework activities have not been completely outsourced to the market. For example, most people today still clean their dishes, their houses and their clothes by themselves. The existing market alternatives, such as commercial laundries or cleaning personnel, are utilized by only a fraction of consumers and are not provided on a large-scale industrial basis. These housework activities have 'remained' in the home, yet they are now carried out with the help of much more sophisticated – and usually electric – devices. What characterizes these devices is that they complement rather than substitute human labor. In fact, they modify the way in which certain housework activities are carried out and the kind of results yielded from a qualitative perspective. The transformation process described here, by which the material conditions of doing housework have been significantly altered, is not confined to the United States; it has taken place in a similar form in other industrialized countries as well.

This monograph aims at identifying the driving forces behind the mechanization of the private household and the corresponding changes in consumption behavior over the past 200 years. Taking the activity of clothes washing as a concrete object of inquiry, we shall examine the driving forces behind both the adoption and the utilization patterns of laundry technology, particularly washing machines – referred to here as the 'case study'. The stylized facts that we pay particular attention to are technological progress in washing machines from the middle of the nineteenth century onwards, the widespread diffusion of these devices in the twentieth century, the contemporaneous increase in laundry amounts and the growth in residential electricity consumption. These phenomena are subsumed here under the label of 'cleanliness consumption patterns'. They have occurred in similar ways in several Western countries, which is why some generalization is possible and is also intended here. Yet, we focus most strongly on the development that has taken place in the United States.

The case study chosen here, the activity of clothes washing, is an extremely rich case to analyze, which does not only attract scholarly attention at present (cf. Hartmann, 1974; Cowan, 1983; Matthews, 1987; Mohun, 1999; Strasser, 2000[1982]; Hessler, 2001) but has already been the subject of debate in the nineteenth century. Back then, laundry washing was the most detested household chore, when only the simplest tools for achieving cleanliness were available, namely a simple washboard and homemade soap (Giedion, 1948; Cohen, 1982; Hardyment, 1988). Moreover, in the absence of electricity and plumbing, all water had to be carried into and out of the house. Laundry washing apparently earned more complaints than any other household task in the nineteenth century (Strasser, 2000[1982], p. 104). At that time, leading intellectuals even considered laundry washing as the homemaker's biggest problem and sought ways to relieve women from this burden (e.g. Cowan, 1983; Matthews, 1987). In recent writings by historians of technology, doing the laundry is referred to as 'backbreaking' labor (Buehr, 1965, p. 61), a 'horrible task' (Cohen, 1982, p. 4) and 'the most toilsome of the housewife's tasks' (Giedion, 1948, p. 550).

Consider the following description of a typical washday in nineteenth-century America (Strasser, 2000[1982], p. 105):

> One wash, one boiling, and one rinse used about fifty gallons of water – or four hundred pounds – which had to be moved from pump or well or faucet to stove and tub, in buckets and wash boilers that might weigh as much as forty or fifty pounds. Rubbing, wringing and lifting water-laden clothes and linens, including large articles like sheets, tablecloths, and men's heavy work-clothes, wearied women's arms and wrists and exposed them to caustic substances. They lugged weighty tubs and baskets full of wet laundry outside, picked up each article, hung it on the line, and returned to take it all down.

Given that hardly any tools were available for doing laundry back then, it is no surprise to hear that clean clothes were not given much attention by the majority of consumers. In fact, consumers possessed few clothes and changed them only rarely. At the same time, there was the wealthy middle class who outperformed the majority of consumers in terms of financial resources and cleanliness of appearance (Ashenburg, 2007, p. 169). These levels of cleanliness, however, were not the result of their own labor; instead, the richer consumers usually delegated laundry washing to servants or made use of laundresses (Cohen, 1982, p. 91). Thus, depending on status and residence, households differed strongly in the nineteenth century concerning the material conditions of doing housework – a difference that lasted until the middle of the twentieth century, when household appliances like washing machines reached high ownership rates (Matthews, 1987; Hardyment, 1988) and consumers came to display similar levels of cleanliness (Hartmann, 1974, p. 279; Vanek, 1978).

In fact, with the diffusion of technically advanced tools during the twentieth century, consumers have increased the amount of clothes washed (e.g. Cowan, 1983; Silberzahn-Jandt, 1991; Strasser, 2000[1982]; Shove, 2003b). Already with the advent of the electricity–driven washing machine in the 1920s, clothes were changed more often (Wilson, 1929; Hewes, 1930; Strasser, 2000[1982], p. 268). This trend continued throughout the twentieth century. Nowadays, U.S. consumers wash about three times the amount that was common in the 1950s (Shove, 2003a). In view of the rise in laundry quantities, the consumption act of clothes washing is an example of technological progress having coincided with a growth in technology utilization. It is part of a larger phenomenon, referred to as the 'Cowan paradox' of rising household standards (Mokyr, 2000), named after the influential contribution of Ruth Schwartz Cowan on housework practices (Cowan, 1983, p. 100):

> Our commonly received notions about the impact of the twentieth-century household technology have thus deceived us on two crucial grounds. They had led us to believe that households no longer produce anything particularly important, and that, consequently, housewives no

longer have anything particularly time-consuming to do. Both notions are false, deriving from an incomplete understanding of the nature of these particular technological changes. [...] The nature of the work has changed, but the goal is still there and so is the necessity for time-consuming labor.

In fact, despite the development of superior household technology, the time devoted to housework was constant over the first decades of the twentieth century (Vanek, 1974) and declined remarkably only in its second half (Aguiar and Hurst, 2007). Naturally, this development is not self-evident. The literature identifies several driving forces which have also been related to the case study of cleanliness consumption: shifts in the labor division between the market and the home, growth in personal income during industrial development, technical progress in household technology that reduced the inputs of human labor and time, reduced availability of domestic servants, social emulation, changing ideologies of housework and of the status of being a housewife, knowledge progress as to the understanding of infectious diseases and changing perceptions of cleanliness (cf. e.g. Cowan, 1983; Matthews, 1987; Mokyr, 2000; Strasser, 2000 [1982]; Shove, 2003b).

The rich collection of stylized facts gathered by sociologists and economic historians has not yet given rise to an overarching theoretical account analyzing the transformation in domestic production activities (cf., however, the contribution of Reid, 1934). In the economics discipline, such an overarching framework has been developed by Gary Becker, who put forth the 'household production function approach' (Becker, 1965; Michael and Becker, 1973; cf. Chapter 2 for a detailed description). The household production theory is rooted in the neoclassical economic tradition and thus based on the assumptions of perfect information, maximizing behavior and nonsatiation. In addition, consumer preferences remain a 'black box'. Changes in behavior are thus exclusively explained with regard to changing relative prices. More in detail, the household production function approach relates the increasing demand for household technology to rising wages and opportunity costs of time: the higher the wage rate, the more costly it is to spend time in unpaid housework activities. Market goods are thus purchased in order to make feasible the expansion of market work by substituting these goods for the household's time. This line of reasoning is referred to as the 'time substitution hypothesis'. Naturally, the point of departure of Becker's account, that housework is a time-intensive, unpaid form of work which women might reduce once they enter the labor force, has also attracted much attention in the sociological literature (e.g. Nickols and Fox, 1983; Bellante and Foster, 1984; Weagley and Norum, 1989). In addition, Becker's theory has been drawn upon by economic historians for studying the phenomena we address here (Mokyr, 2000; de Vries, 1994; de Vries, 2008).

Certainly, the household production function approach has great heuristic potential for economic research by pointing to the interrelatedness of such diverse phenomena as the household's labor supply decision, the demand for durable goods and services, time allocation patterns and the organization of nonmarket production activities. Moreover, in view of the increased female labor force participation in the second half of the twentieth century (Goldin, 1986; Costa, 2000), the adoption of washing machines for their time saving nature is a plausible explanation. Still, with reference to the Cowan paradox, one might ask: Why did consumers also increase the utilization of washing machines by washing more clothes than before? Why have higher laundry amounts been preferred over the alternative of saving even more housework time by keeping a given cleanliness level? Furthermore, the fact that the market for washing machines is saturated nowadays, with these goods being present in nearly every U.S. household, sheds some doubt on the opportunity cost expla-nation. Apparently, working women and full-time housewives are equally equipped with these devices. What is the housewife's incentive to purchase this device when she does not have a reservation wage in mind? Put differently, if wages had not risen during the twentieth century – increasing the opportunity costs of housework as opposed to market work – would we still have observed the given diffusion process of washing machines?

Although the time substitution hypothesis sounds plausible at first sight, the opportunity cost argument might be insufficient in that it does not capture the essential phenomena underlying the complex process of the mechanization of the home over the past 200 years. We argue that additional conjectures – beyond time substitution – are needed in order to understand why, in historical terms, a specific consumption path has been chosen. In this monograph, we tackle the following overarching research questions:

- Which factors have driven the diffusion of washing machines in the twentieth century?
- Why has the proliferation of washing machines throughout the twentieth century coincided with increasing laundry quantities?
- Why do the majority of consumers make use of washing machines instead of laundry services for ensuring cleanliness?
- Why are cleanliness consumption patterns so very similar today?

The aim of this analysis is precisely to explain why specific consumption trends have occurred, while scrutinizing if changes in relative prices are sufficient to explain changes in consumer behavior. We posit that these research questions cannot be answered without substantial hypotheses on the consumer motiva-tions underlying the consumption of cleanliness.

1.2 The Evolutionary Economic Approach

When analyzing long-term changes in consumption patterns, one cannot abstain from putting forth hypotheses about the general causes and directions of preference change (cf. Witt, 2001). A central assumption of our analysis is that consumers share some set of preferences because of their common genetic basis, a set of preferences which can be identified and whose patterns of change show some regularities. In long-run shifts in consumption patterns, we expect to see manifestations of these shared motivations to engage in consumptive activities. In addition, we need to be concerned with consumer learning processes. Learning processes address the way in which consumers get in contact with new goods in the first place, why they regard them as utility-providing and whether the social environment fosters or constrains changing consumption patterns. In that regard, our analysis differs from the more descriptive way in which sociologists, economic historians and historians of technology have tackled the subject. It also differs from the established neoclassical approach, the 'household production function approach', by making assumptions about the content of consumer preferences and by rejecting the utility-maximization hypothesis. In Becker's theory of the household, consumer motivations remain a black box, as the concept of the household's ultimate goals – household 'commodities' – is underspecified (Gronau and Hamermesh, 2006). Changes in household production processes, particularly the substitution of the household's time for goods, are predicted independent of the arguments of the utility function.

As will be shown in this monograph, the essential driving forces behind the rising technological endowment of the home and the demand for washing machines are not changing relative prices but innate consumer needs and consumer learning processes of how to satisfy those needs by engaging in suitable consumption activities. For this purpose, historical facts will be interpreted in view of a psychologically informed consumer theory, namely the 'theory of learning consumers' by Ulrich Witt (2001), which studies the motivational aspects of long-term changes in consumption patterns and their interdependencies with consumer learning processes (cf. Chapter 2). More generally, the analysis aims at demonstrating that only a heterodox economic approach offers a comprehensive explanation of this historical process. The research objective is to trace back the major historical trends of the evolution of cleanliness consumption to an individualistic perspective, i.e. back to the motivational forces and learning capabilities that are at work at the individual level.

The approach taken in this book belongs to the field of evolutionary economics, more precisely, the 'naturalistic' line of research in evolutionary economics (for an overview, cf. Witt, 1987; Witt, 2003). The naturalistic approach is based on the 'continuity hypothesis', i.e. the assumption that there exists ontological continuity between human natural evolution and cultural evolution, including economic evolution. It views modern man with its cognitive and behavioral dispositions as the outcome of Darwinian evolution, whose forces have strongly shaped our biological and psychological makeup. Our evolutionary heritage is reflected, not only in human behavior in everyday life, but in economically relevant contexts. From psychological and biological research, we can learn about these behavioral foundations. Taking them into account should therefore substantially enhance our understanding of human behavior and long-term economic development.

Drawing upon Witt (2001), we analyze consumption behavior with regard to consumers' motivational basis and the driving forces behind changes therein. The central concepts of this analysis are thus consumer basic needs, their properties of satiation and consumer learning processes. That way, we do not leave the utility function 'black boxed', but make the motivational aspects of consumer behavior a central element of our analysis of the evolution of cleanliness consumption. We understand needs in the sense of Witt (2001), who equates them with the so-called 'primary reinforcers' of behavioral psychology (Millenson, 1967, p. 368). Examples are the need for caloric intake, stabilizing body temperature, cognitive arousal and health, but also for social recognition. Those needs belong to the genetic makeup of humans and are therefore shared among them. Individuals are motivated through their basic needs to engage in consumptive activities and they satisfy these needs by consuming goods and services of appropriate quality and quantity.

Witt assumes that, in principle for each need, a specific yet temporary satiation level exists, which can be reached by appropriate consumption activities. In simple terms, the consumer has had 'enough sleep', 'enough to eat' or 'is warm enough', and so on. Although the satiation level of a need itself is, in most cases, a nonobservable theoretical construct, it can be learned from surveys which motivations are related to a specific consumption activity. Moreover, actual consumption patterns are observable in expenditure statistics and consumer surveys. A further central hypothesis is that needs themselves show different satiation properties and that some needs are specifically said to be rather 'hard to satiate' in comparison with other needs. One of these basic needs, which is mentioned by Witt (2001) as being difficult to satiate, is the need for social recognition. Expenditures on a consumption activity are more likely to grow when this activity appeals to the need for social recognition than without this social significance. More generally, differences in satiation properties of basic needs might be a central driving force behind differential growth in different expenditure categories.

At center stage of this analysis stand the associations which consumers hold with regard to specific consumption activities. Drawing upon Witt, we assume the consumption of a good to be closely related to the consumer understanding regarding the consumer needs appealed to by this exact good. One could speak here of consumer beliefs or consumption knowledge about 'means-ends-relationships'. As a result of consumer learning processes, consumer associations evolve; they are malleable over time. Such learning processes can be cognitive or noncognitive in nature. Noncognitive, more elementary learning processes are based on sensory feedback mechanisms only and correspond to individual trial-and-error learning. For cognitive learning processes, social factors play a central role. The mechanisms will later be described in more detail (cf. Chapter 2). Note that consumer associations do not necessarily correspond to the true, objective relationship between consumption goods on the one side and the satisfaction of needs on the other. In addition, learning processes need not lead to an improvement in consumer behavior from the perspective of consumer welfare. To illustrate this point, let clothes be washed for hygienic concerns and let consumers hold false beliefs in that they think that more washing is necessary from a health perspective than what is actually the case. As a result, consumers will wash too much, thereby triggering adverse effects such as allergies. Over time, this discrepancy between beliefs and the true causal relationship might change but will not necessarily diminish. Because of false assumptions, actual consumption patterns might not be appropriate for realizing need satisfaction, although needs are the motivational force behind consumption behavior.

At first sight, these explanations might suggest that our research shows some overlap with the neoclassical literature on quality uncertainty, ranging from Akerlof's (1970) central contribution on the 'market for lemons' to the conceptual works of Nelson (1970) and Darby and Karni (1973). When uncertainty and incomplete information as to the quality of consumer goods are acknowledged, consumer behavior can be interpreted as the 'discovery process' of the technical makeup of existing products. However, this strand of literature differs strongly from our approach, as we do not analyze the case of asymmetric information and also do not take into account the rationale of producers and sellers. Instead, in the tradition of Carl Menger (1950[1871]), we deal with the process by which, in larger leaps of knowledge progress, all members of society explore the usefulness of certain goods and activities for satisfying their needs (cf. also Mokyr, 2002, Chapter 1). We thus focus on a very fundamental epistemological process.

We assume the historical evolution of cleanliness consumption over the past 200 years to be the result of the interplay of supply and demand side factors, namely technical changes in washing technology on one side and motivational driving forces and learning capabilities on the other. Our analysis is thus conceptually rooted in what we will refer to here as 'the learning approach' to consumption behavior, although we connect to other strands of literature where necessary and suitable. The subject of this study is to analyze to which extent, when and why the associations related to the consumption act of clothes washing have been malleable over time. We hypothesize that whenever the associations that a consumer holds with regard to a specific product change, a change in behavior is likely to occur, i.e. the consumption of that product (purchase, use) is likely to be shifted upward or downward with an increase in positive or negative associations, respectively.

The evolutionary specificity of the approach taken here is reflected first, in its long-term perspective on changing consumption patterns and second, in the reconstruction of historical phenomena by means of a psychologically informed theory of consumer behavior (individualistic foundation). The concrete selection of the evolutionary economics literature included and the weight given to it was guided by the aim of this analysis, which is twofold. On the one hand, we seek to contrast evolutionary consumer theory with neoclassical consumer theory and to demonstrate the added value of the evolutionary account with its emphasis on uncertainty and consumer learning processes. Drawing up the specific case study of cleanliness consumption, we will show how the evolutionary account better explains the actual historical development. On the other hand, we intend to illustrate that the specific historical development of cleanliness consumption can be traced back to some very general laws of consumer behavior. For this purpose, a conceptual individualistic model needs to be drawn upon with which to confront the manifold historical facts gathered by economic historians and sociologists. In order to keep the conceptual framework realistic, yet as simple as possible, we most strongly base our analysis on one very specific account, the theory of learning consumers, which in itself integrates a large share of evolutionary consumer theory and which is also consistent with relevant psychological insights on human behavior. If we integrated further accounts and concepts from the wide evolutionary economics literature, the conceptual model would become 'overloaded' at the expense of conceptual clarity.

Likewise, with the focus on the close interaction between consumer learning processes on one side and technological progress on the other, this analysis does not cover all facets of cleanliness consumption patterns. Otherwise, the study as a whole would become much more descriptive and 'additive' in nature – yet without being able to do justice to the rich collection of sociological and historical studies on the subject. We have focused on those aspects and conditions of cleanliness consumption that can be related to the individualistic model. In that regard, the historical-geographical context is one explanatory factor for understanding the evolution of cleanliness consumption, while the general laws of consumer behavior allow for some generalization beyond specific historical contexts.

1.3 Terminology

In this section, we define the central terms and the scope of our research. Only a broad picture will be drawn concerning the set of phenomena dealt with and the issues left out. We will be more specific in each of the subsequent chapters.

The subject of this book is any consumer activity undertaken in order to clean consumer clothes, including purchase activities – which are reflected in expenditure statistics and ownership rates of washing machines – and the activity of laundry washing itself for which time-use studies, laundry quantities and residential electricity use are indicators. We subsume these phenomena under the label of 'cleanliness consumption', as related to the 'consumption activity of clothes washing' (synonymously: 'laundry washing'; 'doing the laundry'). By focusing on the preparation of clothing (i.e. not bed linens, tablecloths or other household items), we address that element of cleanliness consumption that is observable, perhaps conspicuous, in the interaction between consumers. In what follows, we will speak of clean clothes or cleanliness synonymously.[2]

The analysis covers the adoption and utilization patterns of washing machines, whereas the use of commercial laundries and other forms of services plays a minor role. At present, doing the laundry involves the purchase and use of an electric automated washing machine and the accompanying use of electricity, water and detergent. However, 200 years ago, a washing machine resembling the modern product had neither been in use nor in existence. Thus, depending on the time period studied, tools other than the modern washing machine will also be looked at, which is why we choose to speak of 'washing technology' or 'laundry technology' more in general.

We draw upon the household production function approach as a conceptual point of departure throughout this study. For the activity of clothes washing – in comparison with, say, using vacuum cleaners or refrigerators – the terminology of a household production process fits very well. First of all, laundry washing is a quite complex activity that makes use of several factor inputs which can be combined in various ways. Second, laundry washing is a two-stage process of washing the clothes first and wearing them afterward. Thus, laundry washing can be interpreted as an intermediate activity for the satisfaction of more fundamental consumer preferences. This conceptualization will be helpful as it allows for a simple distinction between productive and subsequent consumptive activities within the household production framework. We thus characterize the conceptual nature of cleanliness consumption as follows: cleanliness in the form of clean clothes is the outcome of a household production process in its physical form, a 'commodity' in the terminology of Michael and Becker (1973). Clean clothes, in turn, appeal to consumers' ultimate goals and have instrumental value for more fundamental consumer preferences. In our framework, these ultimate household goals will be equated with 'basic needs' in the sense of Witt (2001). Clean clothes are assumed to better serve consumer basic needs than the original input that went into the production process, i.e. dirty clothes. This implies that it is not washing machines themselves that satisfy consumer needs, but the commodities which are produced with the help of washing machines. Let us summarize these basic definitions:

> Definition of cleanliness consumption: Cleanliness consumption is any consumer activity undertaken in order to clean consumer clothes, covering the purchase and utilization of laundry technology. Cleanliness, in the form of clean clothes, is the outcome of a household production process. Clean clothes have instrumental value for more fundamental consumer preferences, namely basic needs in the sense of Witt (2001).

Although we apply the terminology of the household production process as a starting point, we do not characterize clothes washing as an activity of much cognitive involvement. Quite the opposite, doing the laundry might be dominated more strongly by habits, which is the perspective taken in sociological writings on the subject (cf. Shove, 2003a). In addition, we do not buy into the neoclassical assumptions of static preferences, perfect information and maximizing behavior.

1.4 Overview of the Book

The basic structure of this book looks as follows. The theoretical and conceptual basis of the analysis is introduced in Chapter 2. In Chapter 3, we trace the emergence of the social norm of cleanliness in the nineteenth century. Chapters 4–6 address the twentieth-century conditions of cleanliness consumption and examine the driving forces behind the diffusion of washing machines. Chapter 7 turns to current patterns of cleanliness consumption and the possibility of reducing the energy requirements of clothes washing via energy efficiency progress. A summary of the central findings is given in Chapter 8.

In Chapter 2, we describe the theoretical underpinnings and the conceptual framework of our analysis. We begin with a description and critical assessment of the neoclassical account for analyzing housework, the 'household production function approach'. We then set up a psychologically informed account – the learning approach – as our alternative for analyzing changes in household production processes. We illuminate some basic principles that might drive the adoption and utilization patterns of household technology. Furthermore, we formulate our core arguments in the form of hypotheses, which will be taken up again in the subsequent chapters. More in detail, we first turn to Gary Becker's household production function approach and its major testable implication, the time substitution hypothesis, which links the adoption of capital goods such as household appliances to rising opportunity costs of time. A great part of the discussion revolves around Becker's treatment of preferences, which is critically assessed, particularly the exclusion of 'preferences for the use of time', the nonsatiation assumption and the hollow concept of household 'commodities'. We will argue that preferences play an important role in actual human behavior and substantiate our claim by presenting insights from motivational and behavioral psychology. We then introduce the 'theory of learning consumers' by Ulrich Witt as an alternative to Becker's account, which is compatible with the psychological body of literature reviewed. Witt's account is insightful for our analysis for two major reasons. First, the theory suggests a material specification of preferences in the form of basic needs. Second, Witt puts forth conjectures about the principles by which the motivations for consuming products evolve and translate into changes in consumption patterns – referred to as 'learning processes'. Drawing upon this framework, we will set up a psychologically informed account for analyzing changes in household production processes. We will thus show that the concept 'preferences for the use of time' can be given a behavioral interpretation.

Chapter 3 deals with the origin of the social norm of cleanliness which is currently in place in industrialized countries. It explains how and why the social norm has come into being, whereby the status-signaling property of clean appearance was eliminated. The analysis draws upon the central body of literature on norm emergence and connects its major insights with the learning approach. We find the process of norm emergence to be related to the solution of an externality problem: demanding from each other to be clean or cleaner was believed to hold in check the spread of infectious diseases, which was still a major problem during times of industrialization and urbanization in the United States and United Kingdom. Consumers gave up cleanliness as a mode of social distinction, and cleanliness became a 'must' for all consumers who wanted to take part in social life. Chapter 3 thus provides an explanation for the assimilation of cleanliness consumption patterns over time while showing that the establishment of the consumer mass market for cleanliness products is not the result of processes of social emulation. From Chapter 3, we further learn that the consumption of products such as soap, detergents and laundry equipment is connected to a social norm and to the basic need for social recognition. The case study exemplifies the path dependency of consumption patterns, i.e. the cumulative nature with which historical circumstances affect consumption patterns in the long run. In terms of its contribution, Chapter 3 sheds light on the role of basic consumer needs and processes of consumer learning in the formation of social norms. Moreover, we introduce a new case study, namely, cleanliness consumption, into the literature on norm emergence.

In Chapters 4, 5 and 6, we analyze the driving forces behind the widespread diffusion of washing machines in the twentieth century from three different angles: a technology study, an explorative advertisement analysis and a literature review. We examine the explicative potential of two alternative hypotheses, namely the 'time substitution hypothesis' and the 'drudgery avoidance hypothesis'. The time substitution hypothesis links the adoption of washing machines to rising opportunity costs of time, which raise the shadow price of clothes washing at home and trigger the purchase of washing machines as a substitute for the household's input of time. It will be referred to as the time substitution motive. The drudgery avoidance hypothesis relates the adoption of washing machines to the innate human disposition to avoid heavy physical effort. We derive the hypothesis based on, first, psychological insights showing that the avoidance of heavy physical effort is an innate behavioral disposition, and second, from the observation that laundry washing still demanded such effort in the nineteenth century. It will be referred to as the physical labor saving motive.

In Chapter 4, we take a look at the major phases of progress in laundry technology from the middle of the nineteenth century onwards. This approach is based on the argument that washing machines will only be adopted for the motives of saving time or physical labor, when technically advanced washing machines indeed make such achievements feasible. Chapter 5 turns to advertisements on washing machines. We examine a specific U.S. women's magazine, the *Ladies' Home Journal*, with regard to the appearance of washing machine advertisements and the reasons given for the purchase of these products. This approach is based on the assumption that long-term shifts in advertisement content reflect changes in shared consumer motivations for adopting washing machines. The analysis is based on a selection of issues and covers a time period of 100 years, from 1888 to 1989. In Chapter 6, we scrutinize the time substitution hypothesis by means of a literature review. The review is mainly focused on econometric cross-sectional studies, analyzing the relationship between the employment status of the wife and the ownership of washing machines and the demand for laundry services. In addition, we evaluate further empirical material which lends itself to an examination of the hypothesis from a longitudinal perspective. In terms of its contribution, Chapters 4 to 6 have shown that the time substitution hypothesis in its original form is not sufficient to fully understand changes in the domestic production of cleanliness over the past 200 years. Although, at a general level, time saving capital goods were substituted for human labor and went hand in hand with an increase in female labor force participation, the actual processes producing this outcome have been much more complex than the household production function approach suggests. At a more general level, we have illustrated that it is useful to take 'preferences for the use of time' into account when studying changes in household production processes.

Chapter 7 studies the phenomenon of the 'rebound effect' on energy efficiency progress with regard to washing machines. Rebound effects occur when products do become more energy efficient but are used more intensively than before – thus partly offsetting achievable energy savings. We challenge the standard approach to analyzing rebound effects, which is neoclassical consumer theory, and argue for a broadening of the theoretical basis. We introduce the concepts of consumer needs, their satiation properties and consumer learning processes, and apply our framework to study the development of cleanliness consumption. With regard to the observation of rising cleanliness standards (the Cowan paradox), washing machines are an example of a technology that has been utilized more intensively while it has become technically more and more advanced. In the neoclassical interpretation, this process is a reaction to reduced costs of using washing machines. In contrast to that, we relate the growth in laundry quantities to the emerging social norm of cleanliness, i.e. consumers' motivational background. Our central hypothesis is that rebound effects will only occur as long as the consumer needs appealed to by a specific consumption activity are not yet satiated. Applying this argument to the consumption of cleanliness, we discuss the satiation properties of the underlying need for social recognition. From the perspective of the basic needs involved, further efficiency improvements in washing machines are not likely to produce higher cleanliness levels as the satiation level of social recognition with respect to cleanliness consumption has probably already been met.

In the last chapter of the book, we depict the historical development of cleanliness consumption over the past 200 years as a whole and refer to the insights gained from the perspective of the psychologically informed learning approach. In addition, we briefly summarize how the argumentation has been laid out in each of the individual chapters.

To be clear on this, we do not believe the subject of the analysis to be 'original', but rather that the approach taken here is (cf. Section 1.2). There is a long-standing research tradition on housework, especially in sociology and economic history but also in economics, without which this book could not have been written. In fact, this scientific inquiry into housework and the mechanization of the home in the industrialized world has much more sophisticated forerunners. Already at the beginning of the twentieth century, the proponents of a movement called scientific housekeeping (or, more generally, home economics) saw housework and particularly doing the laundry as a complex task, about which they wrote manuals, i.e. advice literature, and gave lessons at school. Leading intellectuals sought to enhance the status of being a housewife by working out a scientific basis for proper housework. The home economists had to devote quite some effort to establishing the scientific discipline of the same title. This development took a turn with the advent of Gary Becker's household production function approach, which demonstrated the possibility of applying economic analysis to this realm. In fact, Becker's work on the economics of the family, of which the household production function approach is a core element, has after all won the Nobel Prize in economics. Since the 1970s and 1980s, sociological scholars have increasingly devoted attention to the study of housework, in which they see the yet neglected, inconspicuous counterpart to industrial development and economic growth that in itself is an essential source of value creation – both for the private household and the economy as a whole.[3]

With this book, we hope to demonstrate that, although clothes washing is an activity that everybody does, it is still a fascinating subject for an economic analysis which is part of a long-standing and rich research tradition. To our knowledge, this is the first analysis in the spirit of evolutionary economics. Arguably, the evolutionary perspective can shed some additional light on a subject which has yet almost exclusively been dealt with by neoclassical economists and sociologists. The modest aim of this study is to relate the historical facts to an individualistic account, which is not the standard economic framework but a psychologically informed evolutionary account.

Notes

1   These numbers are taken from a consumer survey carried out by Pew Research Center in 2006 among 2,000 U.S. consumers (question wording: 'Do you pretty much think of this as a necessity or pretty much think of this as a luxury you could do without?'; cf. Taylor *et al.*, 2009).
2   In some of the cited figures, it is not clear which share of laundry is dedicated exclusively to clothing care; such figures are thus to be interpreted as proxies only.
3   Interestingly, the evolution of cleanliness consumption particularly appears to reflect some of the general processes of economic development as happening in the industrial sphere, namely technological progress from mechanization to electrification and automation.

References

Aguiar, M., Hurst, E. (2007): 'Measuring trends in leisure: The allocation of time over five decades', *Quarterly Journal of Economics*, 122 (3), pp. 969–1006.
Akerlof, G. A. (1970): 'The market for "lemons": Quality uncertainty and the market mechanism', *Quarterly Journal of Economics*, 84 (3), pp. 488–500.
Ashenburg, K. (2007): *The Dirt on Clean, An Unsanitized History*, North Point Press, New York.
Becker, G. S. (1965): 'A theory of the allocation of time', *The Economic Journal*, 75 (299), pp. 49–517.

Bellante, D., Foster, A. C. (1984): 'Working wives and expenditure on services', *Journal of Consumer Research*, 11, pp. 700–707.

Buehr, W. (1965): Home Sweet Home in the Nineteenth Century, Thomas Y. Crowell Company, New York.

Cohen, D. (1982): The Last Hundred Years: Household Technology, M. Evans and Company, New York.

Costa, D. L. (2000): 'From mill town to board room: The rise of women's paid labor', *Journal of Economic Perspectives*, 14 (4), pp. 101–122.

Cowan, R. S. (1983): *More Work for Mother*, Basic Books, New York.

Darby, M. R., Karni, E. (1973): 'Free competition and the optimal amount of fraud', *Journal of Law and Economics*, 16, pp. 67–86.

de Vries, J. (1994): 'The industrial revolution and the industrious revolution', *Journal of Economic History*, 54 (2), pp. 249–270.

de Vries, J. (2008): *The Industrious Revolution, Consumer Behavior and the Household Economy, 1650 to the Present*, Cambridge University Press, Cambridge, MA.

EIA (2011): Annual Energy Review 2011, Energy Information Administration, Table 2.6 Household End Uses: Fuel Types, Appliances, and Electronics, Selected Years, 1078–2009 (retrieved from http://www.eia.gov/totalenergy/data/annual/pdf/sec2_21.pdf; 10.09.2016).

Giedion, S. (1948): *Mechanization Takes Command: A Contribution to Anonymous History*, Norton, New York.

Goldin, C. (1986): 'The female labor force and American economic growth, 1890–1980', in Engerman, S. L., Gallman, R. E. (eds): *Long-Term Factors in American Economic Growth, Studies in Income and Wealth*, No. 51, University of Chicago Press, Chicago and London.

Gronau, R., Hamermesh, D. S. (2006): 'Time vs. goods: The value of measuring household production technologies', *Review of Income and Wealth*, 52 (1), pp. 1–16.

Hardyment, C. (1988): *From Mangle to Microwave: The Mechanization of Household Work*, Polity Press, Cambridge, United Kingdom.

Hartmann, H. I. (1974): Capitalism and Women's Work in the Home, 1900–1930, Dissertation, Yale University.

Hessler, M. (2001): *'Mrs. Modern Women', Zur Sozial- und Kulturgeschichte der Haushaltstechnisierung*, Campus Verlag, Frankfurt, New York.

Hewes, A. (1930): 'Electrical appliances in the home', *Social Forces*, 9 (2), pp. 235–242.

Lebergott, S. (1993): *Pursuing Happiness: American Consumers in the Twentieth Century*, Princeton University Press, Princeton.

Matthews, G. (1987): *Just a Housewife: The Rise and Fall of Domesticity in America*, Oxford University Press, New York.

Menger, C. (1950[1871]): *Principles of Economics*, The Free Press, Glenco, IL.

Michael, R. T., Becker G. S. (1973): 'On the new theory of consumer behavior', *Swedish Journal of Economics*, 75 (4), pp. 378–396.

Millenson, J. (1967): *Principles of Behavioral Analysis*, MacMillan, New York.

Mohun, A. P. (1999): Steam Laundries: Gender, Technology, and Work in the United States and Great Britain, 1880–1940, The Johns Hopkins University Press, Baltimore and London.

Mokyr, J. (2000): 'Why "more work for mother?" Knowledge and household behavior, 1870–1945', *Journal of Economic History*, 60 (1), pp. 1–41.

Mokyr, J. (2002): *The Gifts of Athena: Historical Origins of the Knowledge Economy*, Princeton University Press, Princeton, NJ.

Nelson, P. (1970): 'Information and consumer behavior', *Journal of Political Economy*, 78 (2), pp. 311–329.

Nickols, S. Y., Fox, K. D. (1983): 'Buying time and saving time: Strategies for managing household production', *Journal of Consumer Research*, 10, pp. 197–208.

Reid, M. G. (1934): *The Economics of Household Production*, John Wiley & Sons, New York.

Shove, E. (2003a): 'Converging conventions of comfort, cleanliness and convenience', *Journal of Consumer Policy*, 26, pp. 395–418.

Shove, E. (2003b): *Comfort, Cleanliness and Convenience: The Social Organization of Normality*, Berg, Oxford and New York.

Silberzahn-Jandt, G. (1991), *Wasch-Maschine. Zum Wandel von Frauenarbeit im Haushalt*, Jonas Verlag für Kunst und Literatur, Marburg, Germany.

Strasser, S. (2000[1982]): *Never Done, A History of American Housework*, Henry Holt and Company, New York.

Taylor, P., Funk, C., Clark, A. (2009): 'Luxury or necessity? Things we can't live without: the list has grown in the past decade', Working Paper, Pew Research Center, Washington D.C.

Vanek, J. (1974): 'Time spent in housework', *Scientific American*, 231, pp. 116–120.

Vanek, J. (1978): 'Household technology and social status: Rising living standards and residence differences in housework', *Technology and Culture*, 19 (3), pp. 361–375.

Weagley, R.O, Norum P.S. (1989): 'Household demand for market, purchased home producible commodities', *Family and Consumer Sciences Research Journal*, 18 (6), pp. 6–18.

Wilson, M. (1929): 'Use of time by Oregon farm homemakers', *Oregon Agricultural Experiment Station Bulletin no. 256*.

Witt, U. (1987): *Individualistische Grundlagen der Evolutorischen Ökonomik*, J.B.C. Mohr (Paul Siebeck), Tübingen, Germany.

Witt, U. (2001): 'Learning to consume: A theory of wants and the growth of demand', *Journal of Evolutionary Economics*, 11, pp. 23–36.

Witt, U. (2003): *The Evolving Economy: Essays on the Evolutionary Approach to Economics*, Edward Elgar, Aldershot.

2   Consumption Behavior as a Learning Process

2.1 Introductory Remarks

In this chapter, we introduce the theoretical framework with which we will analyze the case study of cleanliness consumption. It is a learning approach to consumption behavior, which to a great extent draws upon the 'theory of learning consumers' by Ulrich (Witt, 2001). The learning approach provides unique hypotheses about changes in consumer behavior. At the same time, it leaves sufficient room to add further concepts and conjectures from other accounts. In the chapters to come, several other strands of literature, including other theories of consumer behavior, will be tackled. Throughout the analysis, we will show how the learning account adds a novel perspective to the subject for each of the more specific questions tackled, i.e. in addition to the valuable insights to be derived from more established frameworks.

The established framework that we deal with most extensively is the 'household production function approach' by Gary Becker (Becker, 1965; Michael and Becker, 1973). It is the most prominent economic approach toward housework. The theory offers a specific hypothesis, the time substitution hypothesis, which is applicable to the case study of cleanliness consumption and can be tested empirically. In fact, the theory has already been applied to the research subject. It is thus the 'natural' benchmark against which to outline the rather novel learning account. We therefore start in this chapter with a description and critical assessment of the household production function approach.

To choose a theory which is very well established and has already been applied to the research field allows for 'continuity' in research and scientific debate. A prehistory of applied research is also very useful in that it demonstrates the feasibility of an empirical test of the theory. At the same time, if only this one very specific account and its theoretical predictions were considered, many important questions might be left unanswered or not even asked in the first place. We will show that, in order to achieve a theoretical reconstruction of the very general stylized facts of the evolution of cleanliness consumption, the household production function approach alone is not sufficient.

We proceed as follows. In the next section, we present the core ideas of the household production function approach and its major testable implication, the time substitution hypothesis (Section 2.2). It follows a critical discussion of Becker's assumption that consumers do not have preferences for the use of time, i.e. consumers only care about the output of household production processes and not about the production process as such. We add some remarks on the utility maximization hypothesis in the face of an evolving consumption environment. Our critique of Becker's account is based particularly on psychological theories of motivation and empirical evidence gathered in the behavioral sciences (Section 2.3). The behavioral findings are then applied to derive implications for technical change (synonymously: technological progress) and consumption behavior. In this context, the theory of learning consumers is introduced and compared with Becker's account in terms of its core elements. Furthermore, the central hypotheses for analyzing cleanliness consumption are presented. Thereafter, we introduce the conceptual framework of the analysis (Section 2.4). Some concluding remarks close the chapter (Section 2.5).

2.2 The Household Production Function Approach

2.2.1 Labor-Leisure Choice Analysis

The basis of the 'household production function approach' or 'household production theory' is the labor-leisure choice analysis. Its core assumption is that utility is not only defined over consumption goods but over leisure time as well (cf. Kooreman and Wunderink, 1997, Chapters 5 and 6). By assumption, work at the labor market is not in itself so rewarding that a compensation has to be paid for forgone leisure time. In addition, consumers face a time constraint. They can spend their limited time either working or enjoying leisure. Consumers thus face a trade-off, both between working time and leisure time and between consumption goods and leisure time. The more time the household spends working, the more income it will earn and the more consumption goods can be purchased. However, leisure time, which is enjoyable in itself, then has to be given up to some extent. Opportunity costs thus stand at center stage of the household's optimization task: the price of enjoying one hour of leisure equals the forgone earnings or the consumption basket which could have been purchased with these earnings. As a consequence of these assumptions, in the labor-leisure choice analysis, the conventional budget constraint is modified into a 'full income' constraint. Full income is the hypothetical amount of income the household could earn if all the time available was spent working. It is a function of the household's time allocation. In the household optimum, the marginal rate of substitution of consumption goods versus leisure time equals the real wage rate. This means that the optimal time allocation between market work and leisure is found when the value of a further unit of leisure forgone equals the utility of a further consumption unit made feasible.

What are the comparative-static implications of the model? When the wage rate rises, the household's constraint in the form of full income is modified as potential earnings increase. Also, the price of leisure is raised in absolute and

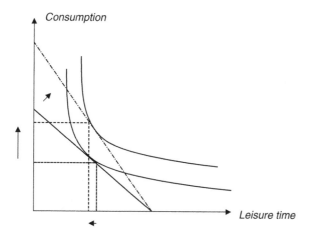

Figure 2.1 Labor-Leisure Trade-Off.

relative terms. Under the assumption that leisure is a normal good, working time is expanded to the disadvantage of leisure. However, the opposite reaction, an expansion of leisure, is also possible. The kind of reaction that eventually occurs depends on the relative magnitude of both income and substitution effects. Those are assumed to depend on the level of the wage rate: the higher the wage rate, the stronger the income effect and the more likely it is that consumers will expand leisure.[1] As the substitution effect is always negative for a normal good and thus goes in favor of a reduction of leisure time, the income effect determines the overall outcome. In the new household optimum, a higher indifference curve will be reached.

Figure 2.1 illustrates how the household optimum is modified by an increase in the wage rate, which makes leisure relatively more expensive compared with consumption goods. Given the shape of the indifference curves depicted here, leisure time is reduced in favor of working time, implying an increase in consumption.

The labor-leisure choice model distinguishes between two categories of time use: market work and leisure. Were household production processes and the category 'housework time' included in that model, it would become much more complicated. Certainly, the central predictions of the model would still hold, i.e. an increase in the wage rate might lead to an increase in labor supply, to its reduction or to no change at all. But in addition to that, changes in household production processes might occur which affect the allocation of time and the purchase of consumption goods. Becker's theory of the household is based on the labor-leisure choice model, yet it modifies it in some crucial points.

2.2.2 Time Substitution Hypothesis

The household production function approach by Gary Becker and Robert Michael (Becker, 1965; Michael and Becker, 1973) is the standard economic framework for analyzing housework. Many of Becker's ideas can already be found in the work of Margaret G. Reid (1934), yet it took Becker's mathematical formalization to increase the popularity of this field of study within the economics discipline (Pollak, 2003). The household production theory modifies neoclassical consumer theory in two decisive points. First, time is recognized to put a constraint on consumer behavior, as does the limited household budget. Second, the utility function is not defined over market goods but over so-called 'commodities', which the household produces itself (including leisure). To depict the transformation of inputs – i.e. time and market goods – into the household production output – i.e. commodities – Becker uses the metaphor of a 'household production technology'. The costs of consuming a certain commodity consist of the expenditures on goods (or on the services derived from durable goods) and the opportunity costs of time per unit of that commodity. The demand for market goods is derived from the household's production objectives. Preferences are assumed to be identical among households as well as fixed (cf. Section 2.2.3). An implicit assumption, in line with the conventional theory of rational choice, is that of nonsatiability in terms of commodities.[2]

The pivotal point of the analysis is how to allocate the limited amount of time between market work and home production activities, and among the production of different commodities. As in labor-leisure choice analysis, market work is only the vehicle for earning income with which goods can be purchased that go into household production processes. This idea is reflected in the full income constraint, which combines time and budget constraints. It implies that the earning potential is limited by time constraints and that all unpaid uses of time have opportunity costs.

In the short run, the optimization calculus proceeds as follows (cf. Pollak, 1969; Pollak, 2003). In a first step, the production opportunity curve is depicted. This is the technically feasible and affordable production set of commodities, given the technological conditions of the household, the prices of input factors and the budget constraint for a given labor supply. Depicting the opportunity curve requires knowledge of the household production function – the technical relation by which material inputs, i.e. market goods and time, are transformed into outputs, i.e. commodities. This calculation yields the shadow prices of commodities, which represent the marginal costs of producing specific commodities and indicate the ratio at which a household can 'transform' one commodity into the other. The production opportunity curve is then related to the household's preferences defined over commodities in order to determine the optimal commodity bundle and the derived demand for market goods with which to produce these commodities. In the household optimum, time and other factors of production are allocated among different production functions (commodities) such that the utilities of the marginal products equalize. The optimal composition of household production is achieved when the ratios of shadow prices of commodities equal the ratios of their marginal utilities.

The central comparative-static implications of Becker's approach concern changes in the wage rate. As it is usually provided that indifference curves are convex, Becker argues that a rise in the cost of time relative to goods would induce a reduction in the amount of time and an increase in the amount of goods used per unit of each commodity. The reasoning is built on an opportunity cost argument: rising wages trigger a rethinking of the given time allocation patterns as spending time in unpaid household activities becomes relatively more expensive in terms of foregone earnings and thus foregone pleasure. If the household did not rearrange its time use in times of rising wages (in general: more paid work, less unpaid work), it would miss the opportunity to earn some extra money, that eventually increases commodity production via time substitution and efficiency gains. This substitution process is predicted independently of the arguments of the utility function.

The time substitution process triggered by changing opportunity costs of time can produce the following effects. First, time allocation among the general time use categories, market work versus housework, might shift – suffering from the same indeterminateness as the labor-leisure choice model. In the 'normal' case, however, in the equilibrium, a lower wage rate coincides with a lower rate of female labor force participation whereas a higher wage rate is accompanied by a higher rate of female labor force participation. Second, the demand for market goods might be altered, shifting toward time saving technologies which enable the expansion of market work at the expense of housework. Third, restructurings in the produced commodity bundle take place, involving shifts in time allocation among different household production activities.

A central implication of the model pertains to substitution processes in the production of commodities resulting from the adoption of technically advanced time saving products, particularly capital goods. With given household production objectives, the adoption of a time saving good will lead to a reduction in the amount of time spent in the respective activity in which the good is used. At the same time, the adoption makes general productivity increases in domestic production feasible. This allows for some expansion of output, i.e. commodities, either in the activity in which the newly acquired capital good is employed or in other activities.

This exposition illustrates that the predictions of the household production theory can be interpreted in two different ways. The first interpretation puts emphasis on the fact that unpaid uses of time become relatively more expensive with rising wages, and that cost considerations trigger outsourcing activities. The second interpretation focuses more strongly on the household's ultimate goals and that rising wages make an expansion of commodity production feasible when additional income is spent on productivity-enhancing capital goods. Given the assumption of nonsatiability, the household always has an incentive to increase its commodity production.

In the Beckerian framework, it is not only changes in the wage rate that provide incentives for adaptations in the organization of household production processes. Modifications will also occur when the price of a production factor (i.e. market goods) is altered; for example, a domestic appliance becomes cheaper. The production process then shifts toward techniques that are more intensive in the use of that factor and toward commodities that use the factor relatively intensively because these commodities become cheaper. This prediction is, of course, in line with the law of demand, and thus compatible with traditional consumer theory. Similarly, a qualitative improvement in a technology already in use in nonmarket production will provide an incentive for its purchase and lead to its more intensive use relative to other production factors.

In sum, Becker's approach suggests analyzing the adoption of any kinds of goods and services in light of their potential to reorganize housework activities, specifically to save time in unpaid nonmarket activities. Triggering factors are changes in the wage rate and in relative prices of input factors and eventually of commodities. The household production theory has one major implication for the analysis of the demand for household appliances:

> H.2.1: Rising wages are an important explanatory factor for the adoption of domestic appliances. Given the nonsatiation assumption pertaining to commodities, an increase in the wage rate is a sufficient condition for the purchase of time saving goods which replace the household's input of time into activities of domestic production (General Long-Run Time Substitution Hypothesis).

Hypothesis H.2.1 is a sufficient condition in that rising wages are predicted to be always followed by reallocations in time use between market work and housework, demanding the adoption of time saving goods in order to maintain or potentially raise the former level of commodity production. It is not a necessary condition, however, as the adoption of time saving goods might also occur for other reasons. Certainly, the same critical arguments as brought forth for the labor-leisure choice model hold here as well. In a strict sense, no clear-cut predictions emerge from the model, as an increase in wages could, in principle, be followed by several responses, depending on the relative magnitude of the income and substitution effect. However, in order to derive a testable implication which can be confronted with empirical data, the 'normal' case can be analyzed. It states that when rising wages raise the price of household production processes (or of commodities, for that matter), time saving capital goods are acquired as a strategy to cut down unpaid uses of time.[3]

A further implication of Becker's account concerns differences in the employment statuses of female household members: given a certain wage rate, working women should have a stronger incentive than nonworking women to adopt time saving devices – as the former should value time higher than the latter – simply because forgone earnings are higher in the former case than in the latter. This yields the following hypothesis:

> H.2.2: Differences in opportunity costs of time are an important explanatory factor for the adoption of domestic appliances. Households with

women participating in the labor force have a stronger incentive to adopt time saving goods compared with households with nonworking women (General Short-Run Time Substitution Hypothesis).

The hypothesis implies that, at a given point in time, we would expect to see a higher ownership level of time saving household appliances for dual-earner households as opposed to single-earner households. Note, however, that the model also predicts that an increase in productivity would always be an incentive to adopt a new device – independent of the changing value of time. This is because commodity production can always be increased, either in the respective activity itself or in another activity, by using a more productive technology. When technological progress turns a product into a time saving device, productivity gains are always implied. Thus, nonemployed women should have the same incentive to purchase this device as do working women. As a decline in the relative price of a technology goes in the same direction by enhancing the efficiency of domestic production processes, a similar argument can be made. These arguments point to the potential limitations of the hypothesis in terms of its explanatory value. However, what we summarized as hypothesis H.2.2 is one of the strong implications of the approach and plays a great role in the empirical analyses carried out on outsourcing decisions in nonmarket production, yet often without reference to the household production theory (cf. Chapter 6).

Applying the Becker framework to our research subject of cleanliness consumption has the advantage of using a well-established elaborate economic approach towards housework which emphasizes some structural interdependencies between market work and domestic production and also provides interesting hypotheses to start from. We will refer to these more in general as the 'time substitution hypothesis'. Even in its basic form, the household production function approach offers great heuristic potential to study such diverse phenomena as labor supply decisions and leisure choice (Heckman, 1974; Lewis, 1975; Wales and Woodland, 1977) as well as the demand for durable goods and services (Abbott and Ashenfelter, 1976; Soberon-Ferrer and Dardis, 1991; Nicol and Nakamura, 1994).[4]

But what if the diffusion of domestic appliances has also happened in times of constant wages and low female labor force participation, and in the absence of technological advances bringing time savings? Certainly, it would not be a rejection of the time substitution hypothesis to find that certain domestic appliances have also started to diffuse before the wage rate has increased or before a certain product has been developed into a time saving device. Becker does not claim that all sorts of observable behavioral changes are to be explained with regard to opportunity costs of time. In reverse, this means that Becker's account provides interesting predictions for certain historical conditions but might not be sufficient to explain the diffusion of household technology, particularly household appliances, in other periods of time, other than by making *ad hoc* assumptions.

2.2.3 Household Production Processes and Consumer Preferences

Becker's model describes how changes in the demand for market goods and the production of commodities are guided by shifts in relative prices. However, both the demand for goods and changes in commodity production might equally be guided by changes in preferences. In this subsection, we provide several arguments for why preferences are important explanatory variables for understanding the demand for household appliances and the rising technological endowment of the home. We specifically emphasize the implications of considering 'preferences for the use of time', namely the household's liking or disliking of specific activities. Based on preferences for time use, it can be differentiated between household activities that are productive and those that correspond to consumption. As we will integrate such preferences into our general framework of consumer behavior, our analysis will be fundamentally different from Becker's account.

As in the traditional theory of rational choice, preferences are assumed to be given and constant in the household production function approach.[5] In fact, the household production function approach has been developed with the aim of eliminating tastes from consumption analysis by introducing differences in household production processes and productive efficiency as explanatory elements. Becker defends this approach on the grounds that knowledge about tastes is limited (Michael and Becker, 1973; Stigler and Becker, 1977). He postulates to develop an analytic framework of consumer choice which excludes preferences as explicative variables and solely relies on monetary variables such as income and relative prices. This objective is met by assuming that households have identical and unchanging preferences. Note that preferences are defined in terms of commodities.

In his later work (Stigler and Becker, 1977) Becker demonstrates more precisely how changes in household behavior are compatible with the assumption of constant preferences or tastes but variable consumption knowledge which affects the household's skills. As in household production theory, preferences are defined in terms of commodities, not market goods. These commodities have shadow prices which depend upon the input costs of market goods and time as well as on the household's technical means and skills in terms of transforming inputs into desired outputs. The household production function is hence determined by both technical equipment and household knowledge. New information, as provided by advertisements or previous experiences in producing a certain commodity, are assumed to raise the skill level. With an increase in skill, the shadow prices of specific commodities fall, which allows for an expansion of the production output at no additional cost. The demand for market goods shifts accordingly. Once consumers have improved their skill with regard to specific commodities, they stick with producing more of them as they can be produced in a relatively more efficient and cheaper manner.

Certainly, Becker provides one possible interpretation of observable changes in behavior, but there are several points to be criticized. Foremost, it appears to be rather arbitrary to assume that new information simply affects skill instead of preferences without substantiating this further. Furthermore, commodities are defined in an inconsistent and *ad hoc* manner. Moreover, information is dealt with in a very abstract way, and apparently, it is assumed to always translate into an improvement of skills. Finally, and most importantly, the production of the commodity sets changes only according to changing relative prices, neglecting preferences and satiation levels (for further points of critique cf. Rosenberg, 1979; Ben-Porath, 1982; Ackerman, 1997, Hodgson, 2003). In that regard, Becker's account, like standard economic theory, is not capable of explaining whether it is a change in constraints or really a preference change that accounts for a shift in the demand curve (Metcalfe, 2001). The concept of a 'household production function' is basically a redefinition of differences in preferences as differences in skills. It is a modification of the labor-leisure choice analysis whose value added can be put into question. Pollak (2003) most prominently criticizes this concept: whether differences in household behavior are attributed to either different preferences or unobservable differences in household technology is not more than a semantic question, he argues (cf. also Rosenberg, 1979).

Certainly, Becker assumes preferences to be constant and identical on one side while allowing again for heterogeneity in household technology on the other. Yet, we do not share Pollak's strong criticism. For specific housework activities, differences in productivity will indeed depend on the presence of electric appliances in the home – which is an element of household technology that is observable via household surveys. Also, preferences are not completely unobservable. Consumer surveys can tell a good deal about the motivational underpinnings of specific activities. Pollak's critique is nevertheless well put for another reason, namely that household technology and consumer preferences are so difficult to disentangle. This problem results from the analytical exposition and the lack of a consistent definition of the central concept 'commodities'. Concerning the analytical exposition in Becker (1965), it is assumed that utility U is dependent upon commodities Z, which are produced with the help of market goods x and time t. Becker writes:

$$U = U(Z[x, t]), \text{ such that } U(x, t).$$

The latter expression is subject to maximization. Thus, the objective household production technology is depicted interchangeably with consumer preferences. One might even argue that utility is eventually defined over market goods and time use – what Becker wanted to avoid. This result stems from the fact that no explicit production function is specified in the analytical model. As a result, the introduction of the two concepts, household technology and commodities, is rather questionable.[6]

In what follows, we will list the shortcomings of the commodity concept and elaborate on its consequences for household production analysis. In the next subsection, we put forth a suggestion of how to enrich the commodity concept, which will allow for a meaningful integration of consumer preferences into the analysis of home production processes. To begin with, simply assuming that commodities provide utility does not tell why this is the case. Certainly, Michael and Becker (1973) address the sources of utility when they refer to Bentham's concept of 'simple pleasures', which include senses, riches, address, friendship, good reputation, power, piety, benevolence, malevolence, knowledge, memory, imagination, hope, association and pain relief (Bentham, 1948 [1789], pp. 33–42). But due to the rather *ad hoc* listing of commodities during the analysis, Becker does not carefully distinguish the cardinal output of production processes, i.e. technological aspects, from ordinal numbers representing preference ordering, i.e. tastes. Hence, commodities such as listening to music are confounded with what might be called 'utilities', such as pleasures of the senses. In the framework, it is not clear where production processes stop and where utility begins (Pollak and Wachter, 1975; Pollak, 2003). Hence, tastes and technology are confounded.

Reid (1934) has suggested the 'third-person criterion' for differentiating among nonmarket activities. This idea has been taken up in accounting frameworks, in that nonmarket productive time is distinguishable from personal time by means of the third-person criterion (Goldschmidt-Clermont, 1993). According to this criterion, an activity is deemed productive if it might be performed by someone other than the person benefiting from it or if its performance can be delegated to someone else while achieving the desired result.[7] Certainly, intuition suggests that watching TV or eating food, for instance, cannot be outsourced to some external subject as this commodity requires consumption by the household itself. In other words, a person cannot satisfy his or her longing for food by having somebody else eating his or her meal. With meal preparation, however, it is exactly the opposite. More in general, one could argue that whenever an input of goods has to be further manipulated in the household to make it more useful for the consumer, but where the household does not derive utility from this 'manipulation', it is a mere productive activity. The latter case would hold, for instance, for meal preparation or doing laundry, if the household did prefer spending its time alternatively but did not have the opportunity to do so. Note that such a statement requires assumptions about preferences. In fact, it hints to the objectivity and generalizability of at least some set of preferences. Otherwise, how should an outsider evaluate which types of activities truly appeal to consumers' needs and which do not? Apparently, it is assumed that at least some preferences are shared among consumers – an assumption that we share, as it can be empirically substantiated (cf. Section 2.3).

Take another example. Commodities are the result of market goods being combined with time. But which of the market goods that function as inputs into production processes are only production factors, and which goods will be transformed into commodities? If, for instance, appliances, electricity and food are 'combined' together with the household's time to prepare a meal, then all of them are labeled 'factors of production' x, although only the processed food will be transformed into a desired commodity z. Thus, assumptions about preferences have to be made in order to distinguish between these distinct entities.

Let us now take a closer look at the situation where the consumer engages in an activity and also enjoys doing it. In contrast to Becker's assumption of an objective value of time, consumers might have preferences for specific activities, such that time spent in different activities is of different value to the consumer.[8] In fact, consumer surveys on 'activity enjoyment ratings' have shown that different activities, i.e. ways to spend time, are felt rewarding or unpleasant to a different extent (Robinson and Godbey, 1997, p. 241). In the surveys, consumers had to indicate to which extent they were 'satisfied' with a certain activity, or 'enjoy' or 'like' a specific activity (the scale varying from 1 to 5 or 1 to 10). The activities listed covered sports, TV, childcare, cleaning and cooking, among others. Interestingly, surveys carried out between 1973 and 1985 found that cleaning activities, i.e. house cleaning, laundry washing and so on, were among the activities rather disliked. Regarding these activities, consumers indicated a level of enjoyment that was below the average of all other activities.

These findings suggest that the analysis of domestic production processes would benefit from making assumptions about the preferences involved. This argument also holds for the following situation. Take two household production activities directed toward the production of two distinct commodities. Assume that technological progress brings about technically more advanced products in both these activities and that a consumer has to decide which one of the technically more advanced devices to acquire. When one product is chosen instead of the other, Becker would conclude that the commodities associated with this product are of higher value to the consumer. But there is also the possibility that both commodities are equally appreciated and that one activity is more detested than the other. The latter explanation refers to preferences for time use.[9] Two possible explanations can thus be brought forth. In order not to miss the explanatory potential for understanding changing consumption patterns, more elements of household production activities need to be taken into account. Thus, whenever Becker's framework is applied to a specific case, as will be done here, assumptions about preferences have to be made concerning both the use of time as well as the content of commodities.

The assumption that household production activities are 'preference free' has been criticized most prominently by Pollak and Wachter (1975), who also derive the analytical implications of this assumption for the analysis of household behavior. They argue that the predictions of the household production function approach depend crucially on the assumptions of constant returns to scale and the absence of 'joint production' – which is what Becker assumes. The assumption of the absence of joint production means that utility is only defined in terms of the output of household production processes and that distinct activities, for instance, time spent cooking and time spent cleaning, are neutral from the perspective of the household. However, the time spent cooking or cleaning might be a direct source of utility or disutility to the household. In this case, household decisions about the allocation of time reflect not only technological conditions but also household preferences as to the use of time.[10] When production processes exhibit joint production, commodity prices do not fulfill their function as proper signals of the household's constraints (input prices and technology). Instead, they depend on the household's tastes concerning the use of time and the chosen commodity bundle. Consequently, the analogy between market prices and shadow prices does not hold anymore. The household is not a 'price taker', and utility can no longer be maximized with regard to commodity shadow prices. With joint production, there no longer exists a straightforward price-demand-function for commodities. Differences in commodity prices thus reflect the household's opportunities as well as its tastes, and there is a gap between the marginal utility value of the domestic product and the market opportunity cost of the homemaker (Chiswick, 1982).

Hence, the central implication of assuming the absence of preferences for the use of time is that time – like other input factors – amounts to only a cost factor. It is an input factor which unfolds clear-cut effects on commodity production, given a specific household technology and household production function. Changes in the value of time affect commodities' shadow prices and thus trigger predictable restructurings of the commodity bundle produced. Were preferences for the use of time existent, then changes in the wage rate could not unfold the same impact on all commodities, differentiated with respect to their time intensity. Instead, the effects were indeterminate. By simply assuming preferences 'away', comparative-static implications can be derived, but they need not have much explanatory power when such preferences do indeed exist and possibly also evolve in the long run.

Preferences might interfere with the outsourcing process in a further dimension, namely insofar that market goods and home-produced goods are not seen as substitutes (cf. Weagley and Norum, 1989).[11] Instead, there might be boundaries for substitution between market goods and home-made goods based on the household's preferences, i.e. its assessment of what is a proper substitute for home production (Brown and Preece, 1987). Arguably, the 'appropriateness' of a substitute is neither an entirely subjective matter nor an objective characteristic of a product. Take children's early education as an example. The homemaker herself might regard raising children as her personal duty and thus not hire a nurse. Her opinion, in turn, might be rooted in a social convention, which she follows to the extent that she cares about her social standing in society (Preece, 1990). Likewise, one can imagine that market work becomes more attractive when societal ideologies degrade housework and being a full-time homemaker. Hence, social agreements as to the appropriateness of certain forms of behavior might interfere with the decision of doing-it-yourself versus employing a market alternative. Gender roles and normative expectations are examples (cf. Berk, 1985; Robinson and Milkie, 1998; Preece, 1990). The household's social surroundings might also affect consumer choice and the structure of the commodity bundle produced at home, i.e. its quantitative and qualitative composition (Brown and Preece, 1987; Preece, 1990, p. 25). As normative expectations and preferences are closely interrelated, an understanding, in which activities normative expectations play a role, and under which conditions their impact on consumer behavior changes, will generate valuable insights into the study of nonmarket production (Preece, 1990).

There is a further point of critique. Assume that the conditions for substitution are given in a certain activity and that a productivity enhancing market good has been acquired. As a concrete example, let the adoption of a washing machine reduce the amount of time that has to be spent for producing one kg of clean clothes. Now that clothes can be cleansed more efficiently, consumers can either clean more clothes than before in the same amount of time, or they can use the freed amount of time to expand the production of commodities other than clean clothes, for instance, spend more time on cooking a meal. In which direction will the expansion of commodity production go? In order to assess consumer reactions to changing relative prices within the household production technology, the shape of the indifferences curves has to be known and assumed to be constant. Otherwise, no predictions as to the income and substitution effects are possible. Material conjectures are needed in order to understand why consumers choose a certain commodity expansion path, while alternative uses of time also exist. One might have to carry out a more detailed case study analysis to get a feeling for the actual mechanisms underlying a specific consumption activity. But once this picture has been developed, it is questionable whether an application of the utility calculus can provide some value added. Naturally, one can always assume well-behaved preferences to have an analytically tractable analysis. However, this need not be an adequate description of reality. And to assume nonsatiation is comparatively weaker than explaining why nonsatiation exists, i.e. why consumers expand cleanliness production, for instance, when these commodities become cheaper. As commodities remain a black box in Becker's account, the theory cannot indicate what it is that people want more of, why that is and how it changes – which, by the way, also holds for other proponents of the 'new home economics' such as Lancaster (1966) and Ironmonger (1972).[12]

It is a general shortcoming of neoclassical consumer theory to be so general that the derived household optimum can be made compatible with a variety of observable behaviors (Hodgson, 2003). Yet, in order to derive concrete, empirically rich hypotheses, which allow observations also to be inconsistent with the model, detailed information on actual consumer preferences, production plans and the decision-making process have to be integrated (Witt, 1987, p. 78). We argue that an important step forward would be achieved when some substantial assumptions about the content of consumer preferences are brought forth – including a definition of the commodity set as well as preferences for the use of time. The value added by introducing the theoretical concepts 'commodity' and 'household production function' into the analysis is overall questionable if these concepts are not given more substance. Especially in a historical view, both preferences and the physical-technological conditions of housework are subject to change. These changes are likely to have implications for consumption behavior. In accordance with Witt (1987), it seems more fruitful to integrate theories about the motivational underpinnings of consumer behavior into consumption analysis instead of eliminating them and their explicative potential.

Our final point of critique concerns the neglect of consumer learning processes by assuming full information and maximization. Even in the (unrealistic) case of a static consumption environment, where the set and type of available products does not change, it is not reasonable to assume that consumers are informed about all existing products in terms of knowing their utility-generating potential and their optimal function within the individual household production technology. More likely, consumers have formed some limited understanding about which kinds of products are able to meet which kinds of consumers' ultimate goals. Thus, when changing opportunity costs of time induce the household to scrutinize the given setup of household production processes, it will take time and effort to figure out how to successfully reorganize the potentially suboptimal domestic production activities. Households might start new exploration processes of the product market. The crucial question is how consumers will decide which kinds of goods will improve their situation, having realized a shift in opportunity costs of time. In order to answer this question, conjectures about the forms and contingencies of consumer-learning processes have to be advanced. The story does not become less complicated when, over time, new products appear on the market, thus increasing the variety to choose from. Consumers cannot be assumed to know *ex ante* the relative advantage of newly emerging products compared with existing product alternatives that might already be part of the household technology. Processes of exploration will thus also take place in that case, mediating the transition from one household production setup to the following one. The outcome of the adjustment process need not be optimal in the sense of a utility-maximizing behavior, however, but rather reflect the contingencies of the actual learning processes. Thus, if the household production function approach claims empirical relevance for long-term development, it needs to be concerned with processes of consumer learning instead of simply assuming full information and utility-maximizing behavior. For both, changing opportunity costs of time as well as qualitative product change are an empirical reality.[13] We turn to the origins and implications of qualitative change in the following section.

2.3 A Behavioral Perspective on Household Production and Technical Change

2.3.1 *'Approach-Avoidance-Conflicts' in Human Behavior*

The household production function approach is a goal-oriented theory of consumer behavior. From the consumer's perspective, it only counts how many commodities are produced and not the means by which this is achieved, for means are relevant only as cost factors straining the budget constraint. But what if consumers have a liking for some housework activities rather than others, as is suggested by the aforementioned findings from consumer surveys (compiled in Robinson and Godbey, 1997)?[14] Then, time allocation is affected by preferences for the use of time and not by the ultimate goals alone. Convincing arguments for including preferences for time use in the analysis of household production processes come from psychological theories of motivation as well as behavioral psychology (cf. Weiner, 1994; Frieman, 2002). In this section, we present evidence for the assumption that people care about how the domestic production process itself is organized, i.e. with what kind of tools it is carried out. This is an important ingredient for the later analysis as we reject Becker's assumption of the absence of preferences for time use. The psychological basis will shortly be reviewed and then applied to study consumption behavior in general and the demand for cleanliness in particular.

Let us now turn to the most elementary aspects of human behavior as described by psychological theories of motivation. Any organism is programmed to maintain a balanced inner state called 'homeostasis'. In fact, all living things possess some internal receptors which monitor the internal environment for the occurrence of imbalances. When imbalances are perceived, the organism is inclined to take corrective action (Frieman, 2002, p. 125). Deprivation states of the organism, in terms of biological basic needs, function as a strong motivating force. They trigger actions which lead to the removal of deprivation. More precisely, they lead to the formation of goals and the mobilization of energy to attain these goals. The tendency of organisms to carry out certain actions is referred to as 'drives' (Hull, 1943). The intensity of the drive depends upon the degree of deprivation. With stronger deprivation, the organism is willing to take into account more obstacles and it will direct more energy towards the removal of deprivation. The strength of deprivation can also give rise to a variable hierarchy among needs in terms of more or less urgent goals. However, although goal achievement is the trigger of behavior ('drive'), the organism need not, at any price, seek to reach the goal (Carver and Scheier, 1990). The body has developed mechanisms, i.e. forms of self-regulation, which lead to the withdrawal from goal achievement when this endeavor becomes too costly or when the outcomes are too difficult to assess. From the viewpoint of natural selection, this makes perfect sense. Thus, some internal mechanism is needed to trace the achievement of goals (or the degree of goal attainment classified as satisfactory – referred to as 'satisficing') and end the activity such that the next relevant goal will be approached (Simon, 1967).

In the psychological literature on motivation, it is commonplace to assume some kind of internal meta-measuring rod that exerts behavioral control in terms of continuing or ending actions. In simple terms, individuals monitor their present actions and compare the qualities of these with internal reference values (Simon, 1967; Frijda, 1988; Carver and Scheier, 1990). The monitoring process is ongoing. By the encounter of adverse conditions implying the feeling of negative affect, the individual stops carrying out a specific action and reassesses the behavior in terms of the likelihood of goal achievement and the effort this will take. These expectations might be based on prior experiences with this action but do not necessarily require much cognitive involvement. In extreme cases, an individual wants a certain task to be completed but has no desire to carry it out him or herself. In such a case, the organism wants immediate goal achievement, i.e. to reach the goal instantaneously. But this is an aspiration too high to be met at all. The internal monitoring system thus recognizes aversiveness as soon as the individual starts to actually carry out this action. An action involving the experience of drudgery, i.e. heavy physical effort, is such a case (Carver and Scheier, 1990, p. 26). Note that drudgery avoidance will be addressed as one of the central motivations behind the diffusion of washing machines (cf. Chapters 4–6).

This situation, whereby organisms experience problems when approaching goals and decide somehow whether to continue or disengage from the respective action, corresponds to a conflict in behavior that might give rise to ambivalent forms of behavior. More in general, individuals often face a so-called 'approach-avoidance-conflict', which occurs when the same action is associated with both rewarding experiences as well as objections (Miller, 1944; Miller, 1959; Lewin, 1951; Elliot and Church, 1997; Elliot, 2006). The conflict is inherent in situations where an organism is driven towards a goal – for instance, obtaining food so as to restore homeostatic equilibrium – but where the action required for goal achievement elicits painful experiences. If two behavioral tendencies stand in conflict with one another, the stronger motivational force will push through (Weiner, 1994, p. 95). A typical experimental setting for analyzing this phenomenon involves rats which are more or less strongly deprived of food. The animals are put in a box, at the end of which some food is placed. The animals clearly have an urge to go for the food, but in order to reach the goal they have to move along a path that is sending electric shocks (cf. Miller, 1959).[15] This experience clearly goes against the organism's basic needs. Arguably, these basic experiments can also shed some light on more complex forms of human behavior (Weiner, 1994, p. 92).[16]

Such conflicts in behavioral tendencies emerge because human behavior follows a general principle by which the positive or negative valence of actions or activities has an impact on the frequencies with which certain behaviors are shown and on whether some actions are taken at all (Frieman, 2002). As substantiated in behavioral psychology, individuals take actions that they find rewarding and seek ways to avoid or reduce in frequency those actions that elicit negative experiences. The 'matching law' and melioration learning in behavioral psychology provide empirical evidence for this conjecture (Herrnstein and Prelec, 1991). This behavioral disposition is innate and is shared among humans:

> H.2.3: Individuals tend to avoid or reduce in frequency those activities that elicit negative sensory feedback, while increasing in frequency those activities that yield positive sensory feedback, i.e. that have positive associations (Behavior Hypothesis).

Certainly, individuals might differ in terms of what they classify as rewarding or painful because of differences in individuals' past experiences. This argument, in fact, is at the core of adaptation level theory (Helson, 1964).[17] At the same time, there also exists a basis for commonalities in classifying situations, activities as well as objects, which stems from the shared genetic basis of humans. First of all, deprivation states, in terms of basic needs, are experienced as painful by all organisms, which is why they show the same behavioral tendency to remove deprivation. Secondly, when in states of deprivation and presented with a so-called primary reinforcer, i.e. an object suited to restore the homeostatic balance, all organisms develop a positive valence toward this object (Lewin, 1951):

> H.2.4: Commonalities in human genetic basis unite individuals in classifying certain activities as either rewarding or unpleasant (Commonalities Hypothesis).

Behavioral psychology has identified, among others, the following basic needs: caloric intake, stable body temperature, the avoidance of pain and upkeep of a healthy body, cognitive arousal, social recognition and so forth. Those needs belong to the genetic makeup of humans and are therefore shared among them. When in states of deprivation, objects and actions appropriate for satisfying these basic needs are primary reinforcers (or unconditioned stimuli, cf. Frieman, 2002; Witt, 2001).[18] The avoidance of pain has been mentioned as a basic human need. Physically painful experiences cause a homeostatic imbalance, mobilizing the individual to find relief from the pain. When a specific action is the source of the painful experience, avoidance behavior is triggered. When a specific stimulus has become associated with unpleasant feelings, fear towards and avoidance of the stimulus is triggered (Weiner, 1994, p. 88). According to Cordes (2005), heavy physical effort classifies as a negatively experienced action, which individuals seek to circumvent. It is a disposition likely to be shared among modern humans as it has evolved during human phylogeny for its evolutionary advantage: in times of limited availability of food, a higher survival chance went to those organisms that economized best on their limited amount of energy.

When the outcome of a specific action is experienced as rewarding but taking the action yields painful experiences, a conflict emerges at the level of basic behavioral dispositions. To resolve such a conflict, several behaviors are possible. First, the individual masters the avoidance tendency and approaches the goal. Second, the individual foregoes the goal in order to avoid the unpleasant experience. The latter can only be a short-run reaction in situations of food deprivation, for example. Third, the individual starts searching for ways by which to attain the goal in a more pleasant way. The latter case corresponds to the situation whereby humans engage in creative activities, the outcome of which are technical means that reduce or eliminate the conflict. We turn to this issue in the following section.

2.3.2 Implications for Technical Change and Product Advertisements

Let us now dwell on the interrelation between consumer motivations and technical change in consumer products and trace how demand-side influences on market development shape the path of technical change and product diffusion over time.

Taking a look back at human early history, one finds that humans have creatively coped with situations of conflict by inventing simple tools (Torrence, 1989). Also, in modern times, patterns of innovative activity and technological creativity might still show some connection to human genetic endowment. Cordes (2005) hypothesizes that one motivation for employing tools and machinery, and thus one driving force of technological evolution and technological creativity, might be the indirect satisfaction of the want to avoid excessive physical activity. Long-term labor saving technological progress in particular, he conjectures, might be related to the shared human motivation to avoid heavy physical effort (Cordes, 2002, p. 94; Cordes, 2005). In line with Cordes (2002), we argue that regularities in long-term technical change (synonymously: technological progress) can be traced back to human shared motivational basis. More specifically, we postulate a close relationship between technological progress and conflicts at the level of basic behavioral drives. In that regard, we view the invention and diffusion of technologies as a strategy to shift the valence of certain activities and to reduce the avoidance tendency in behavior. It is important to note that the switch in behavioral reactions is closely related to specific regional-historical circumstances.[19]

Arguably, this relationship might not only hold for industrial production processes, but for the mechanization of domestic production as well. Let us now relate the motivational underpinnings of technological progress to consumption behavior. Replace the term 'individual' or 'human' by 'consumer' and consider the following line of argument. Assume that consumers share certain basic needs for their common genetic endowment (Witt, 2001) and that these commonalities make consumers experience certain circumstances or situations in a similar way. Then, consumers are also united in identifying certain conditions as pleasant and others as 'problems' ('shared social understandings', cf. Chapter 3). When consumers are united in identifying certain problems and looking for solutions to these jointly experienced problems, there is a potentially large latent demand for specific types of consumption products and hence a strong incentive for producers to carry out innovative searches. This point is in line both with 'demand pull' theory (cf. Mowery and Rosenberg, 1979) and the idea of 'technological paradigms', in that innovative efforts at some point in time are directed toward specific 'problems' ranked as 'relevant' in a society (Dosi, 1982; Loasby, 2001). Naturally, producers have to form an understanding of what it is that consumers want and what they are able to do (Langlois and Cosgel, 1998). The important point is that, in such a case, the producers' conjectures and directions of creative search are highly consistent with the consumers' true problems in terms of experiencing need deprivation with respect to a specific consumption activity. The purchase of consumption goods of appropriate quality and quantity can then be viewed as the individuals' problem-solving strategy. In other words, conflicting motivations trigger not only technological creativity by producers but simultaneous search processes on the part of the consumers. This congruity of producer and consumer actions holds for longer time periods, say 50 years or so. Certainly, the institutional setting constrains or enables technological progress to actually take place (Cordes, 2005).

The recognition of consumption goods as solutions to the problem experienced is contingent upon learning processes on the part of the consumers (Witt, 2001). We will take a closer look at consumer learning in the following subsection. For now, let us dwell on product advertising only, which is one way by which learning is accomplished (Bandura, 1986). From the previous line of reasoning results the following implications for product advertisements. First, advertisements for newly developed consumption goods can be expected to contain some reference to the original problem which has given rise to the creative search and product innovation in the first place, for advertisements are a way for producers to signal that they offer a solution to a specific prominent problem. We have defined such problems as conflicting motivations which are rooted in human genetic endowment and become manifest in specific behavioral contexts or consumption activities. This strand of reasoning yields the following hypothesis (cf. also Chapter 5):

> H.2.5: Producers use advertisements to inform consumers about existing problem solutions. Shifts in advertisement content of a product reflect changes in shared consumer motivations for consuming that product (Advertisement Content Hypothesis).

As a second implication, fluctuations in advertising intensity are historically contingent. They depend upon the urgency of the problem, which the respective product addresses. This point deserves some further comments. First of all, the intensity of the innovative search is historically contingent (Witt, 1993) as it varies with circumstances and the urgency of the problem. When innovative effort and innovative outcomes show a positive correlation (Dosi, 1982), the rate of innovation is also historically contingent. At the same time, producers should have an incentive to increase the visibility of their products in times of potentially high demand, i.e. when consumers show a high propensity to look for solutions to problems shared with others. As a result, fluctuations in advertisement intensity are historically contingent. [20]

Naturally, not all sorts of technical change show some connection to the human biological basis. But when technological progress is indeed directed toward problems that affect basic human needs, long-term changes in advertisement intensity are indicators of the satiation status of this exact need. A drop in advertisement intensity, for instance, corresponds to a satiation of a need – at least temporary – with regard to a specific consumption activity. Naturally,

additional conjectures are needed to explain ongoing technological development in a specific activity beyond the point that, for instance, effort-reducing
motives are met. With these hypotheses, we suggest that technical change at
the level of consumer products follows certain regularities in the long run,
which stem from demand-side influences on market development. Shared consumer motivations are assumed to shape the path of technical change and product diffusion over time. During a given time period, certain need-satisfying
properties should be immanent in all novel or qualitatively modified products.
As our approach is devoted to explaining why all consumer goods should share
certain general properties in the long run, we pay less attention to differences
in the makeup of products and to consumer choice between products at a
given point in time. Yet we do acknowledge that explorative processes might
generate various technological variants of products until the prevailing product
variant emerges (cf. Chapter 4).

The strand of argument developed here shows some overlap with several
strands of the literature that seek to overcome the dichotomy between technology push and demand pull versions of technical change. These strands of
literature emphasize the importance of actors jointly recognizing certain technological problems or challenges and that sufficient homogeneity of expectations is achieved, such that technical problems finally find a solution. Dosi
(1982) has pointed out that neither the supply nor the demand side alone
can adequately explain technological progress and that rather technological
paradigms guide and restrict the path of technical change. Further arguments
can be found in the literature on the sociology of technology, particularly the
social construction of technology (SCOT) (Pinch and Bijker, 1987; Pinch,
1996). The basic idea behind social constructivism is that artifacts are underde-
termined by the natural world and rather are constructions of individuals. The
social constructivist perspective maintains that technologies do not develop
autonomously along the lines of scientific progress ('technological determin-
ism'). Hence, technological progress is not a mere diffusion of new products
within society ('technology push hypothesis'). Instead, social interest groups
have an impact on the path which technological development eventually takes.
This is because goals and problems of potential users shape the final outcome
of the artifact. Still, the approach taken here shows one major difference to
SCOT: the social constructivist literature rather seeks to identify conflicts of
interest between social groups and traces how they eventually have been solved
(e.g. public discourse and social power relations), resulting in a specific type of
artifact, referred to as 'closure'. That way, success stories and market failures of
artifacts can be better understood.

We, on the contrary, provide a foundation for the homogeneity of interests,
stemming from shared innate needs and the joint experience of historical circumstances. We thus push the argument of the demand-side impacts on innovation processes a little bit even further.[21] For that exact reason, several other
accounts dealing with technological progress and product diffusion are not
addressed in more detail, although they show some overlap with our research

objective in one way or another. Product life cycle theory (cf. Abernathy and Utterback, 1978; Windrum and Birchenhall, 1998) and the history of technology (cf. Rosenberg, 1982) more strongly concentrate on production side processes. The diffusion of innovations account (originating with Rogers (1995), formalized in Bass (1969)) focuses on differences in consumer types, whereas we analyze commonalities in dispositions and consumer behavior. When assuming commonalities in consumer motivations for acquiring a certain product, as is done in our account, sequential adoption processes of products are merely a question of disposable income, not of differences in personality traits. Our hypotheses are yet only loosely linked to consumer behavior. We turn to this issue in the following section.

2.3.3 Learning to Appreciate Products

How do changes in motivational states translate into changing consumption patterns? Obviously, a necessary condition for this process is the invention and supply of suitable consumption products. In addition to that, consumers have to learn which products will be able to bring about the removal of deprivation. These issues are the subject of the theory of learning consumers by Ulrich (Witt, 2001), to which we now turn.

Witt's account is specifically insightful in that it deals with what we term preferences for the use of time in the context of the household production theory (Witt himself does not employ this terminology). As in the household production theory, Witt's account acknowledges that consumer behavior takes time, but Witt does not conceptualize time as an input cost that exhibits an influence in the form of a constraint. Instead, time is considered insofar as Witt's approach is a behavioral account which analyzes consumption behavior as activities (for an activity perspective, cf. the works of Linder, 1970; Scitovsky, 1976; and Metcalfe, 2001). The theory of learning consumers opens up towards neighboring disciplines, particularly psychology and social psychology. It is compatible with the findings from the behavioral sciences reviewed earlier and results in a richer and empirically sound description of actual human behavior (for a further account of consumer behavior that draws upon the experimental analysis of behavior, particularly radical behaviorism, cf. Foxall, 1990).[22]

At the same time, Witt's approach shares several conceptual elements with the household production function approach. Like Becker, Witt assumes that demand is derived from higher-order goals. Utility or pleasure are not associated with goods themselves, because goods only have instrumental value. Both approaches introduce a novel concept for such goals: Becker talks about commodities, while Witt defines those ultimate goals as basic consumer needs and learned wants.[23] The novelty of both theories, in contrast to the standard theory of rational choice, is to acknowledge that there exist motivations independent from goods and that it is worthwhile to give these an independent ontological status. Interestingly, both approaches refer to Bentham's idea of 'basic pleasures'. But the household production function account ends half way and does not work out a fully fledged motivational concept. In fact, the commodity concept is still underspecified, despite the welter of research on the subject (Gronau and Hamermesh, 2006). Although Becker defines commodities as the household's ultimate goals, applications of Becker's account associate commodities with the physical output of household production processes, for example, a home-cooked meal (Weagley and Norum, 1989) or clean clothes (Gramm, 1974). From that perspective, commodities are distinct from basic needs in the sense of Witt. In order not to confound these issues, we define consumers' ultimate goals as basic needs while we link commodities to the household production output in its physical form (cf. Section 2.4).[24]

In contrast to Becker, Witt is concerned with developing a systematic approach for analyzing the role of consumer motivations in changing consumption behavior. In fact, it is the feedback between the evolution of products on one side (product innovation, including technical change) and the evolution of motivations on the other that is examined in order to understand market development. Becker's account remains merely at the technological level and focuses on consumption goods which enhance the efficiency of household production processes – i.e. products that consumers should always appreciate, given that commodity production becomes cheaper and consumers are never satiated in terms of commodities. Witt, on the contrary, acknowledges that consumers might be temporarily satiated with regard to specific needs in a specific consumption activity or expenditure category, and analyzes the conditions under which such satiation levels would shift. Witt's account is insightful in that it links technological progress to changing consumption patterns via learning processes. The most striking difference between the two consumer theories thus lies in the treatment of preferences and consumer motivations. By turning to Witt's behavioral account, we can also make explicit assumptions about the content of consumer preferences, including preferences for the use of time.

Before we present the theory of learning consumers in more detail, we shall mention that it is one of the few overarching consumer theories within the field of evolutionary economics, which has dealt much more strongly with the supply side phenomena of economic change. Evolutionary economics criticizes neoclassical consumer theory for its assumptions of full information and optimization and postulates instead the role of uncertainty and learning processes for actual consumer behavior. Most evolutionary economic scholars consider routine-based approaches to household consumption behavior as a realistic and fruitful alternative to the neoclassical account (Langlois and Cosgel, 1998; Loasby, 2001; Metcalfe, 2001; Nelson and Consoli, 2010; Hodgson, 2003). Often, differences in consumer behavior rather than commonalities are subjects of analysis (Loasby, 2001; Metcalfe, 2001). Prominent examples are the routine-based approaches by Metcalfe (2001) and by Nelson and Consoli (2010). Rooted in the evolutionary economic framework, these approaches do share several elements with Witt's account. With regard to our research objective, however, they are not so well suited. In contrast to Witt, Nelson and Consoli (2010) do not provide detailed hypotheses about the forms and processes of consumer learning and they do not distinguish between consumers' ultimate goals on one side and the means for satisfying these goals on the other.[25] Exactly these explanatory elements can be found in Metcalfe's (2001) formal model of adaptive behavior and melioration learning, yet Metcalfe makes no assumptions about the content of consumer preferences.

Let us now turn to the theory of learning consumers in more detail.[26] Witt suggests a material specification of the ultimate goals by assuming that consumer behavior is directed toward the satisfaction of basic needs. Individuals are motivated through their basic needs to engage in consumptive activities. Given that basic needs belong to the genetic makeup of humans, Witt assumes commonalities in consumers' motivational basis. Need satisfaction is achieved by the consumption of specific goods and services of appropriate quality and quantity. In Witt's framework, consumers do not have a priori knowledge about the suitability of consumption goods in achieving their goals. On the contrary, associations between products (means) and the removal of deprivation (ultimate goals) have to be learned first. Although the need satisfaction property is, in principle, an objective attribute of a consumption good, it still has to be explored by the consumer first. Hence, consumer behavior is rather driven by beliefs, i.e. consumer understanding of which good appeals to which consumer need:

> H.2.6: The consumption of a good, covering purchase and use, is closely related to the consumer understanding concerning the type of consumer needs appealed to by this good (Needs Hypothesis).

The account by Witt allows, in principle, for a discrepancy between the 'true', objective relationship between consumption goods and the satisfaction of basic needs on the one hand versus consumer subjective beliefs about this relationship on the other. Changes in consumption behavior would hence occur whenever the objective need satisfaction potential of a good and/or the consumer beliefs regarding this function changes. Witt hence suggests that product innovation, advertisements, public discourse and consumer learning processes can bring about these changes. Note that we will refer to 'consumption activities' more in general to cover both the acquisition and the utilization of a consumption good. We define consumer learning as follows:

> Definition of consumer learning: Consumer learning processes are all the types of behavioral actions that establish new associations (cognitive, non-cognitive) between the satisfaction of consumer needs on one side and consumption activities on the other ('means-ends-relationships').

Learning concerns, first of all, the appropriateness of the types of consumption activities as such. In simple terms, consumers will have to discover which type of goods will appeal to which basic needs. In addition to that, consumers develop beliefs concerning appropriate consumption levels of certain goods. The need satisfaction capacity to be discovered is not an entirely subjective matter, however. First, the common genetic basis which humans share makes some products rather than others suitable for need satisfaction, which will hold for all consumers alike (cf. hypothesis H.2.4). Second, similarities in learning processes emerge whenever consumers encounter similar sources of information – including a certain homogenization of beliefs in intensively interacting consumer groups. Witt (2001) considers these kinds of learning processes as an important condition for the diffusion of qualitatively modified and novel goods.[27]

While the acquisition of pieces of information is a cognitive form of learning, learning can also take noncognitive forms. Also, elementary learning processes can contribute to a better understanding of the need satisfaction quality of goods. In behavioral psychology, two types of noncognitive learning are distinguished: classical (or Pavlovian) conditioning and operant conditioning (Frieman, 2002, Chapter 2).[28] Let us briefly have a look at these mechanisms. Classical conditioning establishes new associations between events and elicits an emotional or physical reaction to a formerly neutral stimulus. The basic approach is to present individuals with two types of stimuli ('events'), one of which will elicit a certain, possibly genetically programmed, response. The other stimulus is neutral in the first place but becomes associated with that other stimulus with repetition, hence producing the same kind of behavioral response. This experimental manipulation, called 'associative pairing', changes the affective evaluation of the formerly neutral stimulus in terms of liking-disliking in the direction of the evaluation of the event that already possesses strong positive or negative values (e.g. a biologically relevant stimulus; cf. Zajonc, 1984; Levey and Martin, 1990; Frieman, 2002, p. 128). The valence of the biologically relevant stimulus is carried over to the originally neutral event as the organism interprets the latter as an indicator of the occurrence of the biologically important event (Frieman, 2002, Chapter 2). In other words, the hedonic valence from an active stimulus becomes transferred to a neutral stimulus (Levey and Martin, 1990). It is therefore a way of changing the motivational significance of events and objects, triggering approach or avoidance tendencies toward the conditioned stimulus (Frieman, 2002, p. 128). At the same time, classical conditioning is a way of drawing causal inferences, i.e. connections between causes and effects that result in mental representations and hence require some degree of cognitive processing (Frieman, 2002, Chapter 5). The learning process might be reflected in changed frequencies of certain behavioral variants.[29]

Operant conditioning or 'instrumental learning' usually occurs simultaneously with classical conditioning (Frieman, 2002, p. 133) and affects the frequency distribution of behaviors. In simple terms, it corresponds to the trial-and-error learning of new behaviors, which has been demonstrated by E.L. Thorndike and B.F. Skinner in experimental settings with animals. The basic idea is that the relative frequency, with which a type of behavior is shown, depends upon the consequences of this exact behavior in terms of positive or negative sensory experiences: actions that are characterized by relatively high rewards will be taken more frequently than actions that yield relatively low rewards (Frieman, 2002, Chapter 7; cf. hypothesis H.2.3). Changes in behavior occur when an individual takes a novel action or encounters a novel stimulus by chance and experiences it as either rewarding or painful, or when the consequences of a given behavior change. Such behavioral consequences are either the removal of a negative stimulus or the presentation of an appetitive stimulus, implying reinforcement, i.e. an increase in the likelihood of the occurrence of that behavior. A decrease in the likelihood of a certain behavior is the result of punishment. For example, individuals learn not to take actions which they have come to associate with unpleasant feelings ('avoidance conditioning'). When a stimulus that triggers avoidance behaviors is taken away, thus increasing the likelihood that a certain behavior will be shown, it is called 'negative reinforcement'. The underlying principle is that different stimuli can be compared in terms of the relative rewards that they elicit and that the consequences of certain behaviors affect the future occurrence of these exact behaviors. Instrumental learning is a way to become more efficient in the search for desired objects and the avoidance of danger, and it holds for the learning of new behaviors. In fact, conditioning learning can give rise to the emergence of complex forms of behavior (cf. the overview given in Foxall, 1990 and Frieman, 2002). Were, at some point in time, no new stimuli to be encountered by the individual, a stable frequency distribution of behaviors would emerge in which the relative frequencies, with which certain actions are taken, are proportional to their relative rewards, referred to as 'matching law' (Herrnstein, 1970).

Witt (2001) argues that these general principles should also apply to changes in consumption patterns, in that consumers seek to avoid activities that they find unpleasant and want to engage in actions that are rewarding. Consumption activities can thus be compared in terms of the relative rewards, i.e. the positive feelings that they elicit. This statement implies more in general that, although consumers are outcome-oriented in that their behavior is motivated by the satisfaction of basic needs, individuals care about how the satisfaction of these needs is achieved. Furthermore, unpleasant experiences in consumption activities trigger search processes on the part of the consumers so to find new ways of attaining their goals. As a result of these search processes, consumers discover which goods can be employed to avoid unpleasant experiences and to achieve the satisfaction of basic needs at the same time. They develop a liking for goods that become associated with goal achievement. The important point is that not only an association towards a consumption good has to be learned, but also the link between the good and need satisfaction.

Once an association between an activity and the satisfaction of a need is formed, the consumption activity is carried out to the extent that a temporary level of satiation is reached. In simple terms, a consumer has had enough sleep, enough to eat, enough to drink and so on, yielding a state of 'homeostatic equilibrium'. When satiation vanishes and inner physiological or psychological states deviate substantially from the homeostatic equilibrium, subsequent acts of consumption are motivated. Thus, the consumer takes a drink, has a meal and so on.

A particularity holds for the satiation property of the basic need for social recognition, which we shall mention here, as this need plays an important role in the later analysis. With social recognition, neither the occurrence of deprivation and satiation are contingent on the individual consumer's behavior only. Instead, the satisfaction of the social needs of consumers is intertwined with the behavior of other consumers: whenever some influential consumers change their behavior in socially significant activities, other consumers will also have to modify their actions. Possibly higher consumption levels than before are necessary to be a socially respected person (cf. Chapter 3). Although social motives might play a role in many more consumption activities, we will examine social recognition only to the extent that it is appealed to by clean clothing and the activity of clothes washing.

Witt (2001) considers consumer learning together with the enabling force of income growth, a necessary condition for the diffusion of qualitatively modified and completely novel goods. Witt distinguishes between different types of goods in terms of how they yield the satisfaction of consumers' needs. In that regard, goods can be divided into two groups: those that show a direct link to need satisfaction (so-called 'direct inputs', e.g. food), and those which are only indirectly linked to consumers' needs. The latter group of goods is termed 'tools'. Tools are said to not be desired for themselves, but for the services they yield when being utilized (washing machines, for instance, can produce clean clothes).[30] This point has implications for the satisfaction of basic needs, described in the next hypothesis:

> H.2.7: The utilization intensity of tools is determined by the satiation properties of the needs underlying its utilization (Tools Hypothesis).

In other words, when analyzing utilization patterns of tools, the needs which are satisfied through the tool's services have to be paid attention to. In addition, the utilization intensity of tools also depends on the number of tools available to the consumer.

To sum this up, changes in type, frequency and the level of consumption are thus the result of both elementary learning processes and the acquisition of new information. In order for an overarching framework to cover both cases of cognitive and noncognitive learning, we employ the general notion of changing 'associations' between means and ends, including changing motivations for consuming products. Alternatively, one might speak of the acquisition of consumption knowledge (cf. Metcalfe, 2001) or consumption capabilities (cf. Langlois and Cosgel, 1998), or improved 'household recipes' (Mokyr, 2002, Chapter 5), but we refrain from using these notions as they have, in our view, too strong a connotation of cognitive learning processes alone. Whenever the associations that a consumer holds with regard to a specific good change, a change in behavior is likely to occur: the demand for that good is likely to be shifted upward or downward with an increase in positive or negative associations, respectively. This might imply a more (increase in positive associations) or less (increase in negative associations) intensive utilization of a good compared with the previous pattern:

> H.2.8: Changes in consumption activities are the result of changing associations on the part of the consumers with regard to these exact activities. Increasing consumption patterns are the result of an increase in positive associations and/or the decline in negative associations concerning a specific consumption activity (Learning Hypothesis).

The set of hypotheses developed in this section will be referred to as 'the learning approach'. The exposition hitherto has shown that the motivational basis of human behavior alone can bring about changes in consumption patterns by affecting the relative frequency with which actions are taken, if some actions are taken at all, and with which instruments an activity is carried out. Theoretically, some stationary behavioral pattern would occur if consumers did not encounter novel stimuli from their environment anymore, including novel consumption goods. However, qualitative product change and an increasing variety of goods over time is a stylized empirical fact which can hardly be neglected when studying the long-term development of a specific consumption activity. The psychologically informed learning account set up in this chapter seems to be a framework suitable for studying the regularities of the long-term development of consumer behavior and household technology. With the set of hypotheses developed here, the evolution of consumption behavior and the related phenomena of technical change, product innovation, advertising and product diffusion can be traced back to an individualistic foundation. Applying the learning approach to a specific case study, the following general questions have to be addressed:

1 What kinds of needs does a specific consumption activity appeal to?
2 What are the satiation properties of these needs?
3 How will consumers learn to associate a particular need with a particular consumption activity?
4 How do consumer learning processes affect the satiation levels of these needs?

The subject of this study is to analyze to which extent, when and why consumer associations related to the consumption activity of clothes washing have been malleable in historical time, shaping the long-term evolution of cleanliness consumption. Before turning to this issue, we introduce the conceptual framework with which we will analyze the case study.

2.4 The Conceptual Framework for Analyzing Clothes Washing

2.4.1 *Motives in Clothes Washing: Health and Social Recognition*

In the previous section, we reviewed some evidence from psychology show-ing that consumers are outcome-oriented in that their behavior is motivated by the satisfaction of basic needs. We also showed that individuals care about how the satisfaction of those needs is achieved and that this concern shows no relation to productivity considerations whatsoever (in the sense that consum-ers strive to be more efficient so to consume even more). More precisely, we made a distinction between actions on one side and goals on the other. We specified the concepts of 'actions taken' and 'goals targeted' as consumption activities and the satisfaction of basic needs, respectively. We maintain this dichotomy as it simplifies the following exposition and relates to the distinction made in Becker's approach between household production processes on one side and ultimate goals on the other. When concrete examples of consumption behavior are examined, the differentiation in 'actions taken' and 'goals tar-geted' is quite intuitive. In fact, in laundry washing, one can easily differentiate between the process of doing laundry and the satisfaction of needs related to clean clothes (see below). As was pointed out earlier, this distinction requires assumptions about consumer preferences. The important point is not to put forth assumptions in an *ad hoc* manner but to derive them from psychological theories of motivation, as laid out in this chapter, and from a detailed case study analysis. Once again, by specifying the consumer's ultimate goals as basic needs in the sense of Witt (2001), we make explicit assumptions about the content of consumer preferences and include preferences for the use of time in our analysis. Thus, despite some overlap in terms of the terminology employed, our approach will be fundamentally different from Becker's.

Let us now turn to the case study of cleanliness consumption and the con-sumer needs involved in clothes washing. Two basic needs are nowadays asso-ciated with clean clothes: health and social recognition. In the medical field, it is common knowledge that the washing of textiles can contribute to hygiene via disinfection. Effectiveness, however, depends upon the type of textiles and laundering practices: higher temperatures and ample rinsing of clothes substan-tially reduce the number of microorganisms (Nichols, 1970; Terpstra, 1998). More recently, the disinfectant potential of laundering has been neglected – on the one hand, because of changes in the properties of textiles; on the other hand, out of ecological concerns (Sattar *et al.*, 1999; Statens Institutt for Forbruksforskning [SIFO], 2003). If hygiene is insufficient, however, fabrics can have negative health effects. For example, infections can spread through 'cross-contamination' when bacteria are transmitted from clothing to hand (Neely and Maley, 2000). A lack of hygiene can also cause an infestation of the body louse on clothing, thereby transmitting pathogenic bacteria (Raoult and Roux, 1999). A recent consumer survey in several European countries (SIFO, 2003) confirms the close interrelation between health and cleanliness.

In sociology, it is commonplace that, in choosing their level of cleanliness, consumers look to the opinions of others (e.g. Preece, 1990), for the notion of cleanliness itself is a social construct (Cowan, 1983; Douglas, 1984).[31] Cleanliness, being a social construct, means that society defines when a consumer can be considered 'clean' – it is not self-evident. The relevance of social recognition is also indicated by the aforementioned survey, which also shows that clothes are washed both for health reasons and for social motives. When asked how much they agree with the statement that 'it is embarrassing to wear clothes with a body odour', a large share of respondents in several European countries 'fully agreed' (Greece: 80 per cent; Netherlands: 80 per cent; Norway: 74 per cent; Spain: 95 per cent). Apparently, cleanliness, particularly the absence of body odor, appears to be a social norm in many industrialized countries today. Cleanliness is expected of everyone and there exists a mutual understanding of what this means (Douglas, 1984). As cleanliness is a concern for every member of society, it affects consumption patterns – in choosing their level of cleanliness, consumers look to the opinions of others. According to the survey, the satisfaction of the needs for health and social recognition is related to clean clothes, i.e. to the outcome of the activity of clothes washing, not to doing laundry itself (cf. also Section 2.4.2). Drawing upon these insights, we assume the ultimate reason for carrying out the activity of clothes washing to be the satisfaction of these exact needs:

H.2.9: The activity of clothes washing is directed towards the satisfaction of the basic needs for health and social recognition (Cleanliness Hypothesis).

The innate needs of health and social recognition are stable elements in consumer behavior. They make up a structural component in laundry washing in that dirt and the smell of unclean clothes are associated with innate fears of illness and pain as well as social disdain, thus triggering behaviors directed toward the avoidance of pain and social ostracism. At a given point in time, a temporary satiation level of these consumer needs exists (as appealed to by clothes washing). To begin with, a specific level of cleanliness could be defined which ensures that health concerns are met from an objective, scientific perspective. This cleanliness level could be measured in terms of the number of microorganisms on a piece of textile. It could, but need not, be identical with the cleanliness level prescribed by society. In fact, the very notion of consumer learning suggests that what is considered appropriate cleanliness by a group of consumers need not correspond with the level actually necessary to avoid negative health effects. Thus, we assume the existence of a distinct social standard of cleanliness:

Definition of social standard of cleanliness: The social standard of cleanliness is the level of consumption of cleanliness which has to be demonstrated in order to receive social recognition, i.e. to satisfy the need for social recognition.

In order to function as a motivating force of consumer behavior, the social standard must be visible and observable and/or communicated between consumers in one way or another. It is thus more closely related to visual aspects and the smell of clothing and by and large reflected in laundry quantities per time interval, such as per year.[32] The relevant peer-group standard of cleanliness as well as consumer's awareness of the hygienic effects of clean clothing are not fixed, but malleable. The extent to which the motivations of health and social recognition become manifest in consumer behavior might undergo changes over time. We assume the significance of these needs in terms of influencing laundry patterns to result from consumer learning processes and to be contingent upon historical and regional circumstances. Tracing back the evolution of the consumption of cleanliness to these innate motives, we thus have to control for the systematic changes in the importance of these motivations in the form of a rising hygienic awareness and changing social normative expectations.

2.4.2 Analogy of Household Production Processes

Although there are fundamental differences between the market economy and the home economy in terms of reward structures, work structures and value structures (Brown and Preece, 1987), drawing upon the household production function approach as the conceptual framework for analyzing laundry washing certainly is quite straightforward. To begin with, laundry washing today can be viewed as a rather complex activity. It makes use of several 'production factors' – washing machines, energy, water and detergent – which can be employed in various ways. Different types of fabrics and pieces of clothes also require special treatment. Thus, in comparison with other activities taking place in the home, for instance, producing heat by putting on the heater, clothes washing is certainly a more sophisticated task. Not seldom are clothes ruined after having been subjected to inappropriate forms of washing, which is why expensive garments are often sent for dry cleaning. We thus employ the metaphor of a household production process as a useful starting point for conceptualizing the activity of clothes washing.

Drawing upon the assumption that clothes washing is directed towards the satisfaction of the needs for health and social recognition, productive and consumptive processes in laundry washing can be distinguished. In simple terms, the satisfaction of consumer needs is achieved by having clean clothes, not by participating in the activity of doing the laundry. Take an engineering perspective and assume a sequential household production process, where an original item becomes converted into a more 'useful' output at the end of the process (for related concepts, cf. Buenstorf, 2004).[33] Goods can be said to become more useful when they better satisfy the household's ultimate goals, here, consumer basic needs. Hence, the household production process up to that point would correspond to a productive activity. With regard to the case study, doing the laundry would be classified as a productive endeavor. It yields clean clothes as the output of a household production process in its physical form. Drawing upon Becker's terminology, clean clothes could be denoted a commodity. This physical product, in turn, appeals to consumers' basic needs and is better suited to serve them than the original item – dirty clothes – that went into the production process (cf. Figure 2.2).

Certainly, it should not be denied that, to some consumers, the pure possession of a washing machine might be a source of pleasure. Collectors of antique washing machines, to be found on the Internet, are a case in point. Our argument rather is that a contribution to the satisfaction of the aforementioned needs can neither be achieved through the possession of the machine alone nor through the simple activity of doing laundry. The services of washing machines are not directly utility-providing in the sense that the process of washing clothes is not yet the consumer's ultimate goal. Instead, the consumer eventually wants to have, say, clean shirts and pants, which are able to satisfy some basic needs. In that regard, the services provided by washing machines are more of an indirect nature, which is why these devices could be labeled a 'tool' in the terminology of Witt's account, particularly an 'indirect tool'.

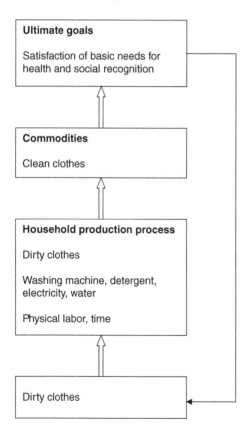

Figure 2.2 Household Production of Cleanliness.

Note that this assumption does not rule out the significance of washing machines with regard to preferences for the use of time. We argued that substitution processes in household production processes do not only result from productivity considerations, but also from preferences for the use of time and that the willingness to substitute might stem from the fact that an activity brings negative associations and that the consumer might seek ways to avoid this activity. Consumption goods might thus be acquired in order to change the valence of certain activities as having positive or negative associations. We therefore do not assume that the absence of positive associations means that laundry washing is a 'neutral' activity, i.e. 'value free', or that it has always been neutral from the perspective of consumers. On the contrary, the evaluation of clothes washing might undergo changes over time, depending exactly on the technical equipment with which the activity is carried out.

We use the metaphor of a household production process as our conceptual benchmark. But would it also be helpful to assume that laundry washing follows a utility maximization calculus, given some (unspecified) utility function? Given the exposition in the preceding sections, it should be clear that both the assumption of complete information as well as the utility-maximization perspective are rejected here. Assume that clothes get damaged within the activity of clothes washing. Could this finding be interpreted as evidence against optimization? Possibly not. When the notion of perfect knowledge is replaced by, say, subjective beliefs, suboptimal household production outcomes are compatible with the theory. Alternatively, if information costs are taken into account, it can be argued as follows: it was an optimal decision for the household to risk that clothes will be damaged instead of spending more time on researching optimal clothing care. Especially when the costs of time and search for information are relatively high in times of high wages – compared with relatively low prices of clothes – it might be a very rational strategy to not spend too much time on washing clothes.[34] In short, there are no means to reject the utility-maximization-hypothesis of neoclassical theory – it is non-falsifiable (Hodgson, 2003). It will thus not deepen our understanding of the subject matter.

We do not assume that explicit knowledge exists concerning the principles by which, for instance, certain laundry techniques are successful in bringing about need satisfaction. Many people probably do not know the chemical principles by which tensides in detergents work. In addition, consumers do not try to optimize detergent use and temperature setting with every act of laundry washing but rather go by 'rules of thumb', which sometimes yield suboptimal outcomes. And, although knowledge in society definitely has increased over time, especially concerning the relationship between hygiene and health (cf. Chapter 3), individual consumers need not possess this kind of information and align their behavior with it. Consumers rather have become conditioned to associate negative feelings with a dirty appearance and smelly clothes that they would feel bad about themselves and are also not willing to tolerate this in other people.

Having said this, what would the deprivation-satiation-mechanism look like? Recall that we have stated earlier that inner physiological or psychological states trigger behaviors that lead to the removal of deprivation. The situation is a little bit different with laundry washing, as consumers apparently act in an anticipatory manner. Consumers do not wait until they are ill or until others let them know their disapproval of their appearance. At the same time, this anticipatory behavior is not to be understood as being guided by explicit expectations being formed and taken into account. Instead, associations are at work which have been learned at an earlier point in time and are reinforced by actual consumer behavior (Witt, 2001; Hodgson, 2003; Nelson and Consoli, 2010). The shape of clothes and their smell rather function as indicators or cues to which the consumer pays attention. This view is closely related to the habit perspective taken in sociological writings on the subject, where doing the laundry is usually depicted as an inconspicuous routine that does not absorb much cognitive effort and involves slowly changing laundry patterns (Shove, 2003a).[35]

2.5 Concluding Remarks

In Chapter 2, we elaborated on the theoretical underpinnings of our research. We derived the conceptual framework and the core hypotheses upon which all subsequent analyses will draw. A great part of the exposition has been devoted to a presentation and critical assessment of Gary Becker's household production function approach, which is the well-established neoclassical account for analyzing technical change in nonmarket production processes and the demand for household appliances. The household production theory is rooted in the framework of rational choice but modifies neoclassical consumer theory in two central points. First, time is introduced as an additional constraint on consumer behavior, next to the budget constraint. Second, preferences are defined, not over market goods, but over commodities. Commodities are produced when market goods are transformed through household production processes. Becker's approach suggests analyzing the adoption of any kinds of goods and services in light of their potential to reorganize household production processes and to enhance their productivity. The triggering factor is an increase in the wage rate, which implies increasing opportunity costs of time and fosters changes in the demand for market goods, specifically capital goods. When capital goods are substituted for the household's time in the production process, an expansion of commodity production and an increase in consumer utility becomes feasible.

The substitution process, triggered by rising wages, is predicted independently of the arguments of the utility function. Becker does introduce a novel concept for preferences – commodities – but does not elaborate on the content of these preferences so that commodities remain a black box in the household production analysis. In fact, the household production theory does not distinguish between commodities on one side and household technology on the other. We have shown that, in order to disentangle technological aspects from the motivational forces of behavior and to separate productive from consumptive activities, assumptions about consumer preferences have to be put forth. Becker generally neglects the impact of preferences or changes therein on changes in household production processes. On the grounds of Becker's account, it thus cannot be understood why consumers choose to produce more of some commodities and not of others once an expansion of commodity production becomes feasible through efficiency progress in household production processes. Becker does not explain what it is that people want more of, why that is and how it changes.

Becker also explicitly factors out that decisions about the allocation of time reflect household preferences as to the use of time. In simple terms, Becker assumes consumers to only care about how many commodities they can produce and not about the way the production objective is achieved. That such preferences for the use of time do not exist is an assumption of central importance for the predictions of the household production theory. Indeed, the clear-cut comparative-static implications of the Becker model depend on the nonexistence of such preferences. But these predictions might not have much explanatory power when households do have likings or dislikings for specific housework activities which affect the production process. In the same manner, the utility maximization hypothesis factors out the explanatory power of actual consumer learning processes for changes in nonmarket activities and the demand for market goods.

The main points of critique raised here concern Becker's treatment of preferences, for preferences do play an important role in actual human behavior, as psychological theories of motivation, as well as behavioral psychology, have shown. The psychological findings reviewed here allow conjecturing that households do not only care about the achievement of production objectives, i.e. commodities, but also about the household technology employed in the production process. While individuals might be motivated to attain a certain goal, they will not seek to reach that goal at any price. In fact, individuals often face so-called 'approach-avoidance conflicts', which occur when an activity is associated both with rewarding experiences as well as objections or even pain. In that case, individuals might forgo goal attainment or they might look for ways to overcome the conflict. Hence, mastering approach-avoidance conflicts in housework activities might be a strong motive for the adoption of household technology.

In view of the collected psychological-behavioral evidence, an important step forward to a better understanding of household production processes would be achieved when some substantial assumptions about the content of consumer preferences were brought forth – including a definition of the commodity concept as well as of preferences for the use of time. In order to elaborate on the explanatory potential of preferences for shifts in the demand for market goods as well as for changes in consumption activities more in general, the theory of learning consumers put forth by Witt (2001) is a starting point.

Witt is concerned with developing a systematic approach for analyzing the role of consumer motivations in (changing) consumption behavior. He examines the feedback between the evolution of consumption goods on one side and the evolution of motivations for consuming these goods on the other. The most striking difference between Witt's and Becker's accounts lies in the treatment of preferences. Witt's account is, in contrast to Becker's theory, compatible with the aforementioned psychological insights into human behavior. It allows for a much richer and more empirically sound description of consumption behavior. More in detail, Witt provides a material specification of preferences in the form of basic consumer needs and assumes consumption behavior to be directed toward the satisfaction of these needs. Basic needs are part of the human genetic makeup and thus represent commonalities in consumers' motivational basis. According to Witt, changes in consumption behavior result from learning processes by which consumers form new associations between consumption activities on one side and the satisfaction of needs on the other. Long-run shifts in consumption patterns thus reflect manifestations of shared consumer motivations to engage in consumption activities.

Drawing upon Witt, we postulated that consumers share some set of preferences for their common genetic basis, that these preferences can be identified and that they evolve according to some regularities. We developed several arguments which illustrate that preferences are a fundamentally important explanatory variable when studying consumption behavior and household production processes. We set up a behavioral account for analyzing changes in household production processes by highlighting some basic principles that might drive the adoption and utilization patterns of household technology. Within that framework, the concept of 'preferences for the use of time' has been given a behavioral interpretation: when human behavior, in general, is guided by the striving for rewarding experiences and the avoidance of pain, then household production processes will also follow this fundamental principle. The behavioral account developed here has been termed 'the learning approach'. It is reflected

Table 2.1 Summary of Hypotheses and Linkages to the Following Chapters

Hypothesis	Chapter
H.2.1: General Long-Run Time Substitution Hypothesis	4, 5, 6
H.2.2: General Short-Run Time Substitution Hypothesis	4, 6
H.2.3: Behavior Hypothesis	3, 4, 5, 7
H.2.4: Commonalities Hypothesis	3
H.2.5: Advertisement Content Hypothesis	5
H.2.6: Needs Hypothesis	3, 4, 5, 7
H.2.7: Tools Hypothesis	7
H.2.8: Learning Hypothesis	3, 4, 5, 7
H.2.9: Cleanliness Hypothesis	3, 4, 5, 7

in the set of hypotheses which are summarized in Table 2.1. The table further indicates in which of the subsequent chapters the hypotheses will be taken up again.

The conceptual framework introduced here is the basis for the subsequent analysis of laundry washing. All following analyses are built on the assumption that the activity of clothes washing is directed toward the satisfaction of the basic needs for health and social recognition, and that clean clothes can be interpreted as commodities in the sense of the physical output of the household production process. In the subsequent chapters, we will trace back the major historical trends of the evolution of cleanliness consumption to an individualistic perspective, i.e. back to the motivational forces and learning capabilities that have been at work at the level of individual consumers. The analysis proceeds in chronological order. We first deal with the conditions in the nineteenth century.

Notes

1 The individual labor supply curve is 'backward-bending', i.e. the household shows different reactions to increasing real wages, subject to the level of the wage rate.
2 Within the household production function approach, the term 'household' refers to a one-person decision unit; a family perspective is not (yet) taken (for the family perspective, cf. Becker, 1981). We will draw upon this terminology to link our analysis to the established economic theory of housework. We will use it interchangeably with the term 'consumer'. No reference to the household as a regional territory 'home' is intended here. When addressing the sociological literature on the subject, the term 'household' comprises the homemaker and other family members.
3 In analogy to the theory of the firm, the adoption of durable goods can be depicted as an investment decision in capital goods (e.g. Diewert, 1974). This aspect of household behavior is not made explicit in the Beckerian account and we do not intend to take it into account either. Becker deals with this issue by assuming that in the case of capital goods used in the production of commodities Z, the x represents services of the market goods employed and not the goods themselves (Becker, 1965). Pollak argues that, in the short run, household technology has to be treated as fixed anyway, which limits the range of possible household reactions to rising wages (Pollak, 1969).
4 Becker's account is frequently applied in context with specific commodities like food (Ekelund and Watson, 1990; Lecocq, 2001) and transportation (Meloni *et al.*, 2004). Becker's theory has also found applications in such distinct fields as sociological analyses of female labor force participation (cf. Coleman [1993] for an overview) and general equilibrium models (Greenwood *et al.*, 2005).
5 In later works, Becker does reject the assumption of the stability of preferences (cf. Becker and Murphy, 1988), but not in the context addressed here.
6 Becker himself is aware of this problem but argues that the household production function approach still seems to provide useful parameters for the analysis of consumption, even though all statements are translatable into statements about the derived utility function (Michael and Becker, 1973).
7 National accounting systems have long since recognized the productive value of housework, viewing households not only as consumption units but as production units also. As far as housework activities represent substitutes for potential market transactions, they are interpreted as productive endeavors contributing to the domestic product and economic growth (e.g. Devereux and Locay, 1992). The value added of household production is recorded in satellite accounts to national accounting frameworks. In this context, the

definition of what counts as 'housework' – for instance, as opposed to leisure activities – is of central importance. The third-person criterion is standard in many national and international accounting frameworks (of the United States, Germany, European Union, United Nations, etc.).

8 The existence of an 'objective' opportunity cost of time, which is malleable with changes in the wage rate, is doubtful (Preece, 1990). Several authors discuss alternatives for how to assess the time value and what the implications of this are (DeSerpa, 1971; Murphy, 1976; Chiswick, 1982; Key 1990). Key, for instance, points out that Becker's approach implies that there exists only a single price of time for all activities, which rules out cross-price effects in the demand for time allocated to alternative activities. DeSerpa measures the value of saving time from an activity as the difference between the value of time in a particular use and the value of time in alternative uses. The idea behind this distinction is that saving time will only be attributed some positive value if the saved time can be transferred to some alternative usage of greater value.

9 Note that pleasure derived from carrying out an activity and pleasure derived from the output of an activity are two distinct incentives of behavior.

10 Preferences for the use of time have been given different names in the literature on household production, for example, 'process utility' (Gronau and Hamermesh, 2006) or 'experiential aspects of time use' (Kaufman-Scarborough, 2006).

11 According to Preece, the substitutability of housework time and goods in the production of commodities receives little support outside of the Beckerian new home economics framework (Preece, 1990, p. 44). Housework is more inflexible than suggested by the theory, such that households cannot marginally adjust their time input into housework or market work, respectively (Preece, 1990, p. 471). Brown and Preece (1987) argue that there are also objective boundaries to substitution between housework and market alternatives as the housewife cannot contract to buy external services in the exact small amounts of time and random hours that she herself actually performs certain duties in the home (around-the-clock family care, i.e. babysitting, cooking, chauffeuring, etc.).

12 Both Lancaster (1966) and Ironmonger (1972) developed accounts which deal with qualitative change in consumer products. Lancaster put forth the concept of 'product characteristics' and argued that it is a product's characteristics rather than the product itself that yields utility. In other words, utility or pleasure are not associated with goods themselves, because goods only have instrumental value. Lancaster further asserted that most goods will have several characteristics and that some of these characteristics will be shared with other products, making them potential substitutes within this specific product dimension. Still, Lancaster does not substantiate what these higher-order goals are and how they affect consumer behavior. As Lancaster does not put forth assumptions about the content of preferences, the characteristics approach can only make a limited contribution to a psychologically informed, evolutionary model of consumer behavior. A similar argument holds for Ironmonger's approach on product innovation and consumer behavior. Ironmonger does give so-called 'wants' an independent ontological status from goods but still continues to think of the want-satisfying potential of goods as something purely technical. Tastes are still determined by exogenous preferences, and changes of tastes are not examined as explanatory factors for changes in consumer behavior.

13 Qualitative product change is constantly happening. It is an empirically observed fact that urges consumers to rethink their consumption patterns – not only because they might miss an opportunity to be better off, but simply because the formerly purchased products might no longer be available in exactly the same form as before.

14 Empirical analyses also find substantial jointness between home production time and leisure time (Graham and Green, 1984; Kerkhofs and Kooreman, 2003).

15 Miller has put forth some propositions concerning what determines the strength of each of the behavioral tendencies and hence the final outcome, i.e. behavioral implications. In general, the avoidance tendency grows faster than the approach tendency, the closer the individual is to the goal. The approach tendency emerges, for instance, in the form of the drive

to obtain food, which can be assumed to remain constant while approaching the goal. The negative experience when moving towards the goal accumulates, thus increasing the desire to escape (Weiner, 1994, p. 92).

16 Practically all economic problems concern trade-offs in decision-making. Alhadeff has developed a microeconomic model, including such conflicting motivations that exceed mere opportunity costs considerations while distinguishing positively defined objectives ('approach behavior') from negatively defined ones ('escape behavior') (Alhadeff, 1982). Similar ideas are to be found in the economics of immediate gratification (cf. Ainslie, 1975; Moore and Loewenstein, 2004).

17 The measuring rod for an action, or more generally, a stimulus, to be categorized as rewarding or painful is the variable 'adaptation level' of the individual (Helson, 1964, Chapter 2). The adaptation level is an operational concept. It represents an indicator for the stimuli experienced by an individual in the past and is 'updated' over time with new experiences. The response triggered by an occurring stimulus depends on the distance of that exact stimulus from the level of adaptation, while a stimulus meeting the adaptation level is neutral from the perspective of the individual. Due to their common genetic basis, humans should show some similarities in the assessment of stimuli, but they might also show differences as a result of individually distinct experiences. In what follows, we concentrate on the commonalities.

18 Primary reinforcers have been identified in experimental psychological research. Psychological findings indicate that, if the satisfaction of these primary reinforcers is hindered, humans are motivated to take actions.

19 Naturally, additional conjectures are needed to explain ongoing technological development in a specific activity beyond the point that, for instance, the effort-reducing motives are met.

20 Admittedly, we employ quite strong assumptions to derive this chain of argument. Although the line of reasoning is consistent, the assumptions can certainly be questioned. As Rosenberg points out, rapid rates of technological progress need not result in rapid market introductions of innovations (Rosenberg, 1982, p. 112). Producers might anticipate that consumers will hold back their demands when they expect rapid technical change to make new products obsolete quickly. In contrast to that, the pace of adoption might increase when product innovation is coming to an end, because potential consumers then have greater confidence that the product will not become outdated immediately (Rosenberg, 1982, p. 118). It goes without saying that the consumer's strategy to hold back consumption will depend on how urgently the type of product is needed. Certainly, changes in the intensity of advertisements could also be put in context with product life cycle theory and its predictions concerning the regular changes in number of firms, size of market, production processes, the emergence of a dominant design and so on (Abernathy and Utterback, 1978).

21 Concerning the case of clothes washing, we contend that consumers recognized the same problems with the prevailing washing technology, namely that the washboard implied unpleasant drudgery and was a time consuming activity. Part of this joint experience can be explained by commonalities in the human genetic basis. That inventors and producers came to know about this situation, leading to shared social understandings, is the result of public discourse triggered by the home economics movement (cf. Chapters 3 and 4).

22 Foxall (1990) developed a framework for the analysis of consumer behavior that is rooted in radical behaviorism, as advanced by B. F. Skinner. Foxall posited that the dominant approach of cognitivism alone cannot yield a full understanding of consumer behavior and that noncognitive forms of behavior, particularly operant conditioning, are able to make a significant contribution to that matter. More precisely, behaviorism can explain a great share of consumer behavior before recourse to some cognitive theories has to be made. Yet, Foxall postulated an integrative approach that comprises both the behaviorist and the cognitivist branch.

23 Witt (2001) uses the terminology of consumer 'wants' instead of 'needs'. He explicitly distinguishes between innate wants and learned wants. As we do not address learned wants here, we will stick to the more familiar term of basic needs in order to denote consumers' ultimate goals.

24 To associate commodities with goods makes more sense when distinguishing between commodities in terms of their time intensity. Consider the need for social recognition. It would be misleading to say that this need was more time intensive, for instance, than the longing for food. However, the (typical) actions taken to achieve need satisfaction might differ in their time intensity.

25 Like Witt (2001), Nelson and Consoli (2010) assume that goods have instrumental value for satisfying consumers' desires – being referred to as 'wants' – and that they are inputs into activities yielding the satisfaction of wants. The household is assumed to develop competences for satisfying these wants, while the actions taken need not be optimal. In contrast to Witt, Nelson and Consoli assume that a household consumption equilibrium exists in which the household carries out the activities which, under a given budget constraint and time constraint, have worked best. The stable patterns of behavior are referred to as 'routines'.

26 For an empirical application of a needs-based approach to consumption behavior, inspired by the analysis by Ernst Engel, see, for example, the quantitative analysis by Chai and Moneta (Chai and Moneta, 2012). Drawing on the assumption that household expenditure categories are closely linked to specific consumer needs, Chai and Moneta study household expenditure patterns from a cross-sectional and a longitudinal perspective. They find household consumption patterns at low income levels to be stable over decades, being dominated by expenditure dedicated to nourishment.

27 The idea of such consumer exploration processes is found in other strands of literature as well (cf. Ruprecht, 2001). The terminology in cognitive psychology is that of 'mental models' being developed (Anderson, 2000).

28 It is important to note that psychological processes cannot be observed themselves, but have to be inferred from observable behavior (Frieman, 2002, p. 7).

29 Associative learning occurs when a formerly neutral stimulus (a certain behavior) coincides sufficiently often with the satisfaction of a basic need (e.g. social recognition) so that the positive feedback from the satisfaction of the need becomes associated with the former neutral stimulus. Social recognition, as a basic need, can bring about such new associations. In other words, if a consumer underwent deprivation in terms of social recognition and learns that he or she receives positive feedback when a specific behavior is demonstrated, this behavior will be shown more frequently in the future. The stimulus becomes eventually rewarding in its own right. A prominent case is money, which has been shown to be a strong secondary reinforcer (Camerer *et al.*, 2005).

30 Many products can easily be categorized based on the criterion if the link to need-satisfaction is direct or indirect. At the same time, most products can easily be differentiated into direct inputs that are 'used up' in the consumption procedure versus tools that are more permanent goods. But there are also some cases where the dichotomy does not hold. Take the consumption of electricity, for example. Electricity certainly vanishes when being consumed. At the same time, energy does not always show a direct link to need satisfaction, as it is consumed in the services it offers in the context of household appliances (e.g. Berkhout *et al.*, 2000). The latter assumption, that electricity provides services, is a standard assumption in analyses on the 'rebound effect' of energy efficiency progress (cf. Chapter 7).

31 Douglas (1984, p. 2) points out that society defines what 'being clean' means: 'As we know it, dirt is essentially disorder. There is no such thing as absolute dirt: it exists in the eye of the beholder'.

32 Although consumers own many more clothes today than 100 years ago, for instance, changes in the clothing stock need not result in a larger laundry amount if clothing consumption behavior remains constant. Assume, for example, that T-shirts are always

washed after having been worn for one day – it might not make a difference then if the consumer possesses ten or twenty T-shirts. An increase in the amount of clothes possessed would only result in a shift in standards of cleanliness if different textiles required different handling, such that more separate washes were necessary. Certainly, laundry quantities are a function of the time interval within which clothes are worn before being laundered again, and the clothing stock of the consumer. However, discussions about changes in clothing stock will be widely neglected in this analysis (for a more detailed analysis, cf. Preece, 1990).

33 This conceptualization is very similar to the suggestion made by Buenstorf (2004) concerning the manipulation of a 'workpiece' by 'energy services' in industrial production processes.

34 In general, the higher the opportunity costs of time, especially in contrast to the prices of clothes, the more likely it is that neither much cognitive effort is involved in doing the laundry nor much money will be invested (time costs, service costs) for bringing the clothes for dry cleaning. The more expensive the clothes, the more likely that either more time will be devoted to washing at home or that the cleaning process is outsourced to a specialized institution.

35 The sociological perspective on housework stands quite in contrast with the neoclassical model. In sociology, laundry washing is a habit that does not absorb much cognitive effort and changes only slowly. In Becker's model, the rational agent is very flexible and constantly seeking an optimized organization of housework. Changes in constraints will thus immediately be reacted to if this will make the household better off. Certainly, the optimization assumption can also be harmonized with the habit perspective: habitual behavior in times of changing constraints is not in conflict with an optimization assumption; it might be optimal to not react to all sorts of changes, for instance, because capital equipment first has to pay off, and so forth.

References

Abbott, M., Ashenfelter, O. (1976): 'Labour supply, commodity demand and the allocation of time', *The Review of Economic Studies*, 43 (3), pp. 389–411.

Abernathy, W. J., Utterback, J. M. (1978): 'Patterns of industrial innovation', *Technology Review*, 80 (7), pp. 40–47.

Ackerman, F. (1997): 'Consumed in theory: Alternative perspectives on the economics of consumption', *Journal of Economic Issues*, 31 (3), pp. 651–664.

Ainslie, G. (1975): 'Specious reward: A behavioral theory of impulsiveness and impulse control', *Psychological Bulletin*, 82 (4), pp. 463–496.

Alhadeff, D. A. (1982): *Microeconomics and Human Behavior: Toward a New Synthesis of Economics and Psychology*, University of California Press, Berkeley.

Anderson, J. R. (2000): *Cognitive Psychology and its Implications*, Worth Publishers, New York.

Bandura, A. (1986): *Social Foundations of Thought and Action: A Social Cognitive Theory*, Prentice Hall, Englewood Cliffs.

Bass, F. M. (1969): 'A new product growth model for consumer durables', *Management Science*, 5, pp. 215–227.

Becker, G. S. (1965): 'A theory of the allocation of time', *The Economic Journal*, 75 (299), pp. 49–517.

Becker, G. S. (1981): *A Treatise on the Family*, Harvard University Press, Cambridge, MA.

Becker G. S., Murphy K. M. (1988): 'A theory of rational addiction', *Journal of Political Economy*, 96, pp. 675–700.

Ben-Porath, Y. (1982): 'Economics and the family–Match or mismatch? A review of Becker's A Treatise on the Family', *Journal of Economic Literature*, 20 (1), pp. 52–64.

Bentham, J. (1948[1789]): *An Introduction to The Principles of Morals and Legislation*, Hafner, New York.

Berk, S. F. (1985): *The Gender Factory*, Plenum Press, New York.

Berkhout, P. H. G., Muskens, J. C., Velthuijsen, J. W. (2000): 'Defining the rebound effect', *Energy Policy*, 28 (6-7), pp. 425–432.

Brown, C., Preece, A. (1987): 'Housework', in J. Eatwell, M. Milgate, P. Newman (eds.) (1987), *The New Palgrave: A Dictionary of Economics*, First *Edition*, Palgrave Macmillan, Basingstoke, United Kingdom.

Buenstorf, G. (2004): *The Economics of Energy and the Production Process: An Evolutionary Approach*, Edward Elgar, Cheltenham, United Kingdom.

Camerer, C. F., Loewenstein G., Prelec D. (2005): 'Neuroeconomics: How neuroscience can inform economics', *Journal of Economic Literature*, 43 (1), pp. 9–64.

Carver, C. S., Scheier, M. F. (1990): 'Origins and functions of positive and negative affect: A control-process view', *Psychological Review*, 97 (1), pp. 19–35.

Chai, A., Moneta, A. (2012): 'Back to Engel? Some evidence for the hierarchy of needs', *Journal of Evolutionary Economics*, 22, pp. 649–676.

Chiswick, C. U. (1982): 'The value of a housewife's time', *Journal of Human Resources*, 17 (3), pp. 413–425.

Coleman, J. S. (1993): 'The impact of Gary Becker's work on sociology', *Acta Sociologica*, 36 (3), pp. 169–178.

Cordes, C. (2002): *An Evolutionary Analysis of Long-Term Qualitative Change in Human Labor*, PhD dissertation, Jena University, Jena, Germany.

Cordes, C. (2005): 'Long-term tendencies in technological creativity – a preference-based approach', *Journal of Evolutionary Economics*, 15, pp. 149–168.

Cowan, R. S. (1983): *More Work for Mother*, Basic Books, New York.

DeSerpa, A. C. (1971): 'A theory of the economics of time', *The Economic Journal*, 81, pp. 828–846.

Devereux, J., Locay, L. (1992): 'Specialization, household production, and the measurement of economic growth', *American Economic Review*, 82 (2), pp. 399–403.

Diewert, W. E. (1974): 'Intertemporal consumer theory and the demand for durables', *Econometrica*, 42 (3), pp. 497–516.

Dosi, G. (1982): 'Technological paradigms and technological trajectories: A suggested interpretation of the determinants and directions of technical change', *Research Policy*, 11 (3), pp. 147–162.

Douglas, M. (1984): *Purity and Danger: An Analysis of the Concepts of Pollution and Taboo*, Ark Paperbacks, London.

Ekelund, R. B. Jr., Watson, J. K. (1990): 'Restaurant cuisine, fast food and ethnic edibles: An empirical note on household meal production', *Kyklos*, 44 (4), pp. 613–627.

Elliot, A. J. (2006): 'The hierarchical model of approach-avoidance motivation', *Motivation and Emotion*, 30, pp. 11–116.

Elliot, A. J., Church, M. A. (1997): 'A hierarchical model of approach and avoidance achievement motivation', *Journal of Personality and Social Psychology*, 72, pp. 218–232.

Foxall, G. (1990): *Consumer Psychology in Behavioral Perspective*, Beard Books, Washington D.C.

Frieman, J. (2002): *Learning and Adaptive Behavior*, Wadsworth, Belmont, CA.

Frijda, N. H. (1988): 'The laws of emotion', *American Psychologist*, 43, pp. 349–358.

Goldschmidt-Clermont, L. (1993): 'The monetary valuation of non-market productive time, methodological considerations', *Review of Income and Wealth*, 39 (4), pp. 419–33.

Graham, J. W., Green, C. A. (1984): 'Estimating the parameters of a household production function with joint products', *The Review of Economics and Statistics*, 66 (2), pp. 277–282.

Gramm, W. L. (1974): 'The demand for the wife's non-market time', *Southern Economic Journal*, 41 (1), pp. 124–133.

Greenwood, J., Seshadri, A., Yorukoglu, M. (2005): 'Engines of liberation', *Review of Economic Studies*, 72, pp. 109–133.

Gronau, R., Hamermesh, D. S. (2006): 'Time vs. goods: The value of measuring household production technologies', *Review of Income and Wealth*, 52 (1), pp. 1–16.

Heckman, J. (1974): 'Shadow prices, market wages, and labor supply', *Econometrica*, 42 (4), pp. 679–694.

Helson, H. (1964): *Adaptation-Level Theory*, Harper & Row, New York.

Herrnstein, R. (1970): 'On the law of effect', *Journal of the Experimental Analysis of Behavior*, 13, pp. 243–266.

Herrnstein, R., Prelec, D. (1991): 'Melioration: A theory of distributed choice', *Journal of Economic Perspectives*, 5 (3), pp. 137–156.

Hodgson, G. M. (2003): 'The hidden persuaders: Institutions and individuals in economic theory', *Cambridge Journal of Economics*, 27 (2), pp. 159–175.

Hull, C. L. (1943): *Principles of Behavior: An Introduction to Behavior Theory*, Appleton-Century-Crofts, New York.

Ironmonger, D. (1972): *New Commodities and Consumer Behavior*, Cambridge University Press, Cambridge, MA.

Kaufman-Scarborough, C. (2006): 'Time use and the impact of technology: Examining workspaces in the home', *Time & Society*, 15 (1), pp. 57–80.

Kerkhofs, M., Kooreman, P. (2003): 'Identification and estimation of a class of household production models', *Journal of Applied Econometrics*, 18, pp. 337–369.

Key, R. (1990): 'Complementary and substitutability in family members' time allocated to household production activities', *Lifestyles: Family and Economic Issues*, 11 (3), pp. 225–256.

Kooreman, P., Wunderink, S. (1997): The Economics of Household Behavior, St. Martin's Press, New York.

Lancaster, K. (1966): 'A new approach to consumer theory', *Journal of Political Economy*, 74, pp. 132–157.

Langlois, R. N., Cosgel, M.M. (1998). 'The organization of consumption', in M. Bianchi (ed.), *The Active Consumer*, Routledge, London, pp. 107–121.

Lecocq, S. (2001): 'The allocation of time and goods in household activities: A test of separability', *Journal of Population Economics*, 14, pp. 585–597.

Levey, A. B., Martin, I. (1990): 'Evaluative conditioning: Overview and further options', *Cognition and Emotion*, 4 (1), pp. 31–37.

Lewin, K. (1951): *Field Theory in Social Science*, Harper, New York.

Lewis, H. G. (1975): 'Economics of time and labor supply', *American Economic Review*, 65 (2), pp. 29–34.

Linder, S. B. (1970): *The Harried Leisure Class*, Columbia University Press, New York and London.

Loasby, B. J. (2001): 'Cognition, imagination and institutions in demand creation', *Journal of Evolutionary Economics*, 11, pp. 7–21.

Meloni, I., Guala, L., Loddo, A. (2004): 'Time allocation to discretionary in-home, out-of-home activities and trips', *Transportation*, 31, pp. 69–96.

Metcalfe, S. (2001): 'Consumption, preferences and the evolutionary agenda', *Journal of Evolutionary Economics*, 11, pp. 37–58.

Michael, R. T., Becker, G. S. (1973): 'On the new theory of consumer behavior', *Swedish Journal of Economics*, 75 (4), pp. 378–396.

Miller, N. E. (1959): 'Liberalization of basic S-R concepts: Extensions to conflict behavior, motivation and social learning', in Koch, S. (ed): *Psychology: A Study of Science*, vol. 2, McGraw-Hill, New York.

Miller, N. E. (1944): 'Experimental studies of conflict', in Hunt, J. V. (ed): *Personality and the Behavioral Disorders*, vol. 1, Ronald, New York.

Mokyr, J. (2002): *The Gifts of Athena: Historical Origins of the Knowledge Economy*, Princeton University Press, Princeton.

Moore, D. A., Loewenstein, G. (2004): 'Self-interest, automaticity, and the psychology of conflict of interest', *Social Justice Research*, 17 (2), pp. 189–202.

Mowery, D. C., Rosenberg, N. (1979): 'The influence of market demand upon innovation: a critical review of some recent empirical studies', *Research Policy*, 8, pp. 103–153.

Murphy, M. (1976): 'The value of time spent in home production', *American Journal of Economics and Sociology*, 35 (2), pp. 191–197.

Neely, A. C., Maley, M. P. (2000): 'Survival of enterococci and staphylococci on hospital fabrics and plastic', *Journal of Clinical Microbiology*, 38, pp. 724–726.

Nelson, R. R., Consoli, D. (2010): 'An evolutionary theory of household consumption behavior', *Journal of Evolutionary Economics*, 20, pp. 665–687.

Nichols, P. S. (1970): 'Bacteria in laundered fabrics', *American Journal of Public Health*, 60 (11), pp. 2175–2180.

Nicol, C. J., Nakamura, A. (1994): 'Labor supply and child status effects on household demands', *Journal of Human Resources*, 29 (2), pp. 588–599.

Pinch, T. J. (1996): 'The social construction of technology: a review', in Fox, R. (ed.): *Technological Change: Methods and Themes in the History of Technology*, Harwood Academic Publishers, Amsterdam.

Pinch, T. J., & Bijker, W. E. (1987): 'The social construction of facts and artifacts: Or how the sociology of science and the sociology of technology might benefit each other', in Bijker, W. E., Hughes, T. P., Pinch, T. J. (eds.): *The Social Construction of Technological Systems*, MIT Press, Cambridge, MA.

Pollak, R. A. 'Conditional demand functions and consumption theories', *Quarterly Journal of Economics*, 83 (1969), pp. 60–78.

Pollak, R. A. (2003): 'Gary Becker's contributions to family and household economics', *Review of Economics of the Household*, 1, pp. 111–141.

Pollak, R.A., Wachter, M. L. (1975): 'The relevance of the household production function and its implications for the allocation of time', *Journal of Political Economy*, 83 (2), pp. 255–277.

Preece, A. (1990): Housework and American standards of living, 1920–1980, PhD sissertation, University of California, Berkeley.

Raoult, D., Roux V. (1999): 'The body louse as a vector of reemerging human diseases', *Clinical Infectious Diseases*, 29, pp. 888–911.

Reid, M. G. (1934): *The Economics of Household Production*, John Wiley & Sons, Inc., New York.

Robinson, J. P., Godbey, G. (1997): *Time for Life, The Surprising Ways Americans Use Their Time*, second edition, The Pennsylvania State University Press, University Park, PA.

Robinson, J. P., Milkie, M. A. (1998): 'Back to the basics: Trends in and role determinants of women's attitudes toward housework', *Journal of Marriage and Family*, 60 (1), pp. 205–218.

Rogers, E. M. (1995): *Diffusion of Innovations*, fourth edition, The Free Press, New York.

Rosenberg, A. (1979): 'Can economic theory explain everything?' *Philosophy of the Social Sciences*, 9 (4), pp. 509–529.

Rosenberg, N. (1982): *Inside the Black Box: Technology and Economics*, Cambridge University Press, Cambridge, MA.

Ruprecht, W. (2001): Towards an Evolutionary Theory of Consumption, Dissertation, Jena University, Germany.

Sattar, S. A., Tetro, J., Springhtorpe, S. (1999): 'Impact of changing societal trends on the spread of infections in American and Canadian homes', *American Journal of Infection Control*, 27, pp. 4–21.

Scitovsky, T. (1976): *The Joyless Economy: An Inquiry into Human Satisfaction and Dissatisfaction*, Oxford University Press, Oxford, United Kingdom.

Shove, E. (2003a): 'Converging conventions of comfort, cleanliness and convenience', *Journal of Consumer Policy*, 26, pp. 395–418.

Simon, H. A. (1967): 'Motivational and emotional controls of cognition', *Psychological Review*, 74 (1), pp. 29–39.

Skinner, B. F. (1953): *Science and Human Behavior*, Macmillan, New York.

Soberon-Ferrer, H., Dardis, R. (1991): 'Determinants of household expenditures for services', *Journal of Consumer Research*, 17, pp. 385–397.

Statens Institutt for Forbruksforskning [SIFO] (2003): *An Investigation of Domestic Laundry in Europe: Habits, Hygiene and Technical Performance*, National Institute for Consumer Research, Oslo.

Stigler, G. J., Becker, G. S. (1977): 'De gustibus non est disputandum', *American Economic Review*, 67 (2), pp. 76–90.

Terpstra, P. M. J. (1998): 'Domestic and institutional hygiene in relation to sustainability. Historical, social and environmental implications', *International Biodeterioration & Biodegradation*, 41, pp. 169–175.

Thorndike, E. L. (2000)[1911]: *Animal Intelligence, Experimental Studies*, Transaction Publishers, New Brunswick, NJ.

Torrence, R. (1989): 'Tools as optimal solutions', in Torrence, R. (ed.): *Time, Energy and Stone Tools*, Cambridge University Press, Cambridge, MA.

Veblen, T. (1994) [1899]: *The Theory of the Leisure Class*, Macmillan, New York.

Wales, T. J., Woodland, A. D. (1977): 'Estimation of the allocation of time for work, leisure, housework', *Econometrica*, 45 (1), pp. 115–132.

Weagley, R.O, Norum P.S. (1989): 'Household demand for market, purchased home producible commodities', *Family and Consumer Sciences Research Journal*, 18 (6), pp. 6–18.

Weiner, B. (1994): *Motivationspsychologie*, third edition, Beltz Psychologie-Verlagsunion, Weinheim, Germany.

Windrum, P., Birchenhall, C. (1998): 'Is product life cycle theory a special case? Dominant designs and the emergence of market niches through coevolutionary learning', *Structural Change and Economic Dynamics*, 9 (1), pp. 109–134.

Witt, U. (1987): 'Familienökonomik – Einige nicht-neoklassische Aspekte', in Todt, H. (ed.): *Die Familie als Gegenstand der Sozialwissenschaftlichen Forschung*, Schriften des Vereins für Sozialpolitik, N. F. 164, Duncker & Humblot, Berlin.

Witt, U. (1993): 'Emergence and dissemination of innovations: Some principles of evolutionary economics', in Day, R. H., Chen, P. (eds.): *Nonlinear Dynamics Evolutionary Economics*, Oxford University Press, Oxford, United Kingdom.

Witt, U. (2001): 'Learning to consume – A theory of wants and the growth of demand', *Journal of Evolutionary Economics*, 11, pp. 23–36.

Zajonc, R. B. (1984): 'On the primacy of affect', *American Psychologist*, 39, pp. 117–129.

3 The Origin of the Social Norm of Cleanliness

3.1 Motivation

To a great extent, consumption behavior is motivated by the desire to appeal to the consumer's social environment. Status-seeking consumption, as well as the compliance with social norms, are manifestations of such a motivation. Whereas luxurious variants of cars or wristwatches might be desired to indicate the superior social status of their owner (Frank, 1999), other consumption goods are merely purchased to demonstrate conformity with referent others (Leibenstein, 1950). A further category of actions or inactions acknowledges social norms such as the nonsmoking norm or the norm of tipping in restaurants.

How and why then would the meaning of a specific consumption act change from being a means to signal the consumer's status to become a means of norm compliance? Theories on status-seeking consumption cannot contribute much to answering this question, as no consumer motivations other than social recognition are considered. In contrast, the literature dealing with the emergence of social norms suggests that changes in normative expectations and behavior stand in context with newly emerging 'problems' or 'dilemmas' within a community (e.g. Demsetz, 1967; Cornes and Sandler, 1986; Ostrom, 2000). In order to understand the transformation of a consumption activity from representing 'status seeking' to being 'norm fulfilling', as it is argued here, one would have to trace how an additional motive – other than social recognition – became associated with the specific consumption act.

Exactly this is the approach to be applied in this chapter to explain the emergence of the social norm of cleanliness in the nineteenth century by which the status-signaling property of cleanliness was eliminated. This chapter draws on Woersdorfer (2010). It will be argued that cleanliness turned from a private into a public good when social networks radically changed in the period of industrialization and urbanization in the Western world, particularly in the United States and the United Kingdom. When infectious diseases put the basic consumer need for health at risk and when consumers understood the association between cleanliness and health, the formation of a social norm of cleanliness was triggered.

We conceptualize cleanliness, in terms of clean clothes, as the outcome of the household production activity of laundry washing (cf. Chapter 2). Clean clothes are assumed to have instrumental value for more fundamental human preferences, i.e. basic consumer needs. With the term 'cleanliness consumption', we refer to the inputs into this household production process, i.e. both expenditures on consumer goods and services, as well as the utilization of the respective goods.

At a more general level, this chapter addresses the evolving associations between consumption goods (or activities) on one side and consumer motivations for consuming these goods on the other (cf. Learning Hypothesis, Chapter 2). In this respect, our approach shows some overlap with Lessig's account of changing 'social meanings' of behavior (and the regulation thereof) (Lessig, 1995; 1996; 1998). Similar to Lessig, the role of shared social understandings for norm emergence is elaborated, starting from the basic assumption that the consequences of consumption behavior have to be learned by consumers. In Lessig's account, social meanings affect consumer behavior because of the consumers' concern for social recognition: whether actions are taken or not depends upon the evaluation of a certain type of behavior in the eyes of others, which is why these evaluations might deliberately be altered. Lessig essentially takes a top-down perspective on norm emergence by focusing on the regulator's motivation and the techniques available for deliberately altering shared social understandings.

Our approach is more general in that it studies the evolution of consumer beliefs about how consumption behavior affects the satisfaction of basic consumer needs. We take a psychologically informed bottom-up approach to norm emergence. At the core of our argument is the assumption that consumer preferences are not entirely subjective, but that consumers have a propensity to share certain motivations due to their genetic inheritance (cf. Chapter 2) (Witt, 2001). Taking into account this material specification of consumer preferences, we arrive at a better understanding of why some norms emerge more easily than others. The joint experience of negative externalities unifies consumers in their search for a solution to the problem, making them more attentive to public campaigns which foster cooperative behavior, reducing the collective action problem involved and eliminating opposition from those consumers whose status is challenged by the formation of new social norms.

The remainder of the chapter is structured as follows. Section 3.2 defines the terms of central importance to our analysis: status-seeking consumption and social norms. In Section 3.3, we introduce our model of norm emergence. Common conjectures from the broader institutional economics literature (i.e. new externalities, mechanisms of social sanctioning and knowledge dissemination) will be complemented by hypotheses we derive from a behavioral consumption theory, the theory of learning consumers introduced earlier (cf. Chapter 2). Section 3.4 summarizes the conceptualization of the consumption of cleanliness and what is assumed to be its major determinants (cf. Chapter 2). Section 3.5 confronts the model of norm emergence with the case study of cleanliness consumption. It is shown when and how the cleanliness norm came into being, thereby replacing the status distinction of clean appearance. Section 3.6 concludes this chapter.

3.2 Status-Seeking Consumption and Social Norms

3.2.1 Status-Seeking Consumption

Economists have long recognized that many consumption decisions are motivated by the desire to receive social recognition, i.e. by the effect that a certain consumption behavior is expected to have on the individual's social environment. It is for the desire to please one's peers that consumers purchase the latest fashion (Leibenstein, 1950; Bernheim, 1994), and it is for the satisfaction derived from being awarded esteem that they acquire a piece of fine art or an expensive watch (Frank, 1989).

The literature on status-seeking consumption originates with Thorstein Veblen's work on 'conspicuous consumption' and Duesenberry's 'relative income hypothesis' (Duesenberry, 1949, Veblen, 1994[1899]). Veblen claimed that individuals accumulate ever more goods in order to possess at least as many goods as others of the same class and to rank high in comparison with the rest of the community in points of pecuniary strength (Veblen, 1994[1899], p. 20). In their striving for status, individuals are said to purchase some commodities, such as jewelry, that serve no other purpose than to demonstrate wealth (ibid, p. 53). According to Veblen, such consumption goods must be both 'wasteful' and visible in order to please 'the observers whose good opinion is sought' (ibid, p. 69). Duesenberry (1949) put forth the dichotomy of absolute versus relative income and/or consumption, claiming that consumption and savings behavior was affected by concerns of social standing. Underlying this dichotomy is the idea that human well-being is a function of both the amount and types of goods affordable as such, as well as in comparison to others.

Research has since then addressed the psychological phenomenon that 'what one person consumes, the other feels forced to consume as well'. As discussed most prominently by Robert Frank, the desire to 'keep up with the Joneses' can lead to a situation in which consumers continually increase their levels of consumption in an effort to out-consume their neighbors (Frank, 1989; 1999). These increases in relative expenditure are met by increased spending on the part of other consumers who seek to defend their relative position in social standing. Striving for status via conspicuous goods is, therefore, a zero-sum game and a 'positional treadmill'.[1]

Game-theoretic analyses have taken up this phenomenon, but do not discuss the possibility of an upper limit for these spirals of spending (e.g. Khalil, 1997; Baumol, 2004). This is in line with Veblen's claim that the desire for status is not satiable (Veblen, 1994[1899], p. 21). In addition, the majority of studies on status consumption externalities analyze the consumption dynamics stemming from interdependent preferences without asking which other motives are met by a specific consumption act (e.g. Carroll *et al.*, 1997; Brock and Durlauf,

2001; Liu and Turnovsky, 2005). However, it cannot be denied that most status goods do have certain properties that are useful to the consumer, apart from providing status distinction (Hirsch, 1976; Veblen, 1994[1899]). In fact, some goods appear to be more positional than others (Frank, 1985; Alpizar *et al.*, 2005). Which 'useful properties' certain status goods possess and which effects they have on consumption patterns are usually not elaborated.

We want to draw attention to the question of which motives other than social recognition or social comparison might be served by a specific consumption behavior, for these other motives might also influence the consumption patterns, as does the motive for social recognition. For example, other consumer motives could lead to satiation phenomena in demand, thus putting an end to spirals of spending. Less obviously, the respective consumption act might become related to a social norm, once the properties of the status good have been explored.

3.2.2 Social Norms

Generally, a social norm can be defined as 'a rule governing an individual's behavior that third parties other than state agents diffusely enforce by means of social sanction' (Ellickson, 2001). When norms are embedded in shared habits of thought and action, they can structure social interactions as subtle, undesigned forces acting upon the individuals' aspirations and dispositions (Hodgson, 2003). According to Opp, constitutive elements of most definitions of norms are behavioral regularity, collective normative expectations and sanctioning (Opp, 2001). Different types of norms can be distinguished, such as norms of cooperation, norms of reciprocity and consumption norms (Elster, 1989). For example, individuals might expect others to refrain from smoking in public places, or it is expected that one cleans up after having had a picnic in a public park. A consumption norm can be defined as 'norms that attach a reputational value to consumer behavior' (Corneo and Jeanne, 1997, p. 334). This concept usually covers the more familiar theme of conformist elements in consumer choices, which do not necessarily stand in context with social dilemmas (Leibenstein, 1950; Bikhchandani *et al.*, 1992). In game-theoretic accounts, norms are interpreted as equilibria in repeated games (e.g. Schotter, 1981) or as rules of the game established in previous interactions (North, 1991). It is another question, though, how these cooperative solutions, or norms, came into being in the first place.

3.2.3 Social Norms Replacing Status-Seeking Consumption

Clearly, the motivations associated with a certain good have an impact on consumption patterns (Witt, 2001). Particularly, there are significant differences between status-seeking consumption on one side and the compliance with social norms on the other. To begin with, when a good serves the purpose of status seeking, expenditures on this good will not necessarily have an upper limit (Veblen, 1994[1989]). By contrast, no straightforward argument supports the assumption that consumption undertaken in order to fulfill other consumers' expectations, i.e. comply with a social norm, will show an inherent tendency to rise. Furthermore, in the case of norm-fulfilling consumption behavior, the social environment determines consumer choices by prescribing what should be consumed and how much of it. For status-seeking purposes, the consumer can choose from a broader set of options, i.e. basically expensive and visible items. Finally, consumption goods, which are related to social norms, rather than status items, might be demanded by a greater number of consumers, giving rise to a standardization of goods.

How and why, then, would the meaning of a specific consumption act change from being a means to signal the consumer's status to being a means of norm compliance? Theories on status-seeking consumption cannot contribute much to understanding this issue, as no motives other than social recognition are considered. Theories on norm emergence, on the contrary, go one step further, suggesting that because of newly emerging externality problems, consumers are motivated to start coordinating their behavior (cf. Section 3.3). Yet, from a theoretical perspective, some issues still remain unresolved. In what follows, we study the driving forces behind changing mutual expectations leading to the emergence of a social (consumption) norm, particularly the social norm of cleanliness. It is argued here that, in order to understand this transformation, one has to trace how and why a consumer motivation other than social recognition became associated with a specific consumption act (cf. Section 3.4).

3.3 The Emergence of Social Norms

In this section, we present our model of norm emergence, which will bring together several strands of literature and draws upon prominent hypotheses from the broader institutional economics literature: first, the Demsetz hypothesis on newly emerging externalities (Demsetz, 1967; Coleman, 1990, Chapter 10); second, works emphasizing the role of social sanctioning and rewarding in establishing norms (Coleman, 1990, Chapter 11; McAdams, 1997; Posner, 1998); and third, the accounts of Lessig and Ellickson, in which highly influential individuals take the lead in supplying norms via public campaigns (Lessig, 1995; Ellickson, 2001). In addition, some conjectures, stemming from the behavioral consumption theory introduced earlier (cf. Chapter 2), will be put forth (Witt, 2001). The resulting framework lends itself to examining why, in a specific historical context, a consumption act changed from a means to signal the consumer's status to a means of norm compliance.

3.3.1 New Externalities

The idea that newly occurring externalities would foster changes in existing property rights regimes has most prominently been propagated by Harold Demsetz (Demsetz, 1967; Alchian and Demsetz, 1973). According to Demsetz (1967), an externality is present when the action of one agent has an effect on the welfare of another without being reflected in the price of that action, and when 'the cost of bringing the effect to bear on the decisions of one or more of the interacting persons is too high to make it worthwhile' (ibid, p. 348). Accordingly, so Demsetz hypothesizes, new property rights will develop whenever the benefits of internalization exceed its costs. An exogenous shock to a stable group, for instance, a technological change or the emergence of a new market (Demsetz, 1967) or an endogenous change in the composition of a group can produce these new externalities in the first place (Coleman, 1990, Chapter 10; Ellickson, 2001).

Demsetz illustrates his arguments by the case study of beaver hunting. He thus examines an example of a public good – a common-pool resource, whose tragic fate according to theory (overexploitation) – results from the discrepancy between individual and collective rationality (Hardin, 1968). In principle, his arguments also hold for the provision of a public good.[2] Recall that a pure public good is characterized by two attributes: first, nonrivalry in consumption, which holds 'when a unit of the good can be consumed by one individual without detracting [...] from the consumption opportunities still available to others from that same unit' (Cornes and Sandler, 1986, p. 6; italics omitted); and second, nonexcludability of benefits once the public good has been provided. Hence, in the context of public goods, externalities exhibit specific properties, namely that individuals have an incentive to free-ride on the provision of these goods as they can benefit from the contribution of others without having to pay for it. The outcome of this individually rational behavior is that, based on private action, the public good will not be provided in sufficient measure.

The two standard solutions to externality problems focus on ways in which the price of the consumption activity can be corrected to reflect its full social cost. Pigou (1920) suggested taxation and public provision of the good, while Coase (1960) advocated the specification and tradability of property rights so that actors are incentivized to privately bargain for monetary compensation. Despite their theoretical appeal, these policy options may fail in many real-world contexts. For example, policy makers might not be able to quantify the externality, or the group of actors involved is too large, causing transaction costs to exceed the welfare gains from internalization (cf. Baumol, 1962; Davis and Whinston, 1962; Buchanan, 1969; for an overview, cf. Ellickson, 1973). In these cases, norms might emerge as alternative, nonmarket and nonmonetary solutions to externality problems (e.g. Demsetz, 1967; Cornes and Sandler, 1986; Coleman, 1990).[3]

A large body of related experimental economic research does indeed hint at the existence of cooperation and reciprocity norms. This research has been devoted to the study of social interactions that are characterized by a social dilemma, such as the provision of a public good where individuals have an incentive to free-ride on others' contributions (e.g. Fehr and Gächter, 2000; Keser and van Winden, 2000; Fehr and Fischbacher, 2004). These experiments reveal that, contrary to what is individually rational, many players do make financial contributions to public goods. Apparently, there exist cooperation and reciprocity norms, which transform prisoners' dilemma type of interactions into coordination games (Camerer, 1997, p. 170). Field studies also indicate a cooperative propensity in humans which hinders the over-consumption of common-pool resources (Ostrom, 2000). This strand of research thus illustrates that social norms do exist and that they often involve the internalization of externalities, hence 'solving' a social dilemma.

Beyond doubt, Demsetz develops a valuable starting point for analyzing both changing property rights regimes and emerging social norms (Opp, 1983, Chapter 3).[4] However, he does not pay attention to the collective action problem that poses itself when agents aim to overcome this behavioral dilemma (Olson, 1965): although everybody would be better off with a norm in place, effectively preventing overexploitation of the common resource, nobody has an incentive to act in a cooperative way as long as other actors cannot be expected to cooperate as well. Demsetz thus commits the functional fallacy of explaining the existence of property rights or norms by their usefulness without addressing the *process* by which these new institutions come into being (e.g. Posner, 1979).

3.3.2 Social Feedback

One attempt to harmonize the findings from experimental research (Fehr and Fischbacher, 2004) as well as field studies (Ostrom, 2000) with the economic model of rational, self-interested individuals is to invoke mechanisms of decentralized social sanctioning in combination with repeated interaction. In fact, sanctioning opportunities often enhance cooperative behavior in experiments (Fehr and Gächter, 2000).[5]

The effect of social sanctioning mechanisms on fostering norm emergence has been pointed out by many scholars (Axelrod, 1986; Coleman, 1990, Chapter 11; McAdams, 1997; Posner, 1998). These approaches share the assumption that individual behavior is affected by the feedback that individuals can expect to receive from their social environment when engaging in a certain behavior. By rewarding cooperative behavior and sanctioning uncooperative behavior, social feedback supports the formation of a social norm of cooperation. However, sanctioning is also a public good, whose costly provision individuals would prefer to be taken care of by others. Axelrod (1986) tackled this issue by introducing meta-norms of sanctioning. Similarly, McAdams (1997) suggested that acts of sanctioning will themselves be socially rewarded and that individuals confer positive esteem on those who support the provision of a public good by sanctioning noncontributors.[6] Posner (1998) may have a similar idea in mind when arguing that sanctioning produces a signal which might pay off for the individual in terms of future cooperative interactions and transactions. Overall, these approaches shift the problem of collective action to higher-order levels without convincingly solving it.

3.3.3 New Information and 'Managers' of Norm Emergence

A more elaborate distinction between individual actors, based on the role they play in the process of norm emergence, is found in Lessig's account of the regulation of 'social meaning' (Lessig, 1995; 1996; 1998) as well as in Ellickson's treatise on the 'market for norms' (Ellickson, 2001).

Ellickson (2001) frames norm emergence analogously to the stylized diffusion process of an innovation within society, whereby actors are modeled as heterogeneous (Bass, 1969; Rogers, 1995).[7] Several types of leading figures promoting norm emergence are distinguished.[8] Among them are scientists whose interest in promoting change stems from their personal motivation to generate new knowledge and make it public. Scientists are assumed to have the best 'technical knowledge' of a subject, i.e. of the situation which is characterized as an externality problem, though scientists themselves are not necessarily best suited to communicate the benefits of change to the public. This is the task of opinion leaders whose actions are motivated by social approval of those who demand the emergence of the new norm.

Although Ellickson's account revolves around the core idea of how social sanctions and rewards bring about new norms when it is assumed that actors put different weight on social esteem, the author also calls attention to the relevance of knowledge change as such. The acquisition of new knowledge about externalities and their probable causes is a potential triggering factor of new social norms. In principle, two cases can be distinguished: new scientific information either makes actors aware of the existence of a certain problem (a), or new information makes them believe that a well-known problem can be solved in a better way by a different behavioral regularity (b). In order to change consumer behavior, new knowledge must diffuse within society. In this context, both the existence of new knowledge as well as its relevance and application have to be communicated in order to receive consumer attention. Ellickson stresses that it matters a great deal for the successful formation of the norm who communicates this new knowledge to the actors involved. Only specific actors have an impact on others' opinions.

Ellickson's framework of norm emergence shares several elements with Lessig's account developed earlier, concerning the regulation of 'social meaning'. In a series of papers, Lessig formulates a positive theory of norm emergence and derives policy implications for the regulation of consumer behavior (Lessig, 1995; 1996; 1998). He develops the idea that the types of behavior shown by people and considered as 'normal' depend upon the social meaning of that behavior, i.e. the shared social interpretations of these actions.[9] Varying meanings affect consumers' mutual expectations. For example, when smoking has a very negative image, you do not expect others to tolerate your smoking. Based on this assumption, Lessig illustrates how changes in behavior can be brought about by deliberately altering the social meaning of certain actions.

The emergence of a social norm is dealt with as a special case (Lessig, 1995). In line with Ellickson, two elements play a central role for norm emergence:

first, new information distributed via public campaigns, and second, central agents promoting the formation of a new norm. The two approaches differ, however, in their concrete assumptions: Ellickson's leading figures promote norm emergence mainly to gain social recognition (e.g. being honorable scientists), whereas Lessig's managers of meaning foster the changing of meanings for other underlying reasons (including status concerns only as a special case). Lessig (1995) illustrates his arguments by a comprehensive case study – the emerging nonsmoking norm in the United States in the second half of the twentieth century (for which he is usually quoted). This norm is the result of public campaigns that distributed information on the health effects of smoking (concerning both the smoker him or herself as well as second-hand smokers), coupled with the creation of a negative image of smokers as 'irresponsible' and 'weak'. Lessig compares this situation with that of the nineteenth century, when smoking was the privilege of men, indicating their superior social status.

Lessig provides valuable and detailed insights into the process of norm emergence while discussing a case of consumption behavior that was once a status signal but became related to a social norm at some point in time. Lessig essentially provides a top-down approach. He shows how some individuals, who have an interest in defending or changing social meanings, can achieve these goals by applying certain techniques of meaning management. As in Ellickson's framework, public campaigns are the main driving forces behind changes in consumer behavior.

However, neither Lessig nor Ellickson provide a full account of the effectiveness of newly distributed information. Ellickson simply relates the effectiveness of these campaigns to whomever communicates the information, whereas Lessig claims that society has to be open to embracing the change. But Lessig does not provide a general starting point for understanding the openness of a community to change, which would amount to a bottom-up approach. Although he acknowledges that not all attempts at meaning regulation are necessarily effective, he does not elaborate on the conditions making processes of social learning more or less likely, particularly in contrast to individual learning. Moreover, Lessig does not explicitly deal with the general factors triggering new attempts to alter social meanings. The concept of shared social understandings mainly applies to a society's agreement on which behavior is 'normal' and what it says about a person deviating from this expected behavior. Thus, Lessig concentrates on only one specific consumer motivation – the consumers' striving for social approval. He assumes that actions, which at some point become related to negative images via public campaigns, will no longer be taken or will decline in frequency in order to avoid social ostracism. The consumers' desire to appeal to their social environment is thus the way through which changed social meanings can have an effect on consumer behavior. In this sense, Lessig includes the idea of social feedback mentioned earlier. However, the idea is not generalized to cover evolving social understandings that affect other consumer needs.

In what follows, we will make a step forward in this direction. Recall that evolving associations between consumption goods on one side and consumer motivations for consuming these goods on the other have previously been termed 'learning processes' (cf. Chapter 2). In the following subsection, we integrate learning processes into the established frameworks of norm emergence by drawing upon the psychologically informed theory of learning consumers (Witt, 2001). We argue that this comprehensive approach will contribute to a better understanding of norm emergence and specifically to a better understanding of the effectiveness of public campaigns which modify social meanings and social norms. At the core of our argument is the assumption that consumer preferences are not entirely subjective, but that consumers share certain motivations due to their genetic inheritance.

3.3.4 Basic Needs and Consumer Learning

Our model of norm emergence draws upon the aforementioned strands of literature that relate new social norms to, first, new consumption externalities; second, mechanisms of social feedback; and third, the relevance of leading figures in communicating new knowledge to other actors. In addition, some original hypotheses will be derived in this subsection. The theoretical framework to be developed can contribute to explaining why, despite the collective action problem involved, social norms can emerge as effective solutions to externality problems. In addition, it will shed some light on what influences the effectiveness of newly distributed information in changing consumer behavior. The resulting model of norm emergence, it is argued here, is equally suited to understanding the transformation of the meaning of a consumption activity from a means of status signaling to a means of fulfilling a social norm. The terminology of 'meaning' is in line with Lessig's understanding, namely that the properties of consumption activities are partly the result of processes of social construction: a group of individuals agrees upon which types of goods function as status signals or what kind of behaviors are norm fulfilling.

In contrast to Lessig, we are not only interested in the process that brings about the change in meaning, but also in asking about the contingencies of these changing associations. We find them in the evolving understandings about the *nonconstructed properties* of goods, i.e. conjectures about the functional relationship between consumption activities and the satisfaction of basic consumer needs other than social recognition. We thus acknowledge the relevance of epistemological barriers and learning processes concerning the content of a social norm. In general terms, we put greater emphasis on analyzing norm emergence as a *learning process* than does the former. We assume that norm formation is strongly affected by individuals' 'mental models' (Denzau and North, 1994), i.e. the interpretation and internal representation of their environment.[10] By taking into account epistemological barriers, a trial-and-error mechanism of change is proposed here. In that regard, our approach differs from the above-mentioned accounts in a number of ways. In our analysis, norms are not understood as behavioral regularities only, which emerge for no apparent reason. At the same time, we do not assume that emerging norms are necessarily effective and provide efficient solutions to externality problems. There are cases where norms emerge only as 'side products' of other measures to solve an externality problem, and where the effective solution cannot be attributed to the norm only (e.g. Posner, 1996).

The core of our argument is formulated in the following hypothesis:

> H.3.1: Individuals share certain basic preferences and derive utility from the same actions due to commonalities in basic human needs. This motivates and enables them to coordinate their behavior for achieving common goals (Commonalities Hypothesis).

The theoretical framework underlying this hypothesis is a behavioral consumption theory, the theory of learning consumers by Ulrich Witt (2001), with its central concept of a consumer basic need. As explained in Chapter 2, consumer needs are depicted as behavioral dispositions of the consumer, motivating him or her to take certain actions. As these basic needs are part of our genetic repertoire, they are universally shared by humans. The common genetic basis of humans gives rise to commonalities in what consumers desire, i.e. what motivates them to take action and from what kind of actions they derive utility. This implies that preferences are not of a completely subjectivist nature, which is one of the core assumptions of standard neoclassical economics.

How is this relevant for the process of norm emergence? Let us imagine that many consumers are affected by a newly occurring endogenous or exogenous shock, such as a newly emerging consumption externality. Let us further assume that this externality problem jeopardizes basic human needs. In view of the commonalities in the consumers' basic preferences, this will have two effects. First, all consumers experience the externality in a similar way, and second, all of them share the common goal to solve the externality problem. This general propensity to share goals makes consumers willing to take coordinated action. Interestingly, the material specification of commonalities in consumer preferences as widely shared, nonsubjectivist basic needs provides an intuitive argument for why payoff structures in prisoner's dilemma games should be symmetric for players: as actors show commonalities in their preferences, they share a motivation to act and they derive the same utility from cooperative solutions.[11]

Externalities are usually defined in an abstract way, as discrepancies between social and private costs, or by pointing to the attributes of the good in question, i.e. nonexcludability of benefits and nonrivalry in consumption. However, intuition suggests that externalities in the form of, say, an open-air concert or the spread of an infectious disease (Cornes and Sandler, 1986, p. 115) have quite different effects on individual welfare. Only the latter seriously jeopardizes the basic need for health. We suggest distinguishing externality problems by the extent to which they affect shared consumer needs and imply the deprivation of basic needs. We conjecture that the emergence of norms is much more likely in the latter than in the former case because of differences in the magnitude of the problem and different degrees of problem awareness. For example, in the case of a spreading infectious disease, individual benefits from vaccination are considerable. Individuals might therefore have a strong incentive to provide the public good of public health by getting vaccinated, although they know that this benefits free riders as well. The social dilemma or collective action problem is much less pronounced in such a case, thus facilitating conditional cooperation. This yields the following hypothesis:

> H.3.2: The emergence of social norms as solutions to newly occurring externality problems is more likely the more strongly the externality affects shared consumer needs (Cooperation Hypothesis).

Despite the high willingness of consumers to cooperate in order to solve the externality problem, actual behavioral changes may not occur when consumers are lacking an adequate problem-solving strategy. In game theoretic studies, the outcome of repeated social interactions ultimately depends on the frequency with which *well-defined* cooperative or noncooperative strategies are chosen. We argue that it is of little help to assume per se that actors will know *ex ante* which behavior counts as cooperative and which does not (in game theoretic terms: the strategy for obtaining the specified payoffs). Such a framework blocks the perspective on the process of norm emergence that might be characterized by trial-and-error mechanisms of change.[12] Externalities might be observable, for example, long before the causes of their emergence are understood and strategies for eliminating the problem are identified. To ask which kind of actions would bring about an internalization of the newly occurring externality is to ask about the *content* of social norms. We frame norm emergence as a process of consumer learning by drawing attention to the effects of changes in knowledge on norm formation:

> H.3.3: When externalities jeopardize shared consumer needs, the learning of strategies for externality internalization (here: the content of the social norm) corresponds to forming new associations between consumption activities and the satisfaction of consumer needs (Content Hypothesis).

The formation of new associations is the subject of the theory of learning consumers (cf. Chapter 2). According to this account, consumer learning of new behaviors can take several forms. Witt (2001) suggests that consumers basically acquire new behavioral repertoires in two ways: either by individual trial-and-error learning or by communicating with and imitating others, i.e. social learning processes.[13] To understand, on an individual basis, the causal connection between certain behaviors and the satisfaction of consumer needs depends first of all on the quality of feedback (Einhorn and Hogarth, 1978), i.e. on how clearly an effect (need satisfaction) can be traced back to a specific cause (consumption behavior) – for example, through sensory experiences. Finding a solution to an externality problem on an individual basis might often prove impossible, as the outcome of an individual's behavior depends upon the joint behavior of the interacting individuals. As a result, consumers might turn to others for help, particularly to those whom they find credible. That way, they can also economize on individual learning costs and react more quickly to new externality problems. In addition, they do not have to generate potentially harmful experiences themselves – think of an individual who is ill and has to find a suitable treatment by him or herself. In general, the more strongly a problem affects a consumer's basic needs (magnitude of the problem) and the more difficult it is to find one's own 'recipes' for problem solving (quality of the feedback), the more likely that the consumer will turn to others for advice. Vice versa, the effectiveness of information provision in terms of changing consumer behavior largely depends on the consumers' problem awareness:

> H.3.4: Knowledge dissemination is more effective, in terms of triggering behavioral adaptations, the more strongly a problem affects the consumer's basic needs and the less likely that he or she can solve the problem through individual learning (Knowledge Hypothesis).

The latter hypothesis implies that, in order to understand why new information produces changes in behavior, it is necessary to open the 'black box' of consumer motivations. Consumer attention to information is selective, and knowledge progress need not always trigger behavioral adaptations. According to Witt, (2001) the process of information acquisition is guided by those needs that the consumer is most deprived of. When many consumers experience deprivation in the same way and when they turn to the same sources of information, similarities in behavior will occur, which leads to a behavioral regularity. By taking into account the role of basic consumer needs in consumer learning processes, we arrive at a better understanding of why information provision will be more effective in some cases than in others. Clearly, this adds to the understanding of norm emergence.

Processes of social learning, including communication with and imitation of other individuals, can also stem from the individual's desire for social approval. Consumers learn new behavioral patterns simply to please their peers. In Witt's conception, consumers learn which consumption activities satisfy the basic need for social recognition. This learning process is brought about by social feedback: whenever the social environment rewards a certain behavior, consumers are inclined to show this behavior more frequently in the future (and vice versa), for they will want to continue receiving the positive rewards from others by fulfilling the latter's expectations.[14] That way, an originally individual consumption activity is turned into a socially determined activity. The social reward obviously depends upon 'doing the right thing' in the eyes of others: both the type of consumption act and the level of consumption which is rewarded with social esteem is socially determined. According to this framework, transformations in consumer behavior occur whenever the social feedback related to a specific consumption activity changes (or, in other words, when the consumption activities that receive positive social feedback vary) and/or when the expected consumption level is altered. This type of learning process obviously depends upon repeated social interactions and visible consumption behaviors.

That social feedback can lead to the formation of (new) behavioral regularities has already been explained in the literature review on norm emergence. Drawing upon Witt (2001), we argue that such a social feedback mechanism can even have long-run implications for consumption patterns, for behaviors exhibited by individuals for social reward will eventually become rewarding in their own right, as consumers start to associate the positive feedback with a specific behavior itself ('associative learning'). This means that consumers will continue to perform these consumption activities, even if positive social feedback occurs only from time to time. Why certain consumption activities rather than others might be subject to social recognition is understood in light of the preceding discussion on norm emergence.

3.4 The Consumption of Cleanliness

This chapter tackles the emergence of the social norm of cleanliness. Cleanliness, in the form of clean clothes, is the outcome of a household production activity, a 'commodity', if you wish (Michael and Becker, 1973). As is explained in Chapter 2, with the term 'consumption of cleanliness', we refer to the inputs into the household production process of laundry washing, covering both consumer expenditures on goods and services as well as the utilization of the respective products. Clean clothes are assumed to have instrumental value for more fundamental consumer preferences – the previously mentioned basic needs.

At present, the majority of households in industrialized countries use washing machines to ensure cleanliness. In the United States, the diffusion degree of this device amounts to about 80 per cent, pointing to a saturated market (EIA, 2011). In the United Kingdom, 92 per cent of all households are equipped with a clothes washer (Rickards *et al.*, 2004). Arguably, similar figures hold for other industrialized countries. The proliferation process of washing machines has its origin at the beginning of the twentieth century; since then, the device has diffused rapidly (cf. Chapter 4). In parallel, laundry quantities have increased substantially: the amounts of laundry per consumer today are multiples of what consumers used to wash fifty (Shove, 2003) or more than a hundred years ago (Klepp, 2003).

Two basic needs are nowadays associated with clean clothes: health and social recognition (cf. Chapter 2).[15] In the medical field, it is common knowledge that the washing of textiles can contribute to hygiene via disinfection. Vice versa, if hygiene is insufficient, fabrics can have negative health effects. In sociology, it is commonplace that, in choosing their level of cleanliness, consumers look to the opinions of others, for the notion of cleanliness itself is a social construct. This means that society defines when a consumer can be considered 'clean' (Cowan, 1983; Douglas, 1984).[16] The relevance of social recognition is also indicated by surveys showing that clothes are washed for health reasons as well as for social motives (cf. Chapter 2). More precisely, cleanliness, particularly the absence of body odor, appears to be a social norm in many industrialized countries today. Whereas cleanliness has now become a concern for every member of society, cleanliness used to be a signal of social status in the past (cf. Chapter 4). In the nineteenth century, few people could afford to spend enough money and time on their outer appearance so as to be clean in terms of the prevailing definition. In fact, depending on status and residence, households differed strongly in terms of possessions, the amount of clothing, the outer appearance and the material conditions of housework (Du Vall, 1998, p. 175; Hardyment, 1988, p. 22; Strasser, 1999, p. 39). The status connotation of cleanliness was still present in many countries, particularly the United Kingdom and the United States, until the middle of the nineteenth century (e.g. Ashenburg, 2007, p. 169).

Apparently, the normative expectations that consumers had of one another changed at some point during the transition from the nineteenth to the twentieth century: everybody started to expect everybody else to be clean, and the level of the individual's consumption of cleanliness became socially determined. As a result, the number of consumers demanding cleanliness and purchasing the respective products, including washing machines, significantly increased. In addition, the status distinction by cleanliness vanished. The explanation of this development will be given in the next section. A central role in this historical transformation process, it is argued here, has been played by the other basic need involved in cleanliness consumption, namely health.

In what follows, we concentrate on cleanliness in the form of clean clothes, ensured by laundering and, to a lesser extent, body hygiene, for this is the case study of interest here. In principle, a great part of our argument can also be applied to other related household production activities such as house cleaning. By focusing on clothing, we analyze norm emergence in situations of repeated social interactions. Certainly, the cleanliness of the consumer's home can also be observed by others when entering it. But cleanliness reflected in the outer appearance, i.e. the absence of odors and/or stains, is more conspicuous in character. It is 'mobile' and something that the consumer 'carries' to all sorts of social interactions such as the workplace, school, and so on. Ultimately, consumers will take what they can most easily and immediately observe as an indicator of the other consumer's overall cleanliness – and as a proxy for his or her health status (cf. Section 3.5). This does not exclude that an emerging norm of cleanliness will 'spread' to other cleaning activities as well.

3.5 The Emergence of the Cleanliness Norm

This section addresses the emergence of the social norm of cleanliness in the Western world. The presentation focuses on the developments that took place in the United Kingdom and the United States, while the very general process described here should also hold for other countries which have gone through a period of industrialization and urbanization in the nineteenth century. We aim to illustrate how processes of social learning triggered the formation of a social norm and thereby removed the status gains which could formerly be derived from cleanliness. A stylized overview of the historical development in the United Kingdom and the United States is given before the facts are interpreted in light of the model of norm emergence developed in Section 3.3.

3.5.1 Stylized Historical Development

During the nineteenth century, major changes took place in the geographic distribution of inhabitants in Britain. It was the time of flourishing industrialization, which triggered large movements of internal migration. Increasing numbers of inhabitants left the rural environment to work in the emerging manufacturing sector (Mathias, 1983, Chapters 5 and 6; Floud, 1994, p. 18). Within the cities, population density was fostered by the absence of cheap public transport, which would have allowed inhabitants to move further away from the workplace (MacKinnon, 1994, p. 280).

The rising population density coincided with bad living conditions in the urban habitat. At that time, the main proximate cause of death among younger people were infectious diseases such as typhoid, cholera and tuberculosis (Baines, 1994). In fact, nineteenth century Britain was shaken by a couple of serious epidemics. Among the most lethal diseases was smallpox (Oxley, 2003). This is a viral infection transmitted by close contact between people via droplet infection (typhoid and cholera, on the contrary, are waterborne diseases). In general, increases in population density raised the likelihood of contracting an infectious disease, independent of the channel of transmission or social class (Oxley, 2003). In addition, the factories built in the 1820s and after accommodated a great number of employees, often working in a dusty or humid environment (e.g. textile mills), thus fostering chronic diseases such as tuberculosis and respiratory diseases. Average height serves as a proxy for the standard of living, and it is estimated to have declined in the first decades of the nineteenth century (Baines, 1994, p. 34).

Similar trends hold for the United States. The share of people employed in agriculture declined from 1810 to 1860, accompanied by migration from rural to urban areas. As in Britain, life expectancy decreased during the first half of the nineteenth century. Migration, interregional trade and the close proximity of inhabitants at the workplace and in the emerging public schools fostered the spread of infectious diseases (Costa and Steckel, 1997). Water supply and sewage systems were inadequate, allowing endemic diseases to spread 'from the slums to the homes of the wealthy' (Fee, 1994, p. 232).

In the nineteenth century, little was known about the actual causes of such lethal diseases as smallpox and plague. Competing theories existed as to their origin.[17] The so-called 'germ theory of disease', relating disease to certain types of microorganisms, was fully established only at the end of the nineteenth century. It is mainly attributed to the pioneering work of Louis Pasteur and Robert Koch, who identified the connection between pathogen microorganisms and disease.[18] The new medical knowledge was brought to the United States by young Americans that had studied bacteriology in Germany, such as William Henry Welch and Alexander C. Abbott (Fee, 1994). Of central importance to the development and acceptance of the germ theory were the microscope and the method of experimental testing: agents of disease could be visualized, replicated and associated with the symptoms of disease. Based on data collection and statistical inference, beliefs about actual causal dependencies between microorganisms and disease turned into objective, 'replicable' knowledge (Cunningham, 1992; Warner, 1992). Hence, the laboratory enabled a knowledge progression which would not have been possible in a personal trial-and-error manner (Mokyr, 2000).

Once these insights became common knowledge, the improvement of sanitary conditions in urban areas became one of the major pillars in the fight against disease. This included cleaning the water supply, establishment of sewage systems, and so on. In addition, quarantine was practiced more extensively than before (Costa and Steckel, 1997). Many of these measures targeted the channels of disease transmission. In terms of prevention, the practice of vaccination became gradually established by codifying it into British law (Oxley, 2003). In the United States, vaccination was complemented by later improvements in medical technology, in particular, the introduction and mass-production of antibiotics between 1930 and 1950 (Costa and Steckel, 1997).

Besides these structural and legal measures, the individual consumer's behavior was also targeted by pointing to the benefits of personal hygiene. The goal was to increase the cleanliness standards of all members of society, independent of class. For that purpose, the new scientific knowledge about the origins of disease and effective measures preventing its proliferation had to diffuse within society. 'Home economists', i.e. female scientists studying housework, were the central agents in public campaigns for hygiene in the United States (Matthews, 1987, Chapter 6; Attar, 1990; Strasser, 2000 [1982], Chapter 11).[19] As leading figures of the 'Hygienic Movement', they were dedicated to raising the hygienic standards of the average consumer. At the same time, they strived for making housekeeping an object of scientific inquiry and sharing their scientific findings with the public (Andrews and Andrews, 1974).[20] Their target audience was homemakers. Home economists distributed their knowledge in the form of household advice books, leaflets and women's magazines as well as teaching (e.g. Cowan, 1976; McClary, 1980; Sivulka, 2001). Often, objective information was paired with moral appeals (Mokyr, 2000, p. 17):

> Homemakers had to be persuaded that they were the primary guardians at the household gate, armed with mop and sponge and charged with keeping out the microscopic enemy. The responsibility of homemakers to keep the domestic environment germ-free was the main logical prerequisite to

'blaming' inadequate maternal care for the high infant and child mortality rates that still plagued the United States and Britain in the late nineteenth century.

Apparently, consumers were not only educated about the impact of hygiene on health; they were also urged to immediately incorporate this new knowledge into their daily practices. That way, consumer health became a matter of personal responsibility. In addition, it was emphasized that individuals expected these higher standards of cleanliness of one another, thus turning cleanliness into a matter of social recognition (Cowan, 1976, p. 16). Particularly, advertisements for soap appealed to feelings of guilt and social ostracism (Cohen, 1982, p. 90). Laundering was seen as an expression of love by the housewife for her family, and mothers who sent their children to school in dirty dresses should have felt embarrassed and guilty (Cowan, 1976, p. 16).

In the middle of the nineteenth century, the Hygienic Movement gained momentum, and the fight against disease turned into a fight against dirt, as such (Mokyr, 2000). In that regard, home economists worked hand in hand with producers of new products and equipment which were said to improve consumers' hygiene, and eventually their health, including laundry equipment and soap. They actively supported the advertising of new products by pointing to their benefits in producing hygiene (Matthews, 1987, Chapter 6). At the beginning of the twentieth century, the use of soap was promoted at schools (Peet, 1952, p. 568). Interestingly, many of the promoted products had already been available before the end of the nineteenth century. The beginnings of the washing machine industry in the United States can be dated back to 1860.[21] In Britain, prices of soap products had already fallen in the first half of the nineteenth century without significantly shifting the demand for soap upwards (Edwards, 1962, p. 135). Only after the intense marketing efforts of producers and home economists did the demand for soap, washing and cleaning equipment, and so on substantially expand (Vinikas, 1992; Mokyr and Stein, 1997). The annual per capita consumption of soap products in Britain, for instance, increased by a factor of six from 3.6 pounds in 1801 to 18.0 pounds in 1912, with major shifts from the 1870s onwards (Edwards, 1962, p. 135).

The moral connotations of housework and hygiene persisted until the beginning of the twentieth century. Middle–class consumers, however, did not have to be convinced of the 'gospel of cleanliness' (Tomes, 1998). They had already maintained fairly high cleanliness standards before the germ theory of disease became fully established (Matthews, 1987, Chapter 2). This is nicely reflected in household advice books, popular novels and advertisements in the media, such as women's magazines. Matthews argues that middle-class consumers practiced a kind of 'cult of domesticity', for which the rise of the genre of the 'domestic novel' in the middle of the nineteenth century – praising the merits of 'good housekeeping' – is an indicator (cf. Chapter 4) (Matthews, 1987, p. 11). Middle- and upper-class consumers were motivated to keep themselves, their clothes and their homes clean for the status gains they derived from this. With more and more consumers ensuring higher standards of cleanliness, the status distinction by clean appearance gradually vanished.

3.5.2 Interpretation from the Perspective of Consumer Learning

In view of the collected evidence, the emergence of the cleanliness norm in the Western world, particularly in the United Kingdom and the United States, can be dated to the period between the middle of the nineteenth and the beginning of the twentieth centuries. This norm emerged when people were urgently looking for ways to solve the problem of the spread of infectious diseases that occurred in the period of industrialization and urbanization. Infectious diseases can be interpreted as an externality (Cornes and Sandler, 1986, p. 115) which emerged with an increased local proximity of consumers. Due to this radical change in social networks, consumer behavior, including the consumption of cleanliness, turned from a private into a public good: issues which had previously been people's private concerns, such as body hygiene and waste disposal, now required coordinated action on the part of consumers.

Of central importance to the emergence of the cleanliness norm was the basic need for health and the deprivation experienced by consumers at that time. Each individual must have realized the problem and can be assumed to have searched for ways of solving it. But consumers were not well equipped to decide how best to achieve improvements in health, for the traditional beliefs as to how disease emerged and how to address it had become obsolete. In principle, each consumer could, by a trial–and–error method, have tried to find out what the best strategies were for improving his or her health. However, as health is a delicate issue, it is not likely that consumers would simply have 'experimented' with such a fundamental aspect of life. The historical overview reveals that behavioral strategies for satisfying the need for health came about by a process of social, not individual, learning.[22] On the one hand, consumers turned to those they regarded as experts in health matters for the fact that they lacked 'personal recipes' for avoiding pain. On the other hand, home economists, both scientists and opinion leaders, were motivated to assure their social standing in society and disseminate their knowledge about the importance of hygiene. Both the search for information and actual information provision probably coincided to a high degree. This alone would bring about similarities in behavioral adaptations. But the social feedback consumers received for their behavior is another crucial element in the transition process that resulted in the cleanliness norm. Due to the germ theory of disease, the public good nature of health was better understood. Consumers formed new beliefs as to the existence and origins of this externality. When it was realized that, in narrow surroundings, individual health translated into the health status of others, measures were taken to coordinate consumer behavior. This was not only done through education, but also by means of social feedback. In fact, information campaigns by home economists and public health officials did not only communicate 'objective' information. In addition, their messages contained strong, moral connotations, pointing to what was expected of consumers by society. References to social ostracism in case of deviating behavior were also part of advertisements. Beliefs were altered as to which behavior was normal and expected. Taken together, these forms of social feedback hint at the emergence of a social norm (Ellickson, 1991).

Upper-class consumers did not need to change their behavior substantially, as they had already kept fairly high standards of cleanliness previously. Household advice books can certainly not be taken at face value in practical terms, but they indicate the importance of cleanliness for the well-to-do. At that time, one could show oneself to be different from the lower classes by being clean: cleanliness was visible – as it still is today – i.e. conspicuous and rare. The lower-class consumers, on the contrary, were deprived of both social recognition and cleanliness. When greater cleanliness was demanded of them, they would not only improve their health, but their social standing as well. Still, to view the increase in the consumption of cleanliness merely as a process of social emulation, i.e. lower class consumers imitating upper-class consumers, would not do justice to the phenomenon at hand. Processes of social emulation are triggered by the need for social recognition, whereas the process analyzed here clearly stems from the basic need for health, of which consumers felt deprived as they faced an externality problem. So the increasing deprivation in terms of health ultimately explains the transformation of cleanliness from being a signal of status to a means to fulfill a social norm. Had a process of social emulation taken place, then upper-class consumers, whose social status was challenged by the efforts of all consumers to improve their cleanliness, might have tried to oppose this undesired trend. In fact, there is evidence of such endeavors in the past, i.e. upper-class consumers defending their social standing through regulations (e.g. Lessig, 1995, p. 1027, on smoking).[23] That upper-class consumers did not become active in this way can be seen as an indicator of the increasing gravity of the externality problem all consumers faced. Due to knowledge change, behavioral adaptations took a certain direction, and social motives guided the learning process. But the consideration of the basic need for health is necessary to understand why expectations changed. By the end, consumers had learned to associate health with visual cleanliness, and norm compliance was manifested in the outer appearance of consumers.[24]

Yet, we do not want to take a functionalist perspective on norm emergence here. Certainly, in the nineteenth century, when infectious diseases were still prominent in the United Kingdom and the United States, a positive effect on health could have been achieved by increasing the cleanliness of the body, clothes and the private habitat. But it is a difficult task to evaluate how far personal hygiene contributed to the eradication of infectious diseases in comparison with the improvements of sanitary conditions as well as the practice of vaccination. For diseases which are transmitted by droplet infection, it is not unlikely that clothing and textiles could have served as vectors of disease transmission. Hence, more intense laundering – as well as other practices of hygiene – could have made a contribution in terms of disinfection. Luckin (1984), for example, sees a connection between increased personal hygiene and the decline of typhus in nineteenth century London (the body louse, which functions as a vector of disease transmission, thrives in dirty clothing). Also, de Vries (1994, p. 264) postulates that changes in household behavior played an essential role:

> Indeed, I would go so far as to claim that it was more through the household productive system than the larger formal economy that the major achievements of industrial society – lower morbidity and mortality, better nutrition and higher education levels, greater comfort – were achieved. None of these 'goods' can be bought off the shelf.

However, the major impact on consumer health is probably to be attributed to vaccination, improvements in public infrastructure and better sewage systems, as well as the introduction of antibiotics (Mokyr, 2000).

3.6 Conclusions

This chapter has addressed the transformation of a consumption activity from a means to signal the consumer's status to a means of norm compliance. As we have shown, this process can only be understood by opening the 'black box' of consumer motivations and by tracing how an additional motive – other than social recognition – became associated with a specific consumption act. The evolving associations between consumption activities on one side and the satisfaction of consumer needs on the other are interpreted as manifestations of consumer learning processes. In line with the hypotheses introduced earlier (Needs Hypothesis, Learning Hypothesis and Commonalities Hypothesis, cf. Chapter 2), Chapter 3 has shown how patterns of cleanliness consumption have been affected by consumer learning processes about the need-satisfaction potential of specific consumption activities.

We have shown how an understanding of the process of norm emergence benefits from a material specification of consumer preferences and of the content of social norms. At the core of our argument is the assumption that consumer preferences are not entirely subjective but that consumers have a propensity to share certain motivations due to their genetic inheritance (Witt, 2001). By linking externality problems to the concept of basic needs, we opened up a psychologically informed perspective on norm emergence that could shed some light on what affects the consumer's willingness to cooperate, despite the possibility of free riders. When externalities jeopardize consumers' needs, the learning of strategies for externality internalization corresponds to forming associations between consumption activities and the satisfaction of consumer needs. To depict norm emergence as a learning process means to reject the assumption that actors know ex ante which kind of strategy or behavior will bring about the internalization of a newly occurring externality. We hypothesize that the more severe the externality problem is in terms of affecting consumer needs and the more difficult it is to find solutions on an individual basis, the more likely that processes of social learning will take place. Consumer attention to public campaigns greatly depends on these two factors.

This is exactly what has happened in the consumption activity of clothes washing: the social norm of cleanliness emerged in the nineteenth century in the Western world and eliminated the status-signaling property of clean appearance. Individual consumption of cleanliness turned from a private into a public good when population density rose in the period of growing industrialization and urbanization. The formation of the social norm of cleanliness was triggered when consumers learned to associate the consumption of cleanliness with health. In contrast to that, processes of social emulation appear to have played a comparatively minor role.

At present, a clean appearance, i.e. visually clean clothing and the absence of smell, is no longer granted status. Instead, cleanliness is associated with consumer health and a social norm. Note that this argument pertains to the outcome of the consumption activity of laundry washing – cleanliness, which has lost its status-signaling potential – not to the products themselves. Public health continues to be a public good today. However, infectious diseases such as smallpox play virtually no role in modern industrialized countries. The potential impact of less-than-clean clothing or insufficient personal hygiene on the provision of this public good is thus much less pronounced today. Still, the social significance of the consumption activity might be maintained in the long-run through repetition of action and self-reinforcing mechanisms.

From a theoretical perspective, Chapter 3 has demonstrated that the assumption of some commonalities in consumer preferences (cf. Chapter 2) enhances our understanding of the emergence of social norms. Moreover, we have proven the compatibility of the body of literature on norm emergence with the psychologically substantiated theory of learning consumers (Witt, 2001). Beyond that, we added a piece to the literature on status-seeking consumption by identifying conditions under which the status-signaling property of a consumption activity will change. Finally, we put forth an example showing that the social significance of a consumption activity need not be an arbitrary property of that activity – although the conditions which gave rise to this social significance might become obsolete, whereas the social significance of the consumption act is maintained beyond that point in time.

Chapter 3 has shown that the social norm of cleanliness has its origin in the Hygienic Movement of the nineteenth century. The major implication of this norm coming into being is an increase in the consumption of goods with which to produce cleanliness, resulting from higher cleanliness aspirations and consumers demanding cleanliness in larger numbers. The origin of the present mass market for products such as soap and laundry equipment can thus be traced back to these particular historical circumstances. In other words, the change in consumer aspirations was a necessary *consumer-side condition* for the increase in cleanliness consumption to occur. For these higher cleanliness aspirations to manifest themselves in substantially different consumption patterns, accompanying processes – particularly at the production side – were crucial as well. In the following chapter, we take a closer look at technological progress in laundry equipment, particularly washing machines, as the most important element of household technology (cf. Chapter 4).

Notes

1 Veblen (1994) [1899] discusses the consumption of positional goods (in the form of conspicuous goods) in the context of status concerns, whereas Frank (1989; 1999) interprets positional goods more from an instrumental perspective: consumption is not so much motivated by the positive social rewards as such (hence a need for social recognition), as by the desire to keep one's social standing.

2 Note that Demsetz's (1967) argumentation deals with the utilization of a public good, the common-pool resource of beavers, whereas our analysis of cleanliness consumption will focus on the provision of a public good.

3 No such dilemma exists when noncontributors can be excluded, at a reasonable cost, from enjoying the benefits of a good in the first place, as is the case for impure public goods (club goods) (Buchanan, 1965).

4 Witt (1987) even argues that the case study of beaver hunting does not provide evidence for the emergence of a property rights regime, but rather for a 'regulated community right' (i.e. communal ownership in combination with curtailment of use), which comes close to the concept of a social norm.

5 Axelrod (1984) illustrated that the 'tit-for-tat' strategy of reciprocity, which starts off from cooperative play in a repeated prisoner's dilemma game, on average yields a higher payoff than other strategies. The fact that individuals do not maximize their payoffs, even in one-shot games where no sanctioning is possible (the 'dictator game'; cf. Camerer and Thaler, 1995), points to the pre-existence of norms of fairness. Some argue that this makes the assumption of purely selfish individuals obsolete (Fehr and Fischbacher, 2004).

6 McAdams (1997) rules out the potential second-order dilemma by claiming that what can be termed the 'social police' derives net benefits from encouraging cooperative behavior and that rewarding these norm enforcers causes zero net costs.

7 For an earlier treatment of the emergence of new institutions within a framework of the diffusion of innovations, cf. Witt (1989) and Witt (1992). When the emergence of an institution depends upon the individuals' choice to adopt or not to adopt a new type of behavior, central agents of collective action might play a decisive role in establishing the critical mass; they have to achieve that a sufficient number of other agents will expect that collective adoption will come about, so that the expectation becomes self-fulfilling (Witt (1989) p. 167). The critical issue for those change agents is to attract the individuals' selective attention in order to modify their knowledge – the basis on which the individuals make their decisions (Witt, 1992). Similarly, Kübler (2001) addresses the case where cooperative behavior itself is nonobservable, and she argues that conditional cooperation would be enhanced if individuals were made to believe that many other actors follow the norm as well.

8 Ellickson (2001) distinguishes three types of actors: a) strongly motivated individuals who would personally gain from the existence of the norm, b) norm entrepreneurs who benefit from being promoters of change (e.g. the 'scientific community'), and c) opinion leaders who promote public action through communication. Ellickson describes an opinion leader as a person to whom other members of the group are unusually prone to defer to in order to avoid being socially out of step. An opinion leader may have earned this trust through prior accomplishments in norm enforcement and/or change (Ellickson, 2001, p. 16).

9 Lessig (1995) defines meanings as 'the semiotic content attached to various actions, or inactions, or statuses, within a particular context' (Lessig, 1995, p. 951). Meanings are 'associations, one idea that gets tied to another' (Lessig, 1995, p. 958). He is interested in those associations that a group of interacting individuals shares.

10 Denzau and North (1994) argue that new experiences which make individuals adjust their interpretation of the environment might result in new institutions, given that these mental models are 'shared' by the interacting individuals.

11 This argument also holds for commonalities in learned consumer preferences. However, we do not address learned preferences here (cf. Witt's (2001) exposition of so-called 'acquired wants').

12 Game theoretic analyses work with abstract representations of structures of social interaction to derive conclusions which can be generalized. The same degree of abstraction holds for experimental research, where cooperative behavior boils down to the distribution of monetary payoffs. The material content of the equilibrium or norm, whose payoffs are known to the actors, is not subject to discussion. In other words, it is unspecified which type of actions or consumption behavior constitute norm compliance.

13 For a more detailed picture of social learning processes, cf. the work of Bandura (1986).

14 This idea of learning by reinforcement is the subject of many learning models, both in psychology as well as economics (cf. Bush and Mosteller, 1955 and Roth and Erev, 1995).

15 It should be kept in mind that both social recognition and health could, in principle, be associated with many other types of consumption acts.

16 Douglas (1984, p. 2) points out that society defines what 'being clean' means: 'As we know it, dirt is essentially disorder. There is no such thing as absolute dirt: it exists in the eye of the beholder'.

17 On the one hand, there were ideas about 'spontaneous generation' of life from lifeless matter as well as the miasma theory of disease, hypothesizing that illnesses were triggered by 'bad air' (Mokyr, 2000). On the other hand, there had been conjectures since the sixteenth century that tiny living entities existed, which could trigger transformations in organic matter.

18 By analyzing the process of fermentation of wine, Pasteur proved the existence of microorganisms in 1857. Koch demonstrated in 1876 that microorganisms could be grown in a pure culture outside the body and that disease could be produced artificially by inoculating animals with the cultures (Osler, 1913).

19 There exist different opinions as to the reasons underlying the home economics movement. Cohen (1982) argues that the better-off middle-class households approached poorer American households at the turn of the twentieth century with a paternalist attitude, but that they were still guided by 'the very best of motives' (Cohen, 1982, p. 88). The poorer urban households were usually immigrants that lived in dirtier environments and lacked education in hygiene and disease prevention.

20 Andrews and Andrews (1974) draw the following comparison: 'In regimenting her time to strict schedules, the housekeeper was to employ the standards of efficiency which industrial efficiency experts like Frederick Taylor applied to strictly commercial enterprises in the early twentieth century'. The corresponding Association of Domestic Science was founded in 1908 (Matthews, 1987, p. 151).

21 By 1873, the United States Patent Office had received over 2,000 applications for such washing machines (Andrews and Andrews, 1974, p. 317).

22 At the beginning of the twentieth century, a large variety of new consumer products became available. As consumers could, in many cases, not rely on former experiences as to how to use certain products (Cowan, 1983, p. 14), they were generally in need of guidance and orientation. In other words, the need-satisfaction potential of many newly advertised products had to be explored.

23 According to Lessig (1995), early nonsmoking regulation focused on maintaining gender inequality, i.e. social status structures. At some point in the nineteenth century, women started to smoke cigarettes (not cigars, like men did). Men feared they would lose their superior social status to women and so they opposed this imitation by legislation, which prohibited the sales of cigarettes: 'Regulation arose originally to defend the social status of the male'. Lessig uses the term 'defensive construction' for this type of meaning regulation. Obviously, imitation and social emulation was not possible in the case that

Lessig studied, because those who would have lost their status position were powerful and determined enough to oppose this trend.

24 Interestingly, white clothes are common today in occupations where hygiene plays an important role, for instance in the medical field. The use of white clothing might be related to the learned association of cleanliness and health: dirt is easily visible on white clothes, allowing the patient to draw (limited) inferences about the hygienic standard of the physician.

References

Alchian, A. A., Demsetz, H. (1973): 'The property right paradigm', *Journal of Economic History*, 33 (1), pp. 16–27.

Alpizar, F., Carlsson, F., Johansson-Stenman, O. (2005): 'How much do we care about absolute versus relative income and consumption?', *Journal of Economic Behavior & Organization*, 56, pp. 405–421.

Andrews, W. D., Andrews, D. C. (1974): 'Technology and the housewife in nineteenth-century America', *Women's Studies*, 2, pp. 309–328.

Ashenburg, K. (2007): *The Dirt on Clean: An Unsanitized History*, North Point Press, New York.

Attar, D. (1990): *Wasting Girls' Time: The History and Politics of Home Economics*, Virago, London.

Axelrod, R. (1984): *The Evolution of Cooperation*, Basic Books, New York.

Axelrod, R. (1986): 'An evolutionary approach to norms', *American Political Science Review*, 80 (4), pp. 1095–1111.

Baines, D. (1994): 'Population, migration and regional development, 1870–1939', in Floud, R., McCloskey, D. (eds.): *The Economic History of Britain since 1700*, Volume 2, second edition, Cambridge University Press, Cambridge, MA.

Bandura, A. (1986): *Social Foundations of Thought and Action – A Social Cognitive Theory*, Prentice Hall, Englewood Cliffs, NJ.

Bass, F. M. (1969): 'A new product growth model for consumer durables', *Management Science*, 5, pp. 215–227.

Baumol, W. J. (1962): 'On taxation and the control of externalities', *American Economic Review*, 62 (3), pp. 307–322.

Baumol, W. J. (2004): 'Red-Queen games: arms races, rule of law and market economies', *Journal of Evolutionary Economics*, 14, pp. 237–247.

Bernheim, D. B. (1994): 'A theory of conformity', *Journal of Political Economy*, 102 (5), pp. 841–877.

Bikhchandani, S., Hirshleifer, D., Welch, I. (1992): 'Learning from the behavior of others: Conformity, fads, and informational cascades', *Journal of Economic Perspectives*, 12 (3), pp. 151–170.

Brock, W. A., Durlauf, S. N. (2001): 'Discrete choice with social interactions', *Review of Economic Studies*, 68, pp. 235–260.

Buchanan, J. M. (1965): 'An economic theory of clubs', *Economica*, 32, pp. 1–14.

Buchanan, J. M. (1969): 'External diseconomies, corrective taxes, and market structure', *American Economic Review*, 59 (1), pp. 174–177.

Bush, R. R., Mosteller, F. (1955): *Stochastic Models for Learning*, John Wiley and Sons, New York.

Camerer, C. F. (1997): 'Progress in behavioral game theory', *Journal of Economic Perspectives*, 11 (4), pp. 167–188.

Camerer, C. F., Thaler, R. (1995): 'Anomalies, ultimatums, dictators and manners', *Journal of Economic Perspectives*, 9 (2), pp. 209–219.

Carroll, C. D., Overland J., Weil D. N. (1997): 'Comparison utility in a growth model', *Journal of Economic Growth*, 2, pp. 339–367.

Coase, R. H. (1960): 'The problem of social cost', *Journal of Law and Economics*, 3, pp. 1–44.

Cohen, D. (1982): *The Last Hundred Years: Household Technology*, M. Evans and Company, New York.

Coleman, J. S. (1990): *Foundations of Social Theory*, The Belknap Press of Harvard University Press, Cambridge, MA.

Corneo, G., Jeanne O. (1997): 'Snobs, bandwagons, and the origin of social customs in consumer behavior', *Journal of Economic Behavior & Organization*, 32, pp. 333–347.

Cornes, R., Sandler T. (1986): *The Theory of Externalities, Public Goods, and Club Goods*, Cambridge University Press, Cambridge, MA.

Costa, D. L., Steckel, R. H. (1997): 'Long-term trends in health, welfare and economic growth in the United States', in Steckel, R. H., Floud, R. (eds.): *Health and Welfare during Industrialization*, The University of Chicago Press, Chicago and London.

Cowan, R. S. (1983): *More Work for Mother*, Basic Books, New York.

Cunningham, A. (1992): 'Transforming plague, The laboratory and the identity of infectious disease', in Cunningham A., Williams P. (eds.): *The Laboratory Revolution in Medicine*, Cambridge University Press, Cambridge, MA.

Davis, O. A., Whinston A. (1962): 'Externalities, welfare, and the theory of games', *Journal of Political Economy*, 70 (3), pp. 241–262.

de Vries, J. (1994): 'The industrial revolution and the industrious revolution', *Journal of Economic History*, 54 (2), pp. 249–270.

Demsetz, H. (1967): 'Toward a theory of property rights', *American Economic Review*, 57, Papers & Proceedings, pp. 347–359.

Denzau, A. T., North D. C. (1994): 'Shared mental models: Ideologies and institutions', *Kyklos*, 47 (1), pp. 3–31.

Douglas, M. (1984): *Purity and Danger: An Analysis of the Concepts of Pollution and Taboo*, Ark Paperbacks, London.

Du Vall, N. (1988): *Domestic Technology: A Chronology of Developments*, G.K. Hall & Co, Boston, MA.

Duesenberry, J. (1949): *Income, Saving, and the Theory of Consumer Behavior*, Harvard University Press, Cambridge, MA.

Edwards, H. R. (1962): *Competition and Monopoly in the British Soap Industry*, Clarendon Press, Oxford.

EIA, 2011: Annual Energy Review 2011, Energy Information Administration, Table 2.6 Household End Uses: Fuel Types, Appliances, and Electronics, Selected Years, 1978–2009; retrieved from http://www.eia.gov/totalenergy/data/annual/pdf/sec2_21.pdf (25.09.2016).

Einhorn, H. J., Hogarth R. M. (1978): 'Confidence in judgment: Persistence of the illusion of validity', *Psychological Review*, 85 (5), pp. 395–416.

Ellickson, B. (1973): 'A generalization of the pure theory of public goods', *American Economic Review*, 63 (3), pp. 417–432.

Ellickson, R. C. (1991): *Order without Law: How Neighbors Settle Disputes*, Harvard University Press, Cambridge, MA.

Ellickson, R. C. (2001): 'The market for social norms', *American Law and Economic Review*, 3 (1), pp. 1–49.

Elster, J. (1989): 'Social norms and economic theory', *Journal of Economic Perspectives*, 3 (4), pp. 99–117.

Fee E. (1994): 'Public health and the state: The United States', in Porter D. (ed.): *The History of Public Health and the Modern State*, Rodopi, Amsterdam and Atlanta.

Fehr, E., Fischbacher, U. (2004): 'Social norms and human cooperation', *Trends in Cognitive Sciences*, 8 (4), pp. 185–190.

Fehr, E., Gächter, S. (2000): 'Cooperation and punishment in public goods experiments', *American Economic Review*, 90 (4), pp. 980–994.

Floud, R. (1994): 'Britain, 1860–1940: a survey', in Floud, R., McCloskey, D. (eds.): *The Economic History of Britain since 1700*, Volume 2, second edition, Cambridge University Press, Cambridge, MA.

Frank, R. H. (1985): 'The demand for unobservable and other nonpositional goods', *American Economic Review*, 75 (1), pp. 101–116.

Frank, R. H. (1989): 'Frames of reference and the quality of life', *American Economic Review*, 79 (2), pp. 80–85.

Frank, R. H. (1999): *Luxury Fever*, The Free Press, New York.

Hodgson, G. M. (2003): 'The hidden persuaders: Institutions and individuals in economic theory', *Cambridge Journal of Economics*, 27 (2), pp. 159–175.

Hardin, G. (1968): 'The tragedy of the commons', *Science*, 162, pp. 1243–1248.

Hardyment, C. (1988): *From Mangle to Microwave, The Mechanization of Household Work*, Polity Press, Cambridge, United Kingdom.

Hirsch, F. (1976): *The Social Limits of Growth*, Harvard University Press, Cambridge, MA.

Keser, C., van Winden, F. (2000): 'Conditional cooperation and voluntary contributions to public goods', *Scandinavian Journal of Economics*, 102 (1), pp. 23–39.

Khalil, E. L. (1997): 'The Red Queen paradox: a proper name for a popular game', *Journal of Institutional and Theoretical Economics*, 153 (2), pp. 411–415.

Klepp, I. G. (2003): 'Clothes and cleanliness', *Ethnologia Scandinavia*, 33, pp. 61–73.

Kübler, D. (2001): 'On the regulation of social norms', *Journal of Law, Economics & Organization*, 17 (2), pp. 449–476.

Leibenstein, H. (1950): 'Bandwagon, snob and Veblen effects in the theory of consumers' demand', *Quarterly Journal of Economics*, 64 (2), pp. 183–207.

Lessig, L. (1995): 'The regulation of social meaning', *University of Chicago Law Review*, 62, pp. 943–1045.

Lessig, L. (1996): 'Social meaning and social norms', *University of Pennsylvania Law Review*, 144 (5), pp. 2181–2189.

Lessig, L. (1998): 'The New Chicago School', *Journal of Legal Studies*, 27 (2), pp. 661–691.

Liu, W.-F., Turnovsky, S. J. (2005): 'Consumption externalities, production externalities, and long-run macroeconomic efficiency', *Journal of Public Economics*, 89, pp. 1097–1129.

Luckin, B. (1984): 'Evaluating the sanitary revolution: Typhus and typhoid in London, 1851–1900', in Woods, R., Woodward, J. (eds.): *Urban Disease and Mortality in Nineteenth-Century England*, St. Martin's Press, New York.

MacKinnon, M. (1994): 'Living standards, 1870–1914', in Floud, R., McCloskey, D. (eds.): *The Economic History of Britain since 1700*, Volume 2, second edition, Cambridge University Press, Cambridge, MA.

Mathias, P. (1983): *The First Industrial Nation: The Economic History of Britain 1700–1914*, second edition, Routledge, London and New York.

Matthews, G. (1987): *Just a Housewife: The Rise and Fall of Domesticity in America*, Oxford University Press, New York.

McAdams, R. H. (1997): 'The origin, development, and regulation of norms', *Michigan Law Review*, 96, pp. 338–433.

McClary, A. (1980): 'Germs are everywhere: The germ threat as seen in magazine articles 1890–1920', *Journal of American Culture*, 3 (1), pp. 33–46.

Michael, R. T., Becker G. S. (1973): 'On the new theory of consumer behavior', *Swedish Journal of Economics*, 75 (4), pp. 378–396.

Mokyr, J., Stein, R. (1997): 'Science, health, and household technology: The effect of the Pasteur Revolution on consumer demand', in Bresnahan, T. F., Gordon, R. J. (eds.): *The Economics of New Goods, Studies in Income and Wealth*, Vol. 58, The University of Chicago Press, Chicago and London.

Mokyr, J. (2000), *The Gifts of Athena: Historical Origins of the Knowledge Economy*, Princeton University Press, Princeton, NJ.

North, D. C. (1991): 'Institutions', *Journal of Economic Perspectives*, 5 (1), pp. 97–112.

Olson, M. (1965): *The Logic of Collective Action*, Harvard University Press, Cambridge, MA.

Opp, K.-D. (1983): *Die Entstehung sozialer Normen*, J.C.B. Mohr (Paul Siebeck), Tübingen, Germany.

Opp, K.-D. (2001): 'How do norms emerge? An outline of a theory', *Mind & Society*, 3 (2), pp. 101–128.

Osler, W. (1913): *The Evolution of Modern Medicine*, Yale University, Yale, CT.

Ostrom, E. (2000): 'Collective action and the evolution of social norms', *Journal of Economic Perspectives*, 14 (3), pp. 137–158.

Oxley, D. (2003): '"The seat of death and terror": urbanization, stunting, and smallpox', *Economic History Review*, 61 (4), pp. 623–656.

Peet, R. (1952): 'Dynamics of the soap industry', *Journal of the American Oil Chemists' Society*, 29 (11), pp. 564–572.

Pigou, A. C. (1920): *The Economics of Welfare*, Macmillan, London.

Posner, E. A. (1979): 'Some uses and abuses of economics in law', *University of Chicago Law Review*, 46 (2), pp. 281–306.

Posner, E. A. (1996): 'Law, economics, and inefficient norms', *University of Pennsylvania Law Review*, 144 (5), pp. 1697–1744.

Posner, E. A. (1998): 'Symbols, signals and social norms in politics and the law', *Journal of Legal Studies*, 27, pp. 765–798.

Rickards, L., Fox K., Roberts C., Fletcher L., Goddard E. (2004): *Living in Britain, Results from the 2002 General Household Survey*, National Statistics, London.

Rogers, E. M. (1995): *Diffusion of Innovations*, fourth edition, The Free Press, New York.

Roth, A. E., Erev I. (1995): 'Learning in extensive form games: Experimental data and simple dynamic models in the intermediate run', *Games and Economic Behavior*, 6, pp. 164–212.

Schotter, A. R. (1981): *The Economic Theory of Social Institutions*, Cambridge University Press, Cambridge, MA.

Shove, E. (2003): *Comfort, Cleanliness and Convenience: The Social Organization of Normality*, Berg, Oxford and New York.

Sivulka, J. (2001): *Stronger than Dirt: A Cultural History of Advertising Personal Hygiene in America, 1975–1940*, Humanity Books, Amherst, NY.

Strasser, S. (2000) [1982]: *Never Done: A History of American Housework*, Henry Holt and Company, New York.

Tomes, N. (1998): *The Gospel of Germs: Men, Women, and the Microbe in American Life*, Harvard University Press, London.

Veblen, T. (1994) [1899]: *The Theory of the Leisure Class*, Macmillan, New York.

Vinikas, V. (1992): *Soft Soap, Hard Sell: American Hygiene in an Age of Advertisement*, Iowa State University Press, Iowa.

Warner, J. H. (1992): 'The fall and rise of professional mystery: Epistemology, authority and the emergence of laboratory medicine in nineteenth-century America', in Cunningham, A., Williams, P. (eds.): *The Laboratory Revolution in Medicine*, Cambridge University Press, Cambridge, MA.

Witt, U. (1987): 'The Demsetz-hypothesis on the emergence of property rights reconsidered', in Pethig R., Schlieper U. (eds.): *Efficiency, Institutions, and Economic Policy*, Springer, Berlin.

Witt, U. (1989): 'The evolution of economic institutions as a propagation process', *Public Choice*, 62, pp. 155–172.

Witt, U. (1992): 'The endogenous public choice theorist', *Public Choice*, 73, pp. 117–129.

Witt, U. (2001): 'Learning to consume: A theory of wants and the growth of demand', *Journal of Evolutionary Economics*, 11, pp. 23–36.

Woersdorfer, J. S. (2010): 'When do social norms replace status-seeking consumption? An application to the consumption of cleanliness', *Metroeconomica*, 61(1), pp. 35–67.

4   Toward the Modern Washday

Major Steps in the Development of Laundry Technology

4.1 Introduction

In Chapter 3, we examined the process by which the social norm of cleanliness came into being in the Western world, particularly in the United States and the United Kingdom, during the period of industrialization and urbanization in the nineteenth century. The emergence of the norm has been explained with regard to the newly established understanding between consumer health on one side and hygiene and a clean outer appearance on the other. At a more general level, Chapter 3 has shown how patterns of cleanliness consumption have been affected by consumer learning processes about the need-satisfaction potential of specific consumption activities (cf. the corresponding hypotheses, which we derived in Chapter 2, namely the 'Needs Hypothesis' and the 'Learning Hypothesis'). As to the terminology employed, we have taken recourse to Gary Becker's 'household production function approach' (Becker, 1965; Michael and Becker, 1973) and defined cleanliness in the form of clean clothes as the outcome of the household production process of laundry washing. The inputs into this household production process, i.e. both expenditures on consumer goods and services as well as the utilization of the respective goods, have been referred to as cleanliness consumption. By showing how consumers have come to associate clean clothes with the basic needs of health and social recognition, Chapter 3 addressed consumer learning processes pertaining to the household production objectives.

In the subsequent chapters, a closer look will be taken at the consumption of a specific product, namely washing machines, which is the most important element of the household production technology for ensuring cleanliness. More precisely, we study the diffusion process of washing machines during the twentieth century, by which the material conditions of doing the laundry were significantly altered. Around 1920, only about 8 per cent of U.S. families possessed a washing machine, while the conventional scrubboard represented the prevailing equipment (Lebergott, 1993, p. 113). At present, four out of five U.S. households are owners of an automatic, electric washing machine, thus forming a saturated market (EIA, 2011).[1] This process of transformation is not confined to the United States; it has taken place in similar forms in other industrialized countries as well.

What have been the driving forces underlying this development? Although higher cleanliness aspirations of a larger number of consumers (cf. Chapter 3) might have been a sufficient condition for the widespread adoption of washing machines, this is not the whole story. We conjecture that two further factors have played a decisive role, namely the consumer motives to save time and to reduce physical labor, particularly drudgery, in the activity of clothes washing.

The motive to save time can be derived from the household production function approach, which is the most prominent economic approach toward housework (cf. Chapter 2). Becker has prepared the ground for a systematic analysis of nonmarket production processes and offers a specific conjecture – the 'time substitution hypothesis' – as an explanation for the mechanization of the home. In Becker's framework, the adoption of consumption goods – such as washing machines – is attributed to changing relative prices, particularly changing opportunity costs of time. Rising opportunity costs of time raise the price of home-produced goods and services and thus urge the household to substitute market goods for its own time in household production processes.

That the adoption of washing machines is motivated by the innate human need for drudgery avoidance is an alternative hypothesis which is in line with psychological findings on human behavior (e.g. Weiner, 1994; Frieman, 2002), a preference-based perspective on technological creativity (Cordes, 2005), and the psychologically informed theory of learning consumers (Witt, 2001) presented earlier (cf. Chapter 2). The conjecture is also compatible with the findings of sociologists and historians of technology who have studied the evolution of the material conditions of laundry washing in great detail (e.g. Giedion, 1948; Cowan, 1983; Matthews, 1987; Preece, 1990; Hardyment, 1988; Silberzahn-Jandt, 1991; Bowden and Offer, 1994; Strasser, 2000 [1982]; Hessler, 2001; Shove, 2003b). The hypothesis can be derived from the basic behavioral principle, according to which the kind and frequency of actions taken depend upon the positive or negative associations consumers hold with regard to specific actions, i.e. consumption activities (cf. 'Behavior Hypothesis', cf. Chapter 2). We will refer to it as the 'drudgery avoidance hypothesis'.

By arguing that historical changes in the domestic production of cleanliness do not only reflect reactions to changing relative prices – the time substitution hypothesis – but also depend on the evaluation of housekeeping activities in the eyes of consumers – the drudgery avoidance hypothesis – we allow the adoption of household production technology to result from 'preferences for the use of time' – a factor missing in the Becker account (cf. Chapter 2). We further make the point that outsourcing decisions affecting the domestic production of cleanliness depend upon the availability and suitability of substitutes for the household's input of time and physical labor, which is a matter of technological progress and relative prices as well as shared social understandings concerning the ideology of housework.

In the following chapters, we confront the aforementioned conjectures (time substitution hypothesis, drudgery avoidance hypothesis) with a collection of empirical observations in order to scrutinize the explanatory power of the variables 'time savings' versus 'physical labor savings' for the evolution of cleanliness consumption during the twentieth century, particularly the diffusion of washing machines. We will, however, not test the hypotheses by means of econometrics.

We begin in this chapter by giving a detailed description of technological progress in washing technology (synonymously: laundry technology) since the middle of the nineteenth century in order to identify if and when savings of time and physical labor in laundry washing have technically become feasible. In the subsequent chapters, we provide insights into the way these technical advances have been advertised and we analyze if there are changes in the relative importance with which advertisements have appealed to the motivations of time savings and drudgery avoidance, respectively (cf. Chapter 5). We also take a closer look at the implications of technical change in the domestic production of cleanliness for consumption patterns and time allocation patterns.

We proceed as follows. Section 4.2 derives the alternative hypotheses of time substitution and drudgery avoidance as triggering factors behind the diffusion of washing machines. Section 4.3 relates these hypotheses to the wider behavioral context. In Section 4.4, we depict, in a very stylized fashion, the major steps of technical change in laundry washing from the middle of the nineteenth century onward. That way we identify changes in the technical possibilities to save time and/or physical labor. In Section 4.5, we pay attention to the demand for domestic servants and the use of commercial laundries as alternative means for ensuring cleanliness. Section 4.6 summarizes the major findings.

4.2 Hypotheses on the Diffusion of Washing Machines

4.2.1 Household Production Processes and the Time Substitution Hypothesis

The core ideas of Gary Becker's theory of the household, its strengths and weaknesses and its major testable implication, the time substitution hypothesis, have been explained in much detail in Chapter 2. In what follows, we will briefly summarize the major elements of this account, including the time substitution hypothesis.

The household production function approach is a neoclassical consumer theory, building on the assumptions of well-behaved preferences, nonsatiation, full information and rational behavior. The pivotal point of the account is the idea that the principles which guide production processes of the firm are also relevant for certain aspects of consumer behavior and can be applied to study the processes taking place in the domestic sphere, i.e. nonmarket activities. Becker thus depicts consumer behavior as a production process of the household, directed toward the achievement of certain production objectives termed 'commodities' – the consumer's ultimate goals. Like in a firm, the household has to decide about the composition and level of the targeted production output and about the employed household technology. The costs of producing certain commodities – referred to as their 'shadow prices' – consist of the expenditures on market goods (or on the services derived from capital goods) and the costs of the household's time input. As time dedicated toward commodity production in household production processes cannot be spent at the (external) labor market, it raises opportunity costs in terms of forgone earnings.

With increasing market wages, spending time in unpaid household production processes becomes relatively more expensive, *ceteris paribus*. In other words, the shadow prices of doing the dishes, cleaning the house and doing the laundry rise with rising wages. Consumers thus have an incentive to increase their labor supply and to purchase market goods which substitute some of the household's time input so to make household maintenance activities more efficient. An increase in opportunity costs of time is a sufficient condition for reallocations in the household's use of time and for expenditures on time saving, productivity-enhancing household technology such as washing machines to occur. As Becker (1965, p. 513) puts it:

> A rise in the cost of time relative to goods would induce a reduction in the amount of time and an increase in the amount of goods used per unit of each commodity.

This predicted substitution process at the level of household production processes implies either more intensive utilization of the given market goods, particularly durable capital goods, and/or the acquisition of further market goods (outsourcing). Following Becker's approach, one would thus analyze the adoption of goods or the purchase of services in light of their potential to make unpaid household production processes more efficient.

Still, although goods are substituted for time in the production of certain commodities, absolute time savings in that exact activity need not occur. Becker does not claim that outsourcing activities necessarily target absolute reductions in the activity in which the new product will be employed. With advanced household technology, particularly time saving domestic appliances, a general expansion of commodity production also becomes feasible, which might at least partially offset the achievable time savings per unit of commodity. This implies that both observations of time savings and constant time use patterns in a specific activity are compatible with Becker's account.

An important assumption in this context is that of nonsatiability in terms of commodities, which is in line with the conventional theory of rational choice: reallocations of time use and outsourcing decisions are assumed to always make sense as they enable an expansion of commodity production in some kind of activity. If households were satiated in terms of the affordable and technically feasible commodity set, increasing shadow prices as a result of higher opportunity costs of time would not trigger the predicted substitution process. It is a major weakness of Becker's approach to not make statements about which kinds of commodities will be produced more. Moreover, as the predicted outsourcing activities are compatible with constant as well as lower inputs of time into a specific activity, it is difficult to gather empirical evidence, on the grounds of which to reject the hypothesis of time substitution. Note that efficiency gains in household production processes occur whenever commodity production becomes cheaper, resulting from a reduction in costly time inputs, declining relative prices of production factors (capital goods), or an improvement in household skills (Stigler and Becker, 1977).

In sum, Becker's approach suggests analyzing the purchase of goods and services in light of their potential to reorganize housework activities, specifically to save time (per unit of commodity), such that commodity production becomes cheaper and can be expanded. Washing machines potentially belong to this category of time saving capital goods. This means that, from a technical point of view, modern washing machines can save some amount of time in clothes washing – compared with the situation of doing the laundry by hand (cf. Section 4.4). Whether absolute time savings actually do occur depends upon the household's behavioral reaction accompanying the outsourcing decision.

For what follows, we leave aside the household's labor supply decision. Although Becker's line of reasoning starts with changing opportunity costs of time, as triggered by rising wages, there is much indeterminacy in the actual effect of rising wages on labor supply – a shortcoming of the general labor-leisure choice analysis (cf. Chapter 2). This problem can be neglected here by starting directly with differences in employment status of the household (both from a cross-sectional and a longitudinal perspective).

Becker's framework has two major implications for the analysis of the demand for washing machines, which we summarize in the following hypotheses (note that these hypotheses draw upon the hypotheses H.2.1 and H.2.2 introduced in Chapter 2):

> H.4.1a: Differences in opportunity costs of time are an important explanatory factor for the adoption of washing machines. Given a certain wage rate, households with women participating in the labor force have a stronger incentive to purchase a washing machine than households with nonworking women, as the former should value time higher than the latter (Short-Run Time Substitution Hypothesis).

> H.4.1b: Changes in female labor force participation over time are an important explanatory factor for the adoption of washing machines. Given the nonsatiation assumption pertaining to commodities, an increase in female labor force participation is a sufficient condition for the purchase of time saving washing machines, which replace the household's input of time into the domestic activity of laundry washing (Long-Run Time Substitution Hypothesis).

Hypothesis H.4.1a suggests that, because forgone earnings are higher for employed women than for nonemployed women, there should be differences in terms of the incentive to adopt washing machines. This hypothesis is one of the strong implications of the Beckerian approach. It plays a great role in the empirical analyses carried out on outsourcing decisions in nonmarket production, yet often without reference to the household production theory, however (we review the respective literature in Chapter 6). Hypothesis H.4.1b is a sufficient but not a necessary condition, as the adoption of washing machines might also occur for other reasons (a closer look at this hypothesis will also be given in Chapter 6). In what follows, we shall refer to these hypotheses more in general as Becker's 'time substitution hypothesis'. When we address consumer motivations for purchasing products (cf. Chapter 5), we alternatively speak of the 'time saving motive' or the 'motive of time substitution'.

The household production function approach has great heuristic potential for economic research by pointing to the interrelatedness of such diverse phenomena as the labor supply decision (especially female labor force participation), the demand for durable goods and services and nonmarket production processes. And in view of the increased female labor force participation in the second half of the twentieth century (Goldin, 1986; Costa, 2000), the adoption of washing machines for their time saving nature is a plausible explanation. However, the fact that the market for washing machines is saturated nowadays, with these goods being present in about four out of five households in the United States, sheds some doubt on the opportunity cost explanation. Apparently, women participating in the labor force and full-time homemakers are equally equipped with these devices. What is the homemaker's incentive to purchase this device, when she does not have to face forgone earnings? Put differently, if wages had not risen during the twentieth century (increasing the opportunity costs of housework opposed to market work) and if women had not increased their labor force participation, would we still have observed the given diffusion process of washing machines?

Apart from making reference to changing relative prices, the household production function approach cannot provide an answer to this question. This shortcoming results from Becker's treatment of preferences (cf. Chapter 2 for a more detailed discussion). Becker does not specify the content of consumer preferences, i.e. for what reasons – apart from efficiency considerations – products might be desired. Moreover, he deliberately excludes 'preferences for the use of time' from his account, i.e. consumers are assumed to not have a liking for spending their time on some activities rather than on others. Utility is only associated with the output of household production processes, i.e. commodities, not the activities themselves. The absence of preferences for the use of time is a crucial assumption for deriving Becker's prediction of time substitution as it implies that the time variable is only a cost factor within the household production process. As a consequence, the potential impact and explanatory value of preferences for the household's outsourcing decision are factored out *a priori*.

While the household production theory provides interesting predictions for certain historical conditions – particularly periods of increasing market wages – it might not be sufficient to explain the diffusion of technology in other periods of time, other than by making *ad hoc* assumptions. So we might need to consider alternative explanations apart from the time substitution hypothesis.

4.2.2 Consumer Motivations and the Drudgery Avoidance Hypothesis

The household production function approach associates consumer preferences with the set of commodities produced – i.e. with the output of household production processes. The production process itself is assumed to be 'preference free'. The adoption of capital goods is thus merely a means with which to increase the production output by achieving efficiency gains in household production technology. Certainly, consumer behavior is directed toward the attainment of ultimate goals, which we defined earlier not as 'commodities' but as the satisfaction of consumers' basic needs in the sense of Witt (2001) (cf. Chapter 2). In that regard, household production processes are deliberately carried out in order to achieve a certain result. However, consumers might as well forego goal achievement when it demands carrying out activities that they experience as unpleasant (cf. Chapter 2).

In that regard, we argue that consumer preferences are not only related to the output of household production processes but to the activities themselves, with regard to which consumers hold positive or negative associations. Likewise, certain goods and services might be desired, as such, for the positive effect the newly adopted goods will have on the activities themselves. In fact, the adoption of tools is one way in which individuals can solve 'approach-avoidance-conflicts' in behavior (cf. Chapter 2). Approach-avoidance-conflicts occur when one and the same activity is associated with rewarding experiences as well as objections: on the one hand, the individual is driven toward a specific goal; on the other, the action required for goal achievement elicits unpleasant or even painful experiences, thus triggering avoidance behavior. The individual thus faces a conflict in behavior. The conflict stems from the general behavioral principle, according to which the kind and frequency of actions taken depend upon the positive or negative associations with those actions (cf. 'Behavior Hypothesis', Chapter 2). Because of strong commonalities in the human genetic basis, the evaluation of actions as pleasant or unpleasant shows some similarities among consumers (cf. 'Commonalities Hypothesis', Chapter 2). As a way of dealing with such a behavioral conflict, the individual might start searching for ways in which to attain the desired goal in a more pleasant way – particularly, when giving up that specific goal is not possible in the long run. In historical times, the invention and diffusion of technologies was a strategy to shift the valence of certain activities and to reduce the avoidance tendency in behavior (cf. Chapter 2).

Our point is that this innate behavioral principle might affect behavior and decision-making in the realm of household production processes as much as – or possibly even more – than do monetary variables, in particular opportunity costs of time. Or to use Becker's terminology: not only commodities but also preferences for the use of time are factors motivating changes in household production processes. In what follows, we thus take a closer look at the kind of motivations associated with the consumption activity of clothes washing in order to identify the inherent approach-avoidance-conflict.

What do we know about the motivational basis of laundry washing? Today, it is known that the washing of textiles objectively and measurably contributes to hygiene via disinfection (e.g. Heicken, 1949; Nichols, 1970; Terpstra, 1998) and thus appeals to the basic need of a healthy, pain-free body. A more recent consumer survey, carried out in several European countries, confirms that hygienic concerns are an important motivational force for doing laundry (SIFO, 2003). The interrelation between health and bodily cleanliness had already been discovered in the middle of the nineteenth century, giving rise to the emergence of the social norm of cleanliness (cf. Chapter 3). Cleanliness is now important for the social standing of a person: consumers expect one another to be clean and they share an understanding of what cleanliness means. By fulfilling society's normative expectations, consumers satisfy their basic need for social recognition.

We base this analysis on the assumption that clothes washing is directed toward the basic needs of health and social recognition, so that the satisfaction of these needs is the ultimate goal behind doing the laundry (cf. 'Cleanliness Hypothesis', Chapter 2). While the positive reward in terms of satisfying these needs is related to the output of the activity of clothes washing, costs have to be taken into account for the production of the desired output.

Let us take a closer look at this situation from the perspective of the household production function approach first. The decisions the household has to make concern both the level of cleanliness produced – the amount of the household production output – and the choice of the instruments – the kind of household production technology – employed. We denote the actual output level of an individual household its individual level of cleanliness (as opposed to a socially shared standard, cf. Chapter 3). This level is, in principle, observable and will be defined here in terms of laundry quantities per time interval, for example, per year. Let us assume that the household targets a specific level of cleanliness. Given this production objective, the household would calculate the shadow prices of clean clothing and estimate the optimal combination of the input factors, taking into account the costs of its personal time (opportunity costs, forgone earnings), technical equipment, water, energy and washing agents. Based on this calculation, the domestic production of cleanliness is carried out, implying a certain allocation of time and a derived demand for market goods.

We argue that this framework misses an important element of the household production process of laundry washing in earlier times, and is thus incomplete. In fact, the motivational background and hence the interpretation of 'costs' of doing the laundry is more complex when the actual reasons of disutility are identified, i.e. the experience of doing the laundry as drudgery. It implies that the household production process is more than a calculative exercise with regard to relative prices and opportunity costs of time. In contrast, in earlier times, the household faced a trade-off in terms of its basic behavioral dispositions – an approach-avoidance-conflict. But let us illustrate first what is meant by the drudgery of doing the laundry.

Before the mechanization of laundry started in the middle of the nineteenth century (cf. Section 4.4), laundry washing was not only a time- but especially a physical labor-consuming job, as it was carried out with hardly any equipment except human physical labor, personal time and soap (the latter often being homemade).[2] Doing the laundry is referred to as 'backbreaking' labor (Buehr, 1965, p. 61), a 'horrible task' (Cohen, 1982, p. 4) and 'the most toilsome of the housewife's tasks' (Giedion, 1948, p. 550) by historians of technology. Hardyment (1988, p. 8) draws the comparison that the old washday was as exhausting as swimming five miles of energetic breaststroke. Contemporaries even went so far as to name clothes washing 'the American housekeeper's hardest problem' (Beecher and Beecher Stowe, 1869, p. 334). From an ironic point of view, the situation could be depicted as follows (Lebergott, 1993, p. 114):

> The 1900 housewife relied on a nonautomatic (and fuel-efficient) wash board. […] Of course, the housewife with a good strong back and shoulders could get several hours of healthy exercise each week washing clothes.

However, doing the laundry was not perceived as an athletic challenge back then. Laundry washing apparently earned more complaints than any other household task in the nineteenth century (Strasser, 2000 [1982], p. 104). Note that the family wash in the United States was usually done once a week, on Mondays, after clothes had been changed on Sunday (Strasser, 2000 [1982], p. 106), while ironing took place the following day (Cohen, 1982, p. 7). The weekly wash was essential to avoid dirt hardening on the fabrics and thus being more difficult to remove (Strasser, 2000 [1982], p. 106). Most households probably also lacked the amount of clothes to do the procedure less frequently. To obtain a first impression, consider the following short description of a typical washing procedure in the second half of the nineteenth century (Buehr, 1965, p. 61; Cohen, 1982, p. 91; Hardyment, 1988, p. 8; Strasser, 2000 [1982], p. 105). First, the dirty clothes were sorted by color, fabric and degree of soiling, and soaked in warm, soapy water overnight. Already for these preparatory steps, water had to be hauled and heated up, which demanded much effort, given that even well-to-do households did not have running water in the home by the nineteenth century (Cohen, 1982, p. 35). In urban environments, water was taken from the well and heated up in a wash boiler on the stove, while rural households, which were in the majority at the end of the nineteenth century, used a fireplace in the backyard (Buehr, 1965, p. 61). In the basements of some urban homes or apartment buildings, an alternative existed in the form of washing sinks (Cohen, 1982, p. 91). The following day, called 'Blue Monday', the used water was drained off and more water had to be carried and heated up before being filled in a wooden tub to which soda and salt were added.

Then began the rubbing of pieces of clothes on the washboard (Buehr, 1965, p. 61). The washboard or scrubboard was invented around 1800 and was the most common tool for cleaning clothes until the turn of the twentieth century (Cohen, 1982, p. 91). The wrought clothes were then boiled on the stove. To agitate the clothes in the tub, a so-called 'washing dolly' was used, which was a pole with one end that looked like a milk stool (Hardyment, 1988, p. 55). Clothes were wrung out by hand before they had to be rinsed several times in another washtub to remove the yellow color the soap had left. At the second stage of rinsing, a blue agent was added to the fluid. According to requirements, starch was applied to the textiles before wringing them out again and hanging them on outside lines to dry. Ironing followed the next day. Due to the lack of electricity or gas in the home, irons had to be heated, either on the open hearth – possibly soiling the iron and thus the textiles – or later, on the stove. Irons were quite heavy devices, weighing up to 8 or 10 pounds. Particularly in the summer, ironing was an extremely unpleasant activity.

Although the expression 'Blue Monday' has its origin in the bluing procedure in the rinsing phase, Cohen (1982) leaves no doubt that women experienced the activity of laundry washing itself as blue. Even at the turn of the century, laundry washing was the 'dirtiest' and the 'most disagreeable' task among all household chores (Cohen, 1982, p. 91), for laundry washing was hard physical work (Strasser (2000 [1982], p. 105):

> One wash, one boiling, and one rinse used about fifty gallons of water – or four hundred pounds – which had to be moved from pump or well or faucet to stove and tub, in buckets and wash boilers that might weigh as much as forty or fifty pounds. Rubbing, wringing and lifting water-laden clothes and linens, including large articles like sheets, tablecloths, and men's heavy work-clothes, wearied women's arms and wrists and exposed them to caustic substances. They lugged weighty tubs and baskets full of wet laundry outside, picked up each article, hung it on the line, and returned to take it all down.

This short overview reveals that the domestic production of cleanliness brought many inconveniences in the form of the heavy physical effort of rubbing clothes, the weight of carrying water and handling the iron and the heat from ironing in the summer, as well as the cold of carrying water during winter plus the damage that soap would do to hands. When carrying out the washing procedure, the household immediately felt a form of physical pain over an extended period of time, resulting from the drudgery involved in clothes washing.

This experience stood in direct opposition to the innate human disposition and motive of drudgery avoidance. Drudgery corresponds to the experience of pain and, probably, the fear of illness, which tends to trigger avoidance behavior (Cordes, 2005; cf. Chapter 2).[3] Hence, to the extent to which the washing activity is connected with drudgery, carrying it out creates a conflict with the motives for doing it. The drudgery of doing the laundry stood in opposition to the benefits of clean clothes, in terms of the satisfaction of the basic needs of health and social recognition. The negative experience of doing the laundry was immediate and opposed the positive feelings that would result from clean clothes. Without modern equipment, nineteenth-century consumers thus faced a *trade-off* in laundry washing between wanting to avoid drudgery and having clean clothes: the consumer could either opt for high standards of cleanliness and take into account the pain of drudgery, or could avoid drudgery and substantially reduce the level of cleanliness.

Note that no such inherent conflict is implied by the opportunity costs of time argument; trade-offs exist only at the level of activities, i.e. the other various uses of time forgone by carrying out the activity of laundry washing.

In view of this exposition, we can identify the motive of drudgery avoidance as an alternative explanation and triggering factor behind the diffusion of technically advanced washing machines in the twentieth century. We derive the following testable conclusions:

> H.4.2a: The adoption of washing machines has been motivated by the behavioral disposition to avoid heavy physical effort (Long-Run Drudgery Avoidance Hypothesis).

> H.4.2b: In the absence of drudgery-reducing washing technology, the household tended to display low levels of cleanliness (Short-Run Drudgery Avoidance Hypothesis).

H.4.2b implies that the higher the targeted cleanliness level, the higher the incentive to adopt a washing machine as a means to avoid the drudgery of doing the laundry. Note also that 'drudgery-reducing technology' is understood here in the most general sense, including both goods and services. In what follows, we shall refer to these two hypotheses more in general as the 'drudgery avoidance hypothesis'.

In this section, we derived two alternative hypotheses on the driving forces underlying the diffusion of washing machines in the twentieth century. Note that the arguments presented here are distinct from the point made in Chapter 3: there, we identified changes in the household production objectives as the factor triggering purchases of cleanliness-related products. It should also be mentioned that rising personal income is the necessary condition for making feasible the switch to more capital-intensive household production processes, enabling households to reduce exposure to drudgery and to save household time.

4.3 The Complex Story of Motives and Constraints in Doing the Laundry

Although the drudgery avoidance hypothesis is not a priori compatible with the household production function approach, proponents of the Becker framework might point out that the same arguments that are elaborated for the allocation of time can be applied to human energy – such that the household production theory also covers effort-reducing technological progress. In fact, both theoretical and empirical analyses drawing upon the household production function approach have not made explicit the distinction between inputs of human time and physical effort into the compound variable 'human labor', but synonymously talk about time or labor (e.g. Pollak and Wachter, 1975; Lovingood and McCullough, 1986). This inadequacy probably has its origin in the labor-leisure analysis, where labor and time are treated as substitutes (cf. Chapter 2).

Certainly, from a biological perspective, human physical energy is limited – as is time – which might give rise to its careful allocation among different purposes. To assume that the human disposition to avoid drudgery is linked to its evolutionary advantage in times of food scarcity (Cordes, 2005) goes in a similar direction. Further support for the analogy to the economic principles of time allocation stems from the fact that human effort is necessarily always present to some extent whenever time is spent in some activity, such that some amount of labor is carried into all uses of time (Michael and Becker, 1973, p. 137). Shifts in the allocation of time, for instance, as a reaction to changing relative prices, thus always imply shifts in the allocation of human energy.

The important point, however, is that the principles by which human physical effort is 'allocated' among its various uses need not be identical to those affecting the allocation of time, and that changes in the allocation decision particularly need not be a reaction to changing opportunity costs of time. Quite the opposite, the guiding principle might rather be the innate behavioral disposition to reduce in frequency those actions that elicit negative experiences, while increasing in frequency those actions that have positive associations ('Behavior Hypothesis', cf. Chapter 2). The willingness to substitute capital goods for human physical labor might thus stem from the fact that an activity brings negative associations and that the consumer might seek ways to avoid this activity. Consumption goods might thus be acquired in order to change the valence of certain activities as having positive or negative associations. As a result, the evaluation of activities might undergo changes over time, depending exactly on the technical equipment with which an activity is carried out. Despite the fact that changes in time allocation patterns always imply some changes in the employment of human effort, we hence assume that the allocation of effort and time each follow different principles.

By advancing the drudgery avoidance hypothesis, we allow the household's substitution processes to result not only from productivity considerations, but also from preferences for the use of time in that the household likes or dislikes certain activities. Still, from the motivational point of view, it is important to note that the time spent doing the laundry and the extent of drudgery experienced (per unit of clean clothes) are two distinct aspects of this activity.

Assume that time needed for doing the laundry (*y*-axis) increases monotonously with the amount of laundry done (*x*-axis). Then, both technological progress and more capital-intensive household production will shift the 'time-laundry amounts' curve downward. Likewise, if the cumulative extent of drudgery experienced (y-axis) increases monotonously with the amount of laundry (x-axis), then both technological progress and higher capital intensity will shift the 'drudgery-laundry amounts' curve downward. The essential point is that the two curves do not shift downward proportionately with technically improved equipment. In historical times, a different technological development in washing machines might be depicted if only time savings or only reductions in drudgery were paid attention to. Vice versa, at a given point in time, the household's choice of cleaning technology affects the mix of drudgery reduction and time savings made feasible. Compare the use of laundry services with a technically, slightly more advanced washing machine. When a laundry service is used to do the cleaning (i.e. a launderette or domestic servant), high savings of both drudgery and time are feasible. When, in contrast to that, the washing machine is employed (mechanization of the task), some reductions in drudgery can be enjoyed while time savings might be comparatively smaller.

The following figure represents the basic argument concerning the technological progress of washing machines over time (cf. Figure 4.1). A similar picture

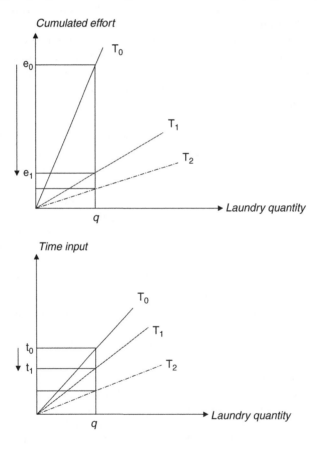

Figure 4.1 Technological Progress in Laundry Washing.

could be drawn where the different T_i values represent different technical variants for a given point in time. Note that the relationship need not be of a linear nature. Assume that for producing a given amount of clothing q, only one kind of washing technology T_0 exists in the starting period, which implies a certain input of time t_0 (e.g. measured in minutes) and physical effort e_0 (accumulated for the amount of laundry items). Then, technological progress (T_1) in the following period allows for a reduction in both inputs of time and effort for producing q. In the example depicted here, the relative reduction in the cumulated drudgery input is larger than that in time savings, while 'relative' pertains to the reduction in one input factor compared with its former input quantity. When, for example, technological progress reduces drudgery by 30 per cent and the time input by 10 per cent, the innovation is more of a physical labor saving kind, implying a modification of the input coefficient. And while an increase in the quantity of laundry might at least partially offset the absolute time savings achievable with a given laundry amount, the effort that is needed to produce this higher output might still be much lower than without technical equipment.

The actual path of technological progress in washing technology from the nineteenth century onward might have affected time and labor savings to a different extent. In the following section, we will take a closer look at the actual historical changes in the household production technology of laundry washing and its implications in terms of the input of time and physical labor required to clean a given amount of laundry. That way, we gather information on the relative importance of time savings versus reductions in drudgery for the proliferation of washing machines in the twentieth century. However, we will not try to quantify the exact effects.

Note that only those devices can be termed 'effort saving' which provide a substantial amount of nonanthropogenic mechanical energy as a substitute for the energy that humans are able to provide in reasonable amounts (Cordes, 2002, p. 20; Buenstorf, 2004, Chapter 4).[4] Throughout the analysis, we use both the expressions 'physical labor' and 'effort'. From the respective context, it should become clear when the expression 'labor' depicts the input of human energy or physical effort alone rather than referring to a production factor, for example, as in the expression 'labor supply'. Often, time and effort will be addressed in parallel when speaking about 'time and labor savings', which should leave little room for misinterpretations. We speak of 'time savings' when a product reduces the required time input per commodity unit, hence enabling time savings in some absolute amount also.

Let us now take a look at the transition in the domestic production of cleanliness from 'Blue Monday' to the fully automated washing machine.

4.4 Technical Advances in Laundry Washing

In this section, we present changes in the domestic production of clean clothes from the perspective of the technical equipment used. The presentation covers technical advances in laundry washing from the middle of the nineteenth century onward and is mainly confined to the United States.[5] The depicted trends apply to other Western countries as well, such as the United Kingdom and Germany, but the development shows a time lag compared with that in the United States (Lebergott, 1993; Silberzahn-Jandt, 1991; Hessler, 2001).

We assert that the overview given here lends itself to providing some insights into how far the time substitution hypothesis or the drudgery avoidance hypothesis are better suited to capture the driving forces underlying the diffusion of washing machines. The central point is that the actual decision whether or not to adopt a certain product for its time or effort saving abilities cannot occur prior to the existence of a marketed product with these exact features.[6] For example, only in historical contexts, when technical change made time savings feasible, is it plausible that the time substitution motive has triggered the adoption of washing machines.

The development depicted here is almost entirely based on secondary literature, particularly sociological literature – the sociology of technology – which studies domestic history and the evolution of material culture (cf. Giedion, 1948; Cohen, 1982; Cowan, 1983; Matthews, 1987; Hardyment, 1988; Strasser, 2000 [1982]). In addition to that, we consulted websites of collectors of antique washing machines and looked up some washing machine patents in order to better understand the technical descriptions and to visualize the actual artifacts.[7] We also took a look into historical material ourselves, by scanning the women's magazine *Ladies' Home Journal* for advertisements on washing machines (in Chapter 5, we describe at length the results of a content analysis of these advertisements, both with regard to the technical change depicted therein as well as the consumer motives appealed to).

Note that, as such, this presentation will deal both with technical advances, as indicated by patents, and with changes in the material situation of the majority of households. Technical inventions necessarily come before the widespread manufacturing of the respective devices and they might precede the actual presence of these products in private households by decades. As patents cannot show when devices actually became commonplace, the focus of this analysis clearly lies on changes in the availability of products as well as the actual situation of doing the laundry. To that end, we include some diffusion and expenditure statistics. However, it is hardly feasible to provide any data on ownership rates of specific types of washing machines differing in terms of their technical characteristics. This is a major shortcoming of the descriptive literature on which this overview is built – a shortcoming which we cannot compensate for here.

The overview of technological progress given here will illustrate that time and effort are two distinct components of the variable 'human labor', and that time savings and effort savings have indeed been prominent at different points in time. Partially, time and effort savings have occurred in parallel but were not similar in magnitude. These findings suggest that, from a historical perspective, the explanatory value of these variables varies substantially. Let us now turn to the evolution of laundry washing in terms of the instruments or household production technology used.

Modern washing machines have a long lineage. The overall technological development of doing the laundry can be divided into four general phases: (1) Blue Monday, (2) mechanization, (3) electrification (including wiring and plumbing of houses) and (4) automation. The situation of *Blue Monday* has already been illustrated when we derived the drudgery avoidance hypothesis (cf. Section 4.2.2). Back then, the core technical means for washing clothes has been the washboard, whose invention dates back to *circa* 1797 (Association of Home Appliances Manufacturers [AHAM], 2009). The washboard remained the major technical equipment for most of the nineteenth century, implying that until about 1920, the American 'washing machine' was the housewife herself (Lebergott, 1993, p. 112).

This situation began to change with the *mechanization* of clothes washing. 'Mechanization' meant that pulling, pushing and pressing by hand became transformed into continuous rotation (Giedion, 1948, p. 47), but that devices were still hand powered by means of a wheel or pump handle. The mechanization of laundry washing fell into the period where industrial production processes became mechanized through the pioneering works of Frank Gilbreth and Frederick Taylor. By carefully studying the sequence of movements of the worker's hand in order to optimize processes, increase precision and allow for repeatability, referred to as 'scientific management', these pioneers prepared the ground for efficiency improvements and standardization in production processes (Giedion, 1948, Chapter 3). Gilbreth also saw applicability of the principles of scientific management in the household sphere, an idea picked up by Christine Frederick in the 1920s when promoting the science of 'household engineering' (Giedion, 1948, p. 522), which belonged to the larger 'home economics' movement (cf. Section 4.5 and Chapter 3).

At the beginning of the mechanization of laundry washing, very distinct technical approaches were applied, all of which appear to have targeted a reduction in physical effort (Giedion, 1948, p. 563). Some of these devices stayed very close to the original mechanism, namely, the rubbing of clothes on scrubboards, while others started off from completely different mechanisms. According to Giedion (1948, p. 550), there were already about 2,000 U.S. patents on washing machines by 1873. The earliest U.S. inventions in washing technology, as is indicated by patents, date back to the middle of the nineteenth century. In Great Britain, inventions date back even to the end of the eighteenth century, but those machines were not yet effective in reducing any drudgery (Giedion, 1948, p. 560).

One device that showed some resemblance to the modern washing machine was the rotary-type washer, invented in 1850, which included a large drum that could be turned by a handle (Buehr, 1965, p. 64). Also around that time, originating with an invention by James T. King in 1851, a technology became available that made use of steam power for rotating the drums (Giedion, 1948, p. 562; Cohen, 1982, p. 93). These devices were too large for private use and were thus confined to commercial applications only, namely the so-called steam or power laundries, where the basic technology remained in use until the beginning of the twentieth century (Mohun, 1999).[8] Steam or power laundries were available from around 1840 and went through a phase of expansion from *circa* 1860–1890 (Cowan, 1983, p. 105; Mohun, 1999). The industry emerged in those regions where there was an initial demand for their services and grew rapidly after the Civil War. Around 1900, steam laundries existed in all major cities and many rural places also (Cowan, 1983, p. 105). The highest demand occurred in the 1920s and after World War II, then sharply declining afterward (Hartmann, 1974, p. 287). For the origin of the washing machine industry in the United States, the demand from the service industry, offering laundry services to the public, played a central role (Giedion, 1948, p. 566).

In general, equipment for laundry facilities was developed quite some decades before several variants suitable for home use became available. The earliest laundry equipment for residential use was designed to imitate the movement of the hand, i.e. the rubbing of textiles on a scrubboard, while translating the back-and-forth movement of the hand into a continuous rotary movement (Giedion, 1948, p. 562; Strasser, 2000 [1982], p. 116). The manual rocking scrubboard is the best example of that principle. Around 1850, a washing machine model was patented, which had actually been popular until the beginning of the twentieth century, called the 'Old faithful' or 'Quick and Easy washer' (Giedion, 1948, p. 563; Strasser, 2000 [1982], p. 116). With this device, clothes were placed between two curved and ribbed surfaces, which were then moved manually by the operator. The advantage of this device was that hands did not have to be put into the water and that more strength could be applied so to achieve better results in terms of cleanliness. Time savings, however, were out of reach as the powering of the device was still done by the operator. As a major disadvantage, clothes were exposed to high mechanical strain, such that more delicate fabrics would still demand hand washing. For this reason, the shape and placement of these frictional surfaces were gradually modified.

Commercial applications have demonstrated that it was sufficient for the laundry to simply swirl in water, especially with the development and accessibility of higher-quality soap. Thus, apart from the aforementioned washer type based on the scrubboard technique, at least four other basic washer types became available at the turn of the twentieth century, each applying a different basic technique to force hot soapy water through fabrics: the dolly, the vacuum washer, the gyrator or agitator type and the cylinder type (Giedion, 1948, p. 562). We would add yet a further category, namely the rocker washer type, where the wooden box itself was swung or 'rocked' back and forth by the operator.

The manual dolly-type washer had the familiar dolly (i.e. 'milk stool'-resembling stick) to agitate the clothes, but it was now operated by rotating a lever or a flywheel gear.[9] The vacuum wash plunger (or vacuum cup washer) used yet another technique. It consisted of a tub into which reached a shaft with funnel-shaped cups or bells. Through the up- and downward movement of the shaft, suction was created such that water was moved through the clothes. The plungers were moved via a hand lever that was connected to a gearing mechanism. A first advertisement of this kind of washer, i.e. a washer based on the principle of 'alternate suction and pressure', appeared in the *Ladies' Home Journal* in 1906 ('Sanitaree Washer').

An agitator-type washer, which was the typological origin of the modern washing machine for private use, was invented in 1869. The device had a cylindrical body and a four-bladed rotor at the bottom of the tub, which drove water through the fabrics and was itself driven by a shaft that passed down through the tub bottom (Giedion, 1948, p. 551). A model of the cylinder type washer, for which records date back to at least 1868, consisted of two tubs: an inner tub (a perforated metal cylinder), which held the clothes and an outer tub filled with water, in which the inner tub revolved. Through the holes in the inner tub, water was forced through the laundry when the inner tub was rotating.

By the end of the nineteenth century, the basic principles of modern washing machines had been established, namely agitator-based washers – nowadays referred to as top-loaders – and perforated tubs, the so-called front-loading washers (Buehr, 1965, p. 67). All these advanced tools were much more costly than the common washboard: at the end of the nineteenth century, nominal washer prices ranged from $2.50 to $4.25, while a washboard cost only 12 or 20 cents (Lebergott, 1993, p. 114; Strasser, 2000 [1982], p. 116). Not surprisingly, therefore, hardly any American household possessed a 'hand and water powered machine' in 1900. Only 1 per cent of households owned such a device, while the scrubboard existed in 98 per cent of households. The remaining 1 per cent of households had no proper equipment at all and resorted to using commercial laundries (Lebergott, 1993, p. 115).[10]

Primitive manual wringers were also introduced at that time, easing the drying of clothes with the help of leverage power. Garments were run through two parallel rollers, which were moved by turning a spring. Nominal prices for wringers varied from $1.30–$3.00 (Strasser, 2000 [1982], p. 116). Although more costly, they were clearly preferred to the wringers attached to wooden simple washers or washtubs as the ordinary tub wringer required about as much effort to hold the tub as to turn the wringer (Lebergott, 1993, p. 114). Flatirons, to be heated on the stove, were most common; however, most people simply wrung out the clothes by hand and ironed them afterward (Buehr, 1965, p. 64).

Cowan (1983, p. 43) claims that, despite the availability of a couple of simple tools for doing laundry and also other housework activities, throughout the nineteenth century no real improvements were achieved in terms of making housework more convenient. In fact, many women suffered from ill health because housework was so burdensome (Cowan, 1983, p. 43). Although mechanization reduced some of the drudgery involved in clothes washing, the largest part of drudgery was not eliminated, especially as water still had to be carried and lifted. The poor insulation of the available simple washers contributed to this state of affairs, as water often had to be reheated during the washing process (Lebergott, 1993, p. 114). Likewise, time savings have, at best, been minor to negligible. First, hygienic improvements were feasible, however: as hands no longer had to be put into the water for scrubbing the clothes, much higher temperatures could be used.

At the beginning of the twentieth century, the *electrification* of the devices marked the next big leap, when the former devices became supplemented by an electric motor to replace the mechanical motion formerly done by hand (Giedion, 1948, p. 556; Buehr, 1965, p. 64). Records indicate that first inventions in the United States were made in 1908, for example, the electricity-powered washing machine, invented by Alva J. Fisher (AHAM, 2009). Electricity supplied the power to run practically every mechanical device, therefore including washing machines (Cohen, 1982, pp. 81). Note that electricity was applied to run the machines, not to heat up the water. Earlier machines were also driven by gasoline, gas, or water power, but none of these techniques were as successful as the electricity-using variant – which is why the following exposition focuses on this specific variant only. When exactly the first electric washing machines for home use appeared on the U.S. market is yet unclear. Several scholars mention the date of 1914 or 1915 (Hartmann, 1974, p. 294; Strasser, 2000 [1982], p. 117). A look into the *Ladies' Home Journal* reveals that a first advertisement of an electric washer appeared already in 1909, addressing the 'Jewel electric washer'. From 1914, the 'Western electric washer and wringer' was intensively advertised in that magazine.

The aforementioned washers were of the cylinder type, i.e. clothes were put into the wooden or metal drum, which turned alternately in one or the other direction. A control at the lower part of the machine engaged the clutch to start the rotation. Usually, a wringer was attached to the device. But other types of washers could also be powered by an electric motor, for example, the mechanized agitator washer. Here, electric power was usually transmitted through a drive shaft at the bottom of the tub. The motor was usually enclosed in a housing, so to separate the grease of the device from the clean clothes. Depending on the type of washing machine, the mechanism to agitate the clothes already had reached a high degree of complexity, involving gears, levers and drive belts.[11]

It goes without saying that safety issues played a great role here as the combination of water and electricity requested handling with caution. Safety problems also occurred with wringers. Next to the detached and larger variants, i.e. mangles, smaller wringers were attached to the washers to remove excess water from the clothes when taking them out of the tub. Safety overload mechanisms were indispensable here as well, but they had not been an element of all devices from the beginning (Lebergott, 1993, p. 114):

> By 1929, the housewife's obsession with 'motorized implements' led her to buy wringers directly attached to the tub. Metal rollers (or vulcanized covers) readily squeezed out the water. Since they occasionally squashed a finger, many women were 'gulled into' buying safer machines with rubber

rollers. [...] Power wringers promised to end the creative task of cranking the wringer. Consumers Union then found 'a great many ... women
catching hands, sleeves and hair in power wringers while drying clothes'.

The sarcastic tone used by Lebergott is due to the fact that not all contemporaries were enthusiastic about the mechanization of housework, although
those critics made up the smallest minority. But this quotation is interesting
for another reason, namely to illustrate how desperately women were looking
for effort-reducing products, that they actually resorted to these potentially
dangerous devices.

In the course of these technical advances, the market for washing machines
began to expand – now as a result of residential demand. Around 1920, about
1,300 companies produced some sort of washing machine.[12] In 1929, the
industry had increased the production value by a factor of six, compared with
1914, and 84 per cent of the newly produced machines were electric. The
net per capita production output of washing and ironing machines increased
by *circa* 62 per cent from 1921–1929, reaching a per capita output of $0.65 in
1929 (Hartmann, 1974, p. 92).[13] By 1920, 8 per cent of households possessed
either a mechanized washing machine or an electric washer; by 1930, a quarter
of American households had already adopted an electric washer (Lebergott,
1993, p. 115). However, scrubboards and wooden tubs were still advertised
and sold in the 1920s, for instance at home economics exhibitions. This means
that not only several washer types but rather different 'generations' of washing
machines existed in parallel for some time.

What are the consequences of the electrification of washing machines in
terms of time and effort savings? Certainly, first, substantial reductions in
drudgery had been realized. However, a great burden still remained, as water
had to be carried and filled manually into the washtub (Cowan, 1976; Strasser,
2000 [1982]). Very little time savings could be achieved as the full attention
of the operator was still required for switching the motor on and off, adding
and removing pieces of clothes, adding soap, adding and removing water and
putting each item through the wringer (Cowan, 1976; Strasser 2000 [1982],
p. 117). Depending on the quality of the machine, one can also imagine that it
was necessary to watch the whole process. Doing the laundry still took about
four hours for the washing process only, i.e. exclusive of ironing and preparation time for starches and the like (Strasser, 2000 [1982], p. 117).

Did electric washers bring any benefits for the cleanliness of clothes, i.e.
the household production output? It can be doubted that the electrification of
washers brought an improvement; it meant that scrubbing of clothes was done
with uniform strength, whereas by hand, the scrubbing intensity could easily
be varied with respect to the nature of the garments. Recall that the same argument also applies to hand-powered machines. Furthermore, the electric motors
were likely to leave stains on the clothes from grease.

Some of the disadvantages associated with the electric motor, in particular,
safety issues as well as the soiling of clothes, were solved with the wiring of

Table 4.1 U.S. Homes with Electricity

Year	Wired households
1907	8
1912	16
1920	35
1930	68
1940	80

Notes: Percentage of homes.
Source: Cowan (1983, p. 81) and Strasser (2000 [1982]), p. 81).

houses. In general, urban families' houses were wired earlier than rural ones. While only 8 per cent of American homes had electric service in 1907, this figure amounted to 80 per cent by 1941 (cf. Table 4.1).

Next to the wiring of homes, the plumbing of houses was a major condition for the elimination of drudgery. Before the establishment of municipal water systems, every bit of water had to be carried into and out of the house. Moreover, it required making a stop in the kitchen whenever water had to be heated up (Strasser, 2000 [1982], p. 86), because the major source of heating for rural areas at the beginning of the twentieth century was the room stove, although there also existed stoves specifically for laundry washing (Cohen, 1982, p. 52). Lebergott (1993, p. 112) has calculated that, around 1900, the homemaker carried 9,000 gallons of water per annum into and out of the house (not only for clothes washing, though). At that point in time, almost half of all U.S. families had to resort to farm wells for their water supply (Lebergott, 1993, p. 118). By 1920, virtually all middle-class urban homes had running cold and hot water in their houses because water heaters were installed in the basement of the house (Cohen, 1982, p. 40). At that point in time, running water meant availability all day long and with sufficient water pressure (Cowan, 1983, p. 87). It took until after World War II for rural homes to also could enjoy this convenience (Vanek, 1978; Cowan, 1983, p. 87). In general, the development in rural areas lagged behind by some 50 years or so (Strasser, 2000 [1982], p. 86). Around 1940, about 70 per cent of American families, independent of income, had indoor running water (Buehr, 1965, p. 80; Lebergott, 1993, p. 101).[14]

These systemic changes in electricity and water supply allowed full use to be made of machines which had been available from the 1920s onward and were equipped with a water pump that drained and later also filled the tub. The advent of hot running water in the home still made a big impact, as electric power had originally been directed toward running the machines only and not for heating the water in the tub (Strasser, 2000 [1982], p. 117):

> For those with the required plumbing (often hot running water as well as cold) and draining facilities, electric machines lightened the washday burden: water running into one tub eliminated all the heavy lifting, and

electrically powered agitation did away with hand cranking and washboard scrubbing.

Only in the 1930s did domestic electric hot water heaters directly fill the tub with hot water. Based on energy expenditure studies, some argue that running water brought an even greater reduction in drudgery than electrification (Cowan, 1976). Clearly, when running water was introduced in the home, time savings occurred as well, as fetching the water from an outside well and the like was no longer required. In relative terms, however, the magnitude of the savings differed strongly: the time savings were rather minor, while the savings of physical labor were substantial. With running hot water, the situation was slightly different, however, as the time needed to heat up the water could be saved.[15]

In the 1920s, a further technical leap happened when spin-dry technology appeared on the market.[16] Although first patents date back to the 1870s (Giedion, 1948, p. 569; AHAM, 2009), this technical novelty could unfold its full effect only in combination with electrification (Giedion, 1948, p. 569). This innovation was directed toward the removal of excess water from the clothing so that the tedious wringing out of textiles by hand or by means of the attached wringer could be eliminated. In the 1920s, washing and drying were usually not carried out within the same tub, but the spin-dryer was attached to the washing machine itself (of the agitator type) to form a single solid unit with it. The dryer, a perforated tub that revolved at high speed, was either powered by a separate electric motor or by the motor of the washer. An alternative to the two-tub machine was also developed at the same time, namely the combined washer-dryer. These machines were able to carry out the two tasks of washing and drying within one device. The machines were usually front-loaded, i.e. of the cylinder type. While speed change was first accomplished by the operator, two-speed electric motors appeared in the 1920s.

In practice, the spin-dryer did allow only for minor time savings as full supervision by the operator was still required in terms of moving clothes and switching the motors on and off. With the combined washer-dryer, washing and drying happened one after the other, which prolonged the overall time period needed to finish a certain amount of laundry. As the wringing of clothes could be dispensed with, the electricity-driven devices diminished the drudgery of clothes washing, as did the two-tub device. In fact, in comparison with carrying out the drying process by means of a mangle or wringer, significant reductions in effort could be achieved. Still, in the 1920s, clothes were not dried to the extent that they could be put directly into the wardrobe. Drying and ironing afterward was usually still done, with the help of the respective means available to the household. In fact, not until the 1950s was it possible to increase the speed to the level required for centrifugal forces to successfully remove excess water. Since the 1960s, wringers, as a tool to dry clothes, have been completely abandoned (Lebergott, 1993, p. 116).

In the course of these technical advances, the demand for washing machines expanded further. The annual units of washing machines sold increased from *circa* 900,000 to *circa* 1.4 million between 1926 and 1935, while the average (nominal) retail price declined from $150 to $60 (Giedion, 1948, p. 568; Cowan, 1983, p. 94).

Further substantial time savings depended on the advent of *automation*, which marks the last final leap in technological progress in washing machines. With the integration of clock-timing mechanisms in washing machines, the necessity of supervision finally ended. Automation meant that, after the completion of a certain task, the operation would automatically stop and begin with the next operation, i.e. washing, rinsing and spin-drying, one after the other. Automation also implied that water was heated inside the tub itself and did not require external filling. Temperature and timing of the process were controlled by the machine itself. Giedion (1948, p. 570) posits that the technical means for full automation were available by 1939. Elsewhere, it is asserted that in 1937 (United States), the first fully automatic clothes washer was already being marketed by the *Bendix* corporation.[17]

Despite the invention of automatic washers, for the majority of U.S. women in the 1940s, the typical American washday still showed much resemblance to the nineteenth-century procedure, including the steps of scrubbing, boiling, bluing, starching and ironing of clothes (Ahern, 1941, pp. 51–64). And as in the pre-electric era, the wash was still done on a weekly basis, i.e. doing the wash on Monday and doing the ironing on Tuesday (Ahern, 1941, p. 49). This becomes clear with regard to the following diffusion statistics: in 1941, 80 per cent of the American population had electricity at home (cf. Table 4.1), while more than 60 per cent of wired households possessed some kind of washing machine (Bowden and Offer, 1994). In other words, a very large share of the population did not make use of washing machines in the early 1940s. Not surprisingly, therefore, the household manual by Ahern (1941, p. 55), published in the 1940s, still mentions the tub, dolly and scrubboard as tools for doing laundry. Although automatic washers were already available in the 1940s, these machines were not widespread by then. Also, in 1952, only 8 per cent of farm households and 21–25 per cent of urban households (employed wives as well as homemakers) owned an automatic washing machine, whereas 90 per cent of farm households and 60–68 per cent of urban households possessed some kind of nonautomatic power machine (Preece, 1990, p. 307). The advanced, automatic washers became standard equipment in American homes only after World War II (Cowan, 1983, p. 94). Until then, for most households, washing by hand and by machine existed in parallel, if only with regard to the fabrics washed and the magnitude of their soiling. For example, dirt not removed by machine washing had to be attended to afterward, using a scrubboard and/or a brush. The use of the washing machine was preferred, however (Ahern, 1941, p. 98).

With the plumbing of houses and improved machinery, both for the cleaning and drying of clothes, a good share of the drudgery of clothes washing had been eliminated. With automation, hardly any more reductions in drudgery could be achieved, such that time savings were the major effect of this innovation.

Following the automation of washing machines, some minor innovations in laundry technology occurred. Combined automatic washer-dryer devices for home use were available by 1953 (AHAM, 2009). Around that time, combined clothes washers and dishwashers were also sold, which required the manual interchange of the inner horizontal tub – a combination no longer available at present. In general, control devices became further refined and basically turned into buttons to be pushed. Semiconductors were incorporated into automatic washers by 1960, while electronic touch-controlled washers were introduced in 1977 (AHAM, 2009). Different laundry programs, with respect to fabric, color, impurity and size of the load, became available with time, thus allowing for further improvements in clothing care by differentiating temperature, length of the wash cycle and rinsing intensity. In parallel, spin speed was further increased and higher washing temperatures became feasible.

Innovations concerning material, shape and color of the machine took place along the way. Already in the 1910s, the wooden tub was replaced by metal to avoid material deformations as a consequence of humidity. As this often left rust stains on the clothes, galvanized or copper tubs were common before enameled steel was used in the 1930s.[18] In general, producers started to pay more attention to the design of products from the 1930s onward. Washing machines became more compact by hiding the mechanism involved (referred to as 'streamlining' by Giedion, 1948, p. 607), thus turning the device into a piece of home equipment. Already the compact electric washing machine required less space than traditional laundry equipment, i.e. the tubs, boiler and wringer together (Hartmann, 1974, p. 322). The very practical consequence of the design initiatives was that washing machines could be fitted in the home much more easily, especially when the standardization of appliance measurements was achieved (Giedion, 1948, p. 616). Since the 1940s, machines have been enclosed in enameled, rectangular cabinets of white color, which is still the standard color today. Before that, many other different shapes and colors existed.[19]

From the 1960s onward, capacity increased substantially (Gordon, 1990, p. 289). Since the 1980s at least, improvements in energy efficiency have been realized (Brenner, 1987). In parallel, improvements in washing power, detergents and softeners took place (e.g. Ruedenauer and Griesshammer, 2004).

The more and more technically improved devices have given rise to growing expenditures on washing machines and a widespread diffusion of these devices (cf. Figure 4.2). In the United States, per capita absolute consumer spending on appliances and electricity increased by more than 2,000 per cent between 1900 and 1990 (Lebergott, 1993, pp. 76). The share of income devoted to laundry equipment per annum has increased substantially from a day's pay in 1900 to a two- to three-weeks' pay in 1990 (Lebergott, 1993, p. 116) – laundry equipment hence being income-superior goods. The retail value of washing machines in the United States more than doubled during the period 1955–1989 from *circa* one billion dollars to two and a half billion dollars.[20]

By 1960, 55 per cent of U.S. households possessed a washing machine; in Great Britain and West Germany, this figure amounted to only 45 per cent and

Figure 4.2 Diffusion of Washing Machines in the United States, 1922–1970.

Source: Bowden and Offer (1994).

Notes: In percent of wired U.S. households.

36 per cent, respectively (Lebergott, 1993, p. 111). At present, the diffusion degree of washing machines in the United States amounts to *circa* 82 per cent of all households (EIA, 2011). Redundancies appear not to exist, i.e. families do possess more than one refrigerator, but not more than one washing machine (EIA, 2011). The market can thus be described as saturated, and mainly characterized by replacement purchases.

From this highly stylized overview, it becomes clear that technological progress over the past 200 years has made clothes cleaning less exhausting and less time consuming. At present, the remaining steps in doing laundry include sorting clothes, loading the machine, adding detergent, choosing the appropriate program, unloading the machine and drying the clothes further by means of a separate dryer or by simply hanging clothes up, for example, in the basement or outside. However, the respective technical advances in washing machines have not reduced the demands on time and physical effort to the same extent. From the beginning, inventions have been directed toward physical labor savings rather than time savings, although mechanization was hardly successful in achieving that goal. It brought neither time savings nor substantial labor savings. With electrification, the first significant reductions in drudgery became feasible, as electric motors substituted the household's hand power. Time savings were still out of reach, as machines still had to be attended to, for instance, by adding pieces of clothing. The advent of electricity in the home did not change this state of affairs, yet it solved the safety issues of the washing procedure and improved the cleanliness of clothes. The elimination of the bulk of drudgery depended on the installation of running water in the home and the invention of spin-dry technology, which put an end to the lifting and carrying of water as well as the wringing out of clothes with the help of a mangle. Substantial time savings in laundry washing have not been feasible until the 1940s, when automation made the supervision of the washing procedure obsolete. We thus conclude that the adoption of washing machines at the beginning of the twentieth century was clearly driven by the motive to reduce the drudgery of doing the laundry – a conclusion in line with the sociological literature, which stresses the burden that clothes washing placed on women (e.g. Hartmann, 1974; Cowan, 1983; Strasser, 2000 [1982]). The time saving motive, in contrast, could not have triggered the diffusion process prior to the advent of automatic washers in the 1940s.

While we have mainly paid attention to changes in household production technology for cleaning clothes, we shall at least mention that the technical advances brought more than labor and time savings. In fact, they enabled cleanliness results not achievable by human work alone. Even if many more individuals devoted their time and effort to clothes washing, but had to resort to the technical means of the nineteenth century, it is doubtful whether they would achieve the same results. In simple terms, clothes are cleaner, from a hygienic perspective, compared with 100 years ago, and the different washing programs allow better clothing care (Gordon, 1990, p. 289). Hence, although this study focuses on the substitution process of machines for human physical labor, the development sketched here is more than a mere substitution process. Through improvements in washing machines – as well as in washing powder – the cleanliness of clothing has been substantially raised. When taking into account that qualitative improvements in terms of hygienic and visual cleanliness have been substantial, it is a small step to conjecture that these factors have also played a role in the diffusion of washing machines. Earlier, we have argued that an emerging social norm of cleanliness might have contributed to an increasing demand for cleanliness-producing goods (cf. Chapter 3). However, the positive effects of sophisticated washing machines on the 'output of domestic production' will be left aside here. We address this point only briefly in the following chapter, where we take a look at the way clothes washers have been advertised over time (cf. Chapter 5).

This overview has further shown that the act of clothes washing belongs to a wider technological system (cf. Shove, 2003a). The entry of electricity and running water in American homes and the convergence of living conditions of urban and rural households were necessary conditions for modern washing machines to unfold their full potential as a time- and physical labor saving tool, just as complementary developments in detergents have contributed to transforming the domestic production of cleanliness. For example, soap powders have been available since the 1920s, eliminating the task of scraping and boiling bars of laundry soap (Cowan, 1976).

A further insight derived from this sketch of the history of technology is that laundry washing cannot be considered a 'neutral' activity in any sense. As the aforementioned statements of contemporaries have indicated, at the time of Blue Monday, doing the laundry was a detested activity full of negative associations. This attitude is not surprising, given the human disposition to avoid painful experiences, including heavy physical exercise. With technological progress, the negative associations should have decreased, as the drudgery element of clothes washing has gradually been reduced and is completely eliminated today. By adopting technically more and more advanced tools, households gradually eliminated the trade-off in clothes washing and thus overcame the inherent approach-avoidance-conflict.

4.5 Laundry Services

For clarity of exposition, we have so far neglected an important aspect of the technical advances in laundry washing, namely shifts in the frequency with which recourse to domestic servants and washerwomen to help out with the laundry was taken. A further alternative existed in the form of commercial laundries. While technical artifacts became more and more advanced, a general decline in the availability of domestic servants and laundresses to get the weekly wash done happened in parallel. From the perspective of the (middle-class) household, this development puts into question that the material conditions of housework have improved over the past century in terms of achieving time and/or physical labor savings (Cowan, 1983, p. 98):

> Washing sheets with an automatic washing machine is considerably easier than washing them with one that has a wringer, itself considerably easier than washing them with a scrubboard and tub. Yet the easiest solution of all (at least from the point of view of the housewife) is to have someone else do it altogether – common practice in many households in the nineteenth century and even in the first few decades of the twentieth. Laundresses were the most numerous of all specialized houseservants; many women who did their own cooking, sewing and housecleaning would have a laundress 'in' to do the wash or, failing that, would send some of it 'out' to be done.

The alternative to doing the laundry at home using more or less technically advanced equipment is to resort to services in the form of domestic servants, washerwomen or commercial laundries – alternatives existent in the nineteenth century and partly also in the eighteenth century. In what follows, we provide some basic facts on changes in the consumption of services over time – a development closely intertwined with the proliferation of washing machines. In fact, the mechanization of the home is closely interwoven with societal change concerning the availability of domestic servants as well as the social standing of being a housewife and the ideology of housework (Giedion, 1948, Chapter 6). By not leaving aside this important 'input factor' of domestic production processes, we give a more adequate and complete picture of changes in household technology to produce cleanliness. In addition to that, we summarize some arguments for why homemakers have increasingly taken to washing machines instead of services, resulting in the current situation of a practically saturated market for washing machines.

We will make the following arguments. First, as the first adopters of washing machines have not been women participating in the labor force but middle-class full-time homemakers, higher opportunity costs of time have not been the triggering factor behind the adoption decision (rejection of the Short-Run Time Substitution Hypothesis, H.4.1a). Second, by adopting washing machines, these consumers did not substitute their own time and physical labor, but the work formerly done by domestic servants. The substitution processes were thus not accompanied by higher female labor force participation rates on the part of the first adopters (rejection of the Long-Run Time Substitution Hypothesis, H.4.1b).[21] Third, through the acquisition of washing machines, middle-class families replaced one drudgery-avoiding 'technology' (domestic servants) with another (Long-Run Drudgery Avoidance Hypothesis, H.4.2a). Fourth, households with higher cleanliness standards had a stronger incentive to adopt washing machines (Short-Run Drudgery Avoidance Hypothesis, H.4.2b). Fifth, the substitutability of factors is interlinked with shared social understandings concerning the ideology of housework. Below, we show that the availability of substitutes has played a decisive role in the proliferation of washing machines – 'availability' referring to the mere existence of alternatives, their affordability and the household's understanding of what counts as a substitute.

In the eighteenth century, most people could at least 'at some time in their lives' rely on some form of assistance with doing the housework, no matter how rich or poor (Cowan, 1983, p. 28). In fact, housework was a joint undertaking of several people at that time, i.e. the housewife had help at least from other family members, more distant relatives, or neighbors (Matthews, 1987, Chapter 1). Many more products had to be 'homemade' back then, so that the housewife alone could not support a whole family with her labor. Only the smallest group of wealthy women were completely free of domestic duties (Matthews, 1987, p. 3).

In the nineteenth century, it was common to have further help in the form of domestic servants, who were usually immigrants and had come to America in large numbers from the 1830s onward (Matthews, 1987, p. 95). The life as a servant in an employer's house was a typical occupation for young women until they got married (Cowan, 1983, p. 28). Starting off as a servant, these people usually remained part of the working class for all of their lives (Matthews, 1987, p. 32). Well-to-do urban families relied on servants to a large extent, but middle-class urban families could also finance at least one full-time servant, who came in every day (Cohen, 1982, p. 1). In British households of the middle class, domestic servants were even more common at that time (Cohen, 1982, p. 8). In the 1850s, there was on average one servant available for ten households, i.e. probably one servant in every tenth home (Matthews, 1987, p. 266).

However, for the majority of women in the nineteenth century, making a living was hard because either a woman was a servant herself or, more likely, she was working in a servant-free home. Due to the hard physical labor, the poor comfort at home and a large number of children, many women could even be considered invalids (Matthews, 1987, p. 30). Working class women were 'overworked and overburdened', and those not overworked could achieve this at the expense of other people's good health: not having servants in the house would have meant 'a career of full-time drudgery' (Cohen, 1982, p. 8). Servants, in turn, had to deal with the most burdensome of chores, including scrubbing floors and doing laundry (Cowan, 1983, p. 29). Apparently, the household sought specifically to avoid doing the laundry, which implies that it was not only unpleasant but probably also more unpleasant than other activities. Note that, independent of the task that the servant was assigned to, the household could achieve the same amount of time savings but could economize on most of the drudgery by having the domestic help take over or support doing the laundry.

But middle-class families still had reasons to complain. Servants were judged to be rather low-qualified help and they were each available for relatively short periods of time. When women got married and had accumulated some cash, they could start their own home in a country where land was abundant. The low quality has been complained about in women's magazines from the Civil War onward, referred to there as 'the servant problem' (Matthews, 1987, p. 97; Cowan, 1983, p. 28). In the late nineteenth century, middle- and upper-class women therefore started initiatives to send 'domestics' to schools for training, such that they would become better acquainted with the American standards of domestic practice (Matthews, 1987, p. 97). The skills of servants attracted much attention as nineteenth-century America was driven by the 'cult of domesticity', characterized by an upward shift in domestic standards (Matthews, 1987, Chapter 2). After the American Revolution, America began to form as an independent nation state and the home obtained a highly politicized role. The ideology of 'Republican Motherhood' established the home as the safe haven in times of social upheaval, as well as the cradle of active and responsible citizens. With the home and the housewife turning into institutions of the highest moral authority as well as responsibility, women found a way to improve their role in society. The claim for increasing the participation of women outside of the domestic sphere was directly derived from their abilities as good housekeepers. From 1908 originates the following statement by Theodore Parker, an influential reformer (cf. Matthews, 1987, p. 88):

> I knew men saying women cannot manage the great affairs of a nation. Very well. Government is political economy – national housekeeping. Does any respectable woman keep house so badly as the United States?

Not surprisingly, therefore, those women whose goal in life was not mere survival, paid much attention to the quality of the housework done by servants.[22] The relationship between maid and 'mistress' was thus of a clear, hierarchical nature: the housekeeper delegated and supervised the work but would not engage in all activities herself. The supervision and organization of servants at that time clearly raised the status of the middle-class housewife if she was successful in maintaining high domestic standards (Matthews, 1987, p. 12). Note that, via the cult of domesticity, a link was formed between status on one side and housewifery and housework standards on the other.

Although domestic servants were portrayed as hindering the accomplishment of domestic perfection, they were still employed. Better education of servants was seen as one way to deal with the problem of low-quality help. In addition to that, leading female intellectuals, foremost Catherine Esther Beecher, sought ways to make housework more efficient by reducing waste of labor. Although Beecher especially did not have political ambitions, she still did not see efficient housekeeping as an end in itself. Beecher wanted to give women self-assurance and confidence by trying to establish housekeeping as a profession ('domestic science'). The basic idea was to render servants unnecessary altogether, such that the homemaker herself could maintain the high household standards depicted in household manuals, advice books and 'domestic novels'. Beecher herself wrote a textbook for female schools in 1841 *(A Treatise on Domestic Economy)*. But Catherine Beecher was not unworldly: she understood that women would not dispense of servants unless manual drudgery was simultaneously reduced (Giedion, 1948, Chapter 6). Especially for doing the laundry, solutions had to be found to make the transition to the servant-free home attractive for middle- and upper-class women. Beecher – like others before her – suggested installing communal laundries, financed by small groups of households.[23] These attempts were not successful, however.

In fact, servants, as well as other forms of services, were in high demand, especially for laundry washing. In the nineteenth century, doing the laundry was the most disliked activity of all and whoever could afford it either delegated it to servants or made use of laundresses, if not on a weekly basis then at least twice a month (Cohen, 1982, p. 91). Despite the high propensity to turn to services, the household's income, in the end, decided to which extent desire and reality actually matched. Depending on status and residence, households differed strongly in the nineteenth century concerning the material conditions of housework – a difference that lasted until the middle of the twentieth century (Vanek, 1978). In general, family status was indicated by the number of servants (Vanek, 1978). The richer families had the possibility to resort to washerwomen or domestic servants to a larger extent, while urban families were ahead of their rural counterparts by decades. At the end of the nineteenth century, the typical American farm family and poorer urban households usually did their own laundry. A prosperous farm woman, however, sent her laundry to a laundress, whose common equipment at that time naturally consisted of washboards and tubs (Cohen, 1982, p. 6). In urban areas, the services of steam laundries could be made use of, which included the picking up and delivery of clothes to the door (Preece, 1990, p. 308).

From the beginning of the twentieth century onward, commercial laundries had started to replace independent laundresses in some towns, for the use of laundry services was also possible in homes without electricity and running water (Preece, 1990, p. 304). But this service was only affordable for the well-to-do middle-class (Cohen, 1982, p. 2). In fact, at the turn of the twentieth century, middle-class urban neighborhoods could be identified by the absence of clotheslines on Monday – exactly because they could outsource this task completely (Strasser, 1999, p. 139). Vanek (1978) maintains that, by 1935–36, all families devoted some share of their income to finance domestic help, but that this share was higher for richer and urban families.

There are different opinions concerning the way consumers took to steam or power laundries. On one side, the use of steam laundries was a way to avoid the 'horrible task' of laundry washing (Cohen, 1982, p. 7). On the other, the quality of clothes washing left much to be desired (Cohen, 1982, p. 2). Cohen (1982) posits that most households of sufficient financial strength still went for the commercial variant, 'no matter how bad it shredded the family clothes and linens'. Poorer households could not regularly afford the services of steam laundries, but might have sent – as an exception – delicate fabrics like men's white dress shirts (Cohen, 1982, p. 93). Possibly more delicate clothing was handled with better care. A study of the 1920s, for example, shows that all families surveyed made use of steam laundries, independent from income, especially for men's shirts and flatwork such as sheets and tablecloths (Cowan, 1983, p. 105).[24]

Recall that the cult of domesticity in the nineteenth century was a middle-class phenomenon. At that point in time, middle- and upper-class consumers were clearly distinguishable from poorer households in terms of possessions, including the amount of clothing and the outer appearance in general (Du Vall, 1988, p. 175; Hardyment, 1988, p. 22). Strasser (1999, p. 39) posits that wardrobes were small until the end of the nineteenth century, and that only well-to-do households had 'more than a few changes of clothing for each season', while many people had one change or nothing at all. Clothing care, apart from laundering, was a frequent task, which only the very richest women did not have to do. Higher cleanliness aspirations of the middle-class went hand in hand with a higher stock of clothing. Although the financial background did eventually decide the extent to which domestic servants were resorted to, the middle class were also much more in need of additional help, for the higher the cleanliness levels targeted, the more drudgery that had to be taken into account.

So, in the first decades of the twentieth century, closed market substitutes were available so that households would not have to do the laundry themselves if they could only afford these services (Hartmann, 1974, p. 276). This situation was significantly altered when the numbers of domestic servants dropped after the First World War (Cowan, 1976).[25] In general, other better-paid occupations attracted former domestic servants. Furthermore, immigration laws became more restrictive in the early 1920s (Cutliffe and Reynolds, 1997, p. 20). The overall number of persons occupied in domestic service fell from about 1.8 million in 1910 to about 1.4 million in 1920, while the number of households increased by about 4 million to 24.4 million (Cowan, 1976, p. 330). Cowan (1976) calculates that the ratio of servants to inhabitants was 98.9 to 1,000 in 1900, whereas by 1920, only 58 paid servants were available for 1,000 inhabitants (Cowan, 1976, p. 330). According to Vanek (1978), the number of paid household workers dropped further, from about 67 per 1000 households in 1930 to 25 per 1000 households in 1970. The problem intensified through the parallel decrease in unpaid domestic help, i.e. 'unmarried daughters, maiden aunts, grandparents' (Cowan, 1976, p. 329). In advertisements for washing machines and other household appliances in the 1920s, servants gradually disappeared as the people depicted doing housework (Cowan, 1976).

Several scholars argue that the proliferation of washing machines and other domestic appliances stood in close context with the decrease in domestic servants (Cowan, 1983; Matthews, 1987; Strasser, 2000 [1982]). In other words, at the same time that many households ceased to rely on domestic servants, they started to purchase electric washers in greater numbers. Advertisements portrayed washing machines as a means to eliminate the need for domestic help (Vanek, 1978). Beyond doubt, the purchase of washing machines certainly was a reaction to the reduced availability and higher price of domestic help. However, it is not the whole story. In addition, the shared social understanding concerning the meaning of housework was in transition. Already at the beginning of the twentieth century, the cult of domesticity was replaced by a more scientific approach to housekeeping, characterized by a stronger emphasis on efficiency considerations (Matthews, 1987, p. 111). We have already mentioned the initiative taken by Christine Frederick to treat housekeeping activities like industrial production processes by targeting efficiency gains in domestic chores. After World War I, yet a different ideology began to form. In fact, housework turned into a means to express the housewife's affection and love for her family. As with the cult of domesticity, households were urged to dispense with domestic servants, although this time not for their low quality but rather because 'tasks of this emotional magnitude could not possibly be delegated to servants' (Cowan, 1976, p. 336). Women were urged to do the housework by themselves, i.e. without making use of servants or services of any kind.[26] In simple terms, serving the children convenience food was not considered an appropriate substitute for a home-cooked meal prepared by the homemaker. Having the laundry done by an outsider possibly also went against this ideology.

Faced with this situation, the adoption of washing machines was the logical response in order to avoid the drudgery of clothes washing. Recall that, in the 1920s, the available clothes washers substantially lightened the washday burden in a wired house with running water, whereas automatic devices had not yet been invented. The first adopters of the improved devices were urban middle-class women, i.e. those with higher available income, higher cleanliness standards and the structural prerequisites in terms of running water at home (Strasser, 1999, p. 113). These housewives took on tasks previously delegated to domestic servants, in a shift toward the adoption of washing machines referred to as 'in sourcing' of work (Cowan, 1983, p. 98; Cutliffe and Reynolds, 1997, p. 20)[27] that raised the absolute time these women spent doing the laundry. Still, without washing machines, the situation would have been worse, i.e. much more physical effort would have been needed to fulfill this household chore. The exchange of one 'factor of production' for another had a further implication in that the homemaker faced a loss in status, i.e. a degradation of her labor: once a supervisor of others' work, the middle-class housewife became an unspecialized worker herself (Cowan, 1976, p. 23).[28]

An important point to note is that washing machines and other devices did not stand in context with higher labor force participation rates on the part of these first adopters. The consumers who purchased this advanced equipment in the 1920s were middle-class women who followed the do-it-yourself logic prescribed by the new ideology of housework rather than replacing their unpaid labor. Cowan (1976) argues that the husband's income could be considered a rough proxy for the social status of the household and that higher income made it less likely that the women entered the labor force, while being able to afford the new appliance.

When power laundries began to notice the competition coming from electric washing machines, they expanded their variety of services from 1915 onward (Hartmann, 1974, p. 286; Strasser, 2000 [1982], p. 119). As a reaction to that, the washing machine industry started to launch advertisements against steam laundries (Strasser, 2000 [1982], p. 120). Still, in the 1930s, commercial laundries were frequented to a much lesser extent than at the beginning of the century, while the ownership rates of electric residential washing machines expanded. This development is probably also intertwined with the transition in the ideology of housework. Further factors possibly contributing to the diffusion of electric clothes washers – as opposed to the alternative household technology, i.e. the demand for services – have to be mentioned. First, the attitudes toward technology were quite favorable at the beginning of the twentieth century (Matthews, 1987, p. 111; Hessler, 2001). Second, washing machines, like other domestic appliances, could be purchased by installment payments, making the purchase also attractive for less wealthy households (Hartmann, 1974, p. 299).[29]

At present, the larger part of U.S. households owns a washing machine, implying that clean clothes are mainly home-produced, although alternative 'roads not taken' have also existed (Cowan, 1983, Chapter 5). Arguably, the present situation has its origin in the processes described here, which reveals a strong path dependency in the consumption of cleanliness.

4.6 Conclusions

In this chapter, we examined the driving forces underlying the diffusion of washing machines in the United States throughout the twentieth century. Two hypotheses were scrutinized, namely the time substitution hypothesis and the drudgery avoidance hypothesis. The time substitution hypothesis, associated with Gary Becker's household production function approach, relates the acquisition of washing machines to differences in opportunity costs of time between working women and nonworking women and to the entry of women into the labor force. We formulated the alternative hypothesis that the adoption of washing machines has been motivated by the behavioral disposition to avoid heavy physical effort and that, in the absence of drudgery-reducing technology, low cleanliness levels would be displayed. Given that the avoidance of drudgery is an innate human disposition and that clothes washing in the nineteenth century was heavy physical labor, we conjectured that consumers faced a trade-off between wanting to have clean clothes on one side and wanting to avoid drudgery on the other.

By looking at the phases of technological progress in washing technology and the wider technological system over the past 200 years, we gathered some empirical material with which to evaluate the explicative potential of these alternative conjectures. We found that more and more technically advanced devices did indeed allow for both time savings and reductions in effort in clothes washing. As the adoption of washing machines made time and physical labor savings feasible, it is plausible that the purchase of these devices has been driven by both these motivations.

At the same time, reductions in physical effort were achievable before time savings became feasible. The early diffusion of washing machines until, say, the 1940s – the advent of automation – thus cannot be explained, or only to a minor extent, with reference to the time saving motive. In addition, we find little support for the time substitution hypothesis when it is taken into account that the earliest adopters of washing machines in the 1920s were the better-off middle-class households who had full-time homemakers. These consumers had the financial means to acquire technically advanced devices, but they did not acquire these products because of higher opportunity costs of time (rejection of the Short-Run Time Substitution Hypothesis) or because they intended to join the labor force themselves (rejection of the Long-Run Time Substitution Hypothesis). Instead, middle-class housewives had to find a replacement for domestic servants, who became more scarce and expensive in the 1920s. These servants had the opportunity to find other, possibly better-paid jobs in the growing manufacturing sector and therefore withdrew from domestic tasks. While resorting to servants as well as other forms of services (washerwomen and commercial laundries) has clearly been an act of outsourcing from the point of view of the middle-class household, the adoption of washing machines in that historical setting was not. Instead, the purchase of these devices implied an in-sourcing of work formerly not done by middle-class housewives themselves. Washing machines substituted the servants' labor rather than the household's own work and included an increase in the absolute time the latter spent washing clothes. Achievable time savings were thus rather 'hypothetical' than 'actual'. Moreover, by choosing washing machines over commercial laundries, middle-class households would forgo even larger time savings, which clearly goes against the time substitution argument and is a paradox for the Beckerian approach.

We interpret the consumption behavior depicted here as evidence in favor of the drudgery avoidance hypothesis and argue that the prospect to solve the conflict in motivations, i.e. between cleanliness (health, social recognition) on one side and drudgery avoidance on the other, has been the essential driving force behind the diffusion of washing machines.

In the nineteenth century, only very simple tools for clothes washing were available. Doing the laundry was 'backbreaking labor', detrimental to health and involving several unpleasant tasks. Well-to-do consumers had the possibility to outsource this task to domestic servants, who would receive payment in return. That way, the wealthy middle class could maintain their higher cleanliness aspirations without having to endure the feeling of drudgery (Short-Run Drudgery Avoidance Hypothesis). The situation was quite different from the perspective of less wealthy households. Poorer consumers showed very low levels of cleanliness and changed their few clothes very rarely (cf. Chapter 3). Hence, they avoided drudgery by basically avoiding clothes washing.[30]

At the beginning of the twentieth century, a few central conditions changed. First, consumers' available income was expanding during times of further industrial development, which made washing machines and other household appliances more easily affordable. Second, with big advances in laundry technology and the wider technological system taking place (electricity, plumbing), the drudgery that had formerly been involved in doing the laundry had practically been eliminated (while time savings were also feasible, especially from the 1940s onward). Hence, the former behavioral trade-off could be overcome once a consumer could afford the improved technology: by adopting a washing machine, the negative association related to clothes washing was eliminated (Long-Run Drudgery Avoidance Hypothesis). These arguments hold specifically for lower class consumers. An additional condition was necessary to make upper-class consumers appreciate these products, namely the decline of domestic servants. Given their high cleanliness standards, upper-class consumers had a particularly strong incentive to buy washing machines as a substitute for domestic help, thus replacing one drudgery-avoiding 'technology' (services) by another (goods).

Note that the findings gathered here point to the relevancy of preferences for the use of time in the behavioral interpretation given earlier for understanding the diffusion of clothes washers. The acquisition of washing machines has been motivated by the negative associations consumers held toward clothes washing, thus making them search for ways to avoid this activity. Technically advanced products were thus acquired in order to change the valence of doing laundry.

The discussion hitherto is valid, independent of the household production objectives, i.e. levels of cleanliness. When actual or potential drudgery is faced, the substitution of washing machines for human physical labor always makes sense in that it solves the conflict of motivations. Yet, the pressure to substitute is stronger, the more intense the conflict is. Earlier, we argued that a social norm of cleanliness came into being at the beginning of the twentieth century, having its origin in the nineteenth-century Hygienic Movement and implying an increase in cleanliness levels for the largest share of the population (cf. Chapter 3). Although they would have had an incentive to purchase washing machines anyway, so to avoid the washday burden, we can assume that the emerging norm was a further triggering factor: with a gradually rising stock of clothing and higher frequency of laundry washing, the trade-off also became more pronounced for the less well-to-do. The upward shift in the social standard of cleanliness thus also contributed to the diffusion of washing machines in the twentieth century.

The result of technological progress in washing machines, growth in income, the decline of servants and the social norm of cleanliness was the homogenization of cleanliness consumption patterns in the twentieth century and the mass market for washing machines. The adoption of technically advanced devices was contingent upon learning processes on the part of the consumers concerning both the availability and functionality of these novel products. Consumers had to become aware of these new devices and their ability to better satisfy consumer needs than former tools. This latter process can be termed 'learning of new associations' (cf. Chapter 2). Learning how to use new products necessarily had to follow. Advertisements for washing machines come to mind as a way in which consumers grasped both the availability and the function of novel goods. In addition to that, advertisements might have had an important role in linking social and technical change and in reinforcing existing ideologies (Cowan, 1976). Households can be assumed to have shown a high propensity for turning to advertisements when more and more production processes of the home were replaced by market alternatives and advertisers supported the learning process, resulting in the acquisition of new products.

In the following chapter, we turn to this matter, i.e. the content of advertisements and the extent to which the motives of time savings and physical labor savings were put in context with technically advanced washing machines. We will thus separate the relative importance of time savings versus the reductions in physical effort from a motivational perspective.

Notes

1 The latest statistics pertain to the year 2009 (EIA, 2011).
2 Soap made at home was based on leftover fats, which were boiled in an iron kettle together with lye made out of wood ashes (Ahern, 1941, p. 14). An actual soap industry, including commercial production, dates back to the thirteenth century in several European countries (Ahern, 1941, p. 3).
3 More precisely, Cordes (2005) assumes an innate human disposition to avoid heavy physical effort 'beyond an individual adaptation level'. Cordes thus argues that individuals differ in terms of categorizing behaviors as unpleasantly effortful, depending on individual experiences. In view of the statements quoted above, it seems safe, however, to assume that individuals experienced clothes washing in a similar way. For our exposition, we thus leave aside differences in individual adaptation levels and focus on the commonalities in households' motivational basis.

4 Human physical labor comprises three subcategories, which are mechanical work, psychomotor skills and demanding handicraft (Cordes, 2002, p. 20). Mechanical work includes human muscular power which is either directed toward lifting, pushing, pulling, or carrying heavy external objects, or applied in order to propel oneself or an object. Reaction time, control precision, or sensory abilities belong to the group of psychomotor skills. Labor of this category does not require high energy expenditures but rather additional, sometimes complex, equipment. Demanding handicraft includes tasks which require high levels of manual and finger dexterity.

5 Although our analysis is confined to the past 200 years, the washing of clothes and other textiles has a much longer tradition in human culture. In earlier times, people washed their clothes by holding them in streams or standing in lake water into which they dipped the textiles before pounding them on rocks (Ahern, 1941, p. 1; Strasser, 2000 [1982], p. 107). According to Buehr (1965, p. 61), this practice was still to be found in some rural places in early nineteenth century North America. A form of soap was discovered as already in use in Roman times (Ahern, 1941, p. 3; DuVall, 1988, p. 191).

6 The consumer's desire for time or effort savings in a specific consumption activity can date back even further and, if recognized by producers, will be an incentive to innovate in that direction (cf. Chapter 2).

7 A particularly rich website is the following one: http://www.oldewash.com (retrieved: 30.09.2016). Patents can be found here: http://uspto.gov (retrieved: 30.09.2016).

8 Our research of the *Ladies' Home Journal* has shown that a steam washer was also available for residential use in 1905 (cf. Chapter 5).

9 AHAM (2009) attributes the invention of the dolly-type washer to William Blackstone, 1874, who later founded a company to produce the Blackstone washer.

10 We would not interpret these figures in the way that only 1 per cent of families made use of services, covering commercial laundries as well as servants. Simple scrubboards have probably also been owned by richer households, who relied on domestic servants to operate them (cf. Section 4.5).

11 For an overview of specific constructions, see the photographs of washer models at http://www.oldewash.com.

12 http://www.oldewash.com/articles/lives.htm (retrieved: 30.09.2016).

13 Other expenditure categories witnessed stronger growth, for example, electric cooking stoves and ranges grew by about 160 per cent in only a 4-year period. However, the per capita output of that exact category is a lot smaller ($0.007). The expenditure category that showed both the strongest growth and the highest per capita output was mechanical refrigerators (Hartmann, 1974, p. 92). Note that the figures are values, i.e. expressed in nominal prices.

14 This analysis takes the middle of the nineteenth century as the starting point. But we are certainly aware of the fact that, further back in history, living conditions in Europe had already been better. In Roman times, for instance, running water had already been available in buildings, at least to supply public baths and toilets (Buehr, 1965, p. 80; Yarwood, 1981, p. 122).

15 We could not find out when the first machines which could heat up the water inside of the tub itself entered the market. Most likely, this technical advancement did not occur until the automation of washing machines. Today's washing machines carry out this procedure, which makes up a large share of the energy used for clothes washing (Ruedenauer and Griesshammer, 2004).

16 AHAM (2009) dates the market introduction of the agitator-based, spinner-type clothes washer to 1926.

17 An advertisement for the Bendix automatic washer that appeared 1945 in the *Ladies' Home Journal* states that the Bendix automatic had been on the market for 8 years already, hence since 1937.

18 http://www.oldewash.com/articles/lives.htm (retrieved: 30.09.2016).

19 Cf. the various photographs at http://www.oldewash.com.

20 Author's compilation from U.S. Bureau of the Census, Statistical Abstract of the United States (http://www.census.gov/library/publications/2011/compendia/statab/131ed.html, retrieved: 30.09.2016).

21 Note that domestic servants had already been part of the (female) labor force. When domestic servants started to take up occupations in other sectors after World War I, they therefore did not expand female labor force participation rates.

22 In the grand total, this argument is right. Educative, religious and charitable activities have been carried out mainly by middle- and upper-class women since the beginning of the nineteenth century. These kinds of activities were the only way for women to take a more active role in social and political life (recall that women did not have the right to vote in the nineteenth century). However, the most outspoken political woman at the center of public attention was Harriet Beecher Stowe, the author of *Uncle Tom's Cabin* (a critique of slavery) in 1851, who lived a rather struggling existence (Matthews, 1987, Chapter 2).

23 One forerunner was Melusina Fay Pierce, who established cooperative housekeeping in Cambridge in 1869. By providing the equipment and a full-time occupation for a few employees, doing the laundry could be avoided while high standards could be maintained (Strasser, 2000 [1982], p. 112).

24 For further information, cf. Hartmann's (1974, p. 280) review of survey information on laundry patterns for 1926 and 1927. Nearly 1,000 homemakers (rural and urban, of different income levels) were surveyed in 1927 by Clark (1928). The study reveals that the majority of households did their own laundry at home, but that 'many of them' also sent laundry out to commercial laundries. Among the items sent out most frequently were men's shirts and collars as well as flatwork (i.e. sheets, tablecloths etc.). Women's clothing was usually washed by the homemaker herself, independent of income. The use of alternatives increased with income (cross-section). Similar results were found by Harte and Gorton (1926), surveying nearly 4,000 urban and rural families, namely that the majority of households did laundry at home.

25 Elsewhere it is argued that the decline in servants had already started earlier, namely in the nineteenth century (Buehr, 1965; Cohen, 1982, p. 8) when the 'chronic labor shortage' of domestic tasks resulted from alternative occupations, implying higher salaries, in the growing mill towns.

26 A similar situation had already happened around 1850, both in North America and Europe (de Vries, 2008, p. 187), when households also believed that the then-available market alternatives to home-cooked meals and the like were not appropriate. As a consequence, women withdrew from the labor market – a shift made possible by the growth in income of the male 'breadwinner'. Again, increases in market wages were not an incentive to increase female labor force participation but to actually reduce it (income effect).

27 Interestingly, some servants could only be kept in their jobs when offered the modern equipment to do so (Hewes, 1930).

28 Although the argument by Cowan (1976) is right, it is surprising that a feminist scholar puts more emphasis on the situation of the homemaker than the servant, for the latter was usually also female. The payment of servants was low, and they hardly had any privacy. From the perspective of female servants, the development was clearly beneficial.

29 According to Hartmann (1974, p. 299), the General Electric (GE) company promoted the diffusion of washers by making installment contracts feasible when retailers sold washers together with the GE electric motor. Note that the possibility of installment buying somewhat weakens the argument that household income was such a decisive factor for the adoption of washing machines (affordability). In the empirical studies to be reviewed later (cf. Chapter 6), however, we show that household income had a significant positive impact on the ownership of washing machines.

30 The material conditions of housework also differed strongly between urban and rural households.

References

Association of Home Appliances Manufacturers [AHAM] (2009): Appliances Milestones. (http://www.aham.org/consumer/ht/d/Items/cat_id/5263/cids/424,5263/pid/1458; retrieved: 18.10.2009).

Ahern, E. (1941): *The Way We Wash Our Clothes*, M. Barrows & Company, New York.

Becker, G. S. (1965): 'A theory of the allocation of time', *The Economic Journal*, 75 (299) pp. 49–517.

Beecher, C. E., Beecher S. H. (1869): *The American Women's Home*, Rutgers University Press, New York.

Bowden, S., Offer, A. (1994): 'Household appliances and the use of time: The United States and Britain since the 1920s', *Economic History Review*, 47 (4), pp. 725–748.

Brenner, T. E. (1987): 'Soaps and detergents: North American trends', *Journal of the American Oil Chemists' Society*, 64 (2), pp. 251–256.

Buehr, W. (1965): *Home Sweet Home in the Nineteenth Century*, Thomas Y. Crowell Company, New York.

Buenstorf, G. (2004): *The Economics of Energy and the Production Process: An Evolutionary Approach*, Edward Elgar, Cheltenham.

Cohen, D. (1982): *The Last Hundred Years: Household Technology*, M. Evans and Company, New York.

Cordes, C. (2002): An Evolutionary Analysis of Long-Term Qualitative Change in Human Labor, Dissertation, Jena University, Germany.

Cordes, C. (2005): 'Long-term tendencies in technological creativity: A preference-based approach', *Journal of Evolutionary Economics*, 15, pp. 149–168.

Costa, D. L. (2000): 'From mill town to board room: The rise of women's paid labor', National Bureau of Economic Research, No. W7608.

Cowan, R. S. (1976): 'The "Industrial Revolution" in the home: Household technology and social change in the 20th century', *Technology and Culture*, 17 (1), pp. 1–23.

Cowan, R. S. (1983): *More Work for Mother*, Basic Books, New York.

Cutliffe, S. H., Reynolds, T. S. (1997): 'Technology in American context', in Cutliffe, S. H., Reynolds, T. S. (eds): *Technology & American History*, The University of Chicago Press, Chicago and London.

De Vries, J. (2008): *The Industrious Revolution, Consumer Behavior and the Household Economy, 1650 to the Present*, Cambridge University Press, Cambridge, MA.

Du Vall, N. (1988): *Domestic Technology: A Chronology of Developments*, G.K. Hall & Co, Boston, MA.

EIA, 2011: Annual Energy Review 2011, Energy Information Administration, Table 2.6 Household End Uses: Fuel Types, Appliances, and Electronics, Selected Years, 1978–2009 (http://www.eia.gov/totalenergy/data/annual/pdf/sec2_21.pdf.)

Frieman, J. (2002): *Learning and Adaptive Behavior*, Wadsworth, Belmont, CA.

Giedion, S. (1948) (1969): *Mechanization Takes Command: A Contribution to Anonymous History*, Norton, New York.

Goldin, C. (1986): 'The female labor force and American economic growth, 1890–1980', in Engerman, S. L., Gallman, R. E. (eds): *Long-Term Factors in American Economic Growth (Studies in Income and Wealth)*, No. 51, University of Chicago Press, Chicago and London.

Gordon, R. J. (1990): *The Measurement of Durable Goods Prices*, University of Chicago Press, Chicago and London.

Hardyment, C. (1988): *From Mangle to Microwave: The Mechanization of Household Work*, Polity Press, Cambridge, United Kingdom.

Hartmann, H. I. (1974): Capitalism and Women's Work in the Home, 1900–1930, Dissertation, Yale University.

Heicken, K. (1949): 'Über die Wertbestimmung chemischer Desinfektionsmittel zur Wäsche- und Kleiderdesinfektion', *Zeitschrift für Hygiene*, 129, pp. 303–331.

Hessler, M. (2001): *'Mrs. Modern Women', Zur Sozial- und Kulturgeschichte der Haushaltstechnisierung*, Campus Verlag, Frankfurt.

Hewes, A. (1930): 'Electrical appliances in the home', *Social Forces*, 9 (2), pp. 235–242.

Lebergott, S. (1993): *Pursuing Happiness: American Consumers in the Twentieth Century*, Princeton University Press, Princeton.

Lovingood, R. P., McCullough, J. L. (1986): 'Appliance ownership and household work time', *Home Economics Research Journal*, 14 (3), pp. 326–335.

Matthews, G. (1987): *Just a Housewife: The Rise and Fall of Domesticity in America*, Oxford University Press, New York.

Michael, R. T., Becker G. S. (1973): 'On the new theory of consumer behavior', *Swedish Journal of Economics*, 75 (4), pp. 378–396.

Mohun, A. P. (1999): *Steam Laundries: Gender, Technology, and Work in the United States* and *Great Britain, 1880–1940*, The Johns Hopkins University Press, Baltimore and London.

Nichols, P. S. (1970): 'Bacteria in laundered fabrics', *American Journal of Public Health*, 60 (11), pp. 2175–2180.

Pollak, R. A., Wachter, M. L. (1975): 'The relevance of the household production function and its implications for the allocation of time', *Journal of Political Economy*, 83 (2), pp. 255–277.

Preece, A. G. (1990): *Housework and American Standards of Living, 1920–1980*, Ph.D. Dissertation, University of California, Berkeley.

Ruedenauer, I., Griesshammer, R. (2004): *Produkt-Nachhaltigkeitsanalyse von Waschmaschinen und Waschprozessen*, Oeko-Institut e.V., Freiburg.

Shove, E. (2003a): 'Converging conventions of comfort, cleanliness and convenience', *Journal of Consumer Policy*, 26, pp. 395–418.

Shove, E. (2003b): *Comfort, Cleanliness and Convenience: The Social Organization of Normality*, Berg, Oxford and New York.

Statens Institutt for Forbruksforskning [SIFO] (2003): *An Investigation of Domestic Laundry in Europe: Habits, Hygiene and Technical Performance*, National Institute for Consumer Research, Oslo.

Silberzahn-Jandt, G. (1991), *Wasch-Maschine. Zum Wandel von Frauenarbeit im Haushalt*, Jonas Verlag für Kunst und Literatur, Marburg, Germany.

Stigler, G. J., Becker, G. S. (1977): 'De gustibus non est disputandum', *The American Economic Review*, 67 (2), pp. 76–90.

Strasser, S. (2000) [1982]: *Never Done: A History of American Housework*, Henry Holt and Company, New York.

Terpstra, P. M. J. (1998): 'Domestic and institutional hygiene in relation to sustainability. Historical, social and environmental implications', *International Biodeterioration & Biodegradation*, 41, pp. 169–175.

Vanek, J. (1978): 'Household technology and social status: Rising living standards and residence differences in housework', *Technology and Culture*, 19 (3), pp. 361–375.

Weiner, B. (1994): *Motivationspsychologie*, third edition, Beltz Psychologie-Verlagsunion, Weinheim.

Witt, U. (2001): 'Learning to consume: A theory of wants and the growth of demand', *Journal of Evolutionary Economics*, 11, pp. 23–36.

Yarwood, D. (1981): *The British Kitchen: Housewifery Since Roman Times*, B.T. Batsford Ltd., London.

5 Consumer Motivations and Washing Machine Advertisements

5.1 Introduction

In the previous chapter, we depicted the development of laundry technology and the wider technological system in the United States from the middle of the nineteenth century onward (cf. Chapter 4). Starting off from the hypotheses that the proliferation of washing machines during the twentieth century was driven by the motives to avoid the drudgery of and substitute the household's time in the activity of clothes washing (drudgery avoidance hypothesis, time substitution hypothesis, cf. Chapter 4), we investigated from an objective, engineering-like perspective when technological progress made reductions in physical effort and time inputs actually feasible. We also examined how the demand for laundry services as an alternative means or 'household production technology' for doing laundry has developed.

Recall that the time substitution hypothesis has been derived from Gary Becker's household production function approach (Becker, 1965; Michael and Becker, 1973; cf. Chapter 2). It argues that differences in opportunity costs of time ('Short-Run Time Substitution Hypothesis') and changes in female labor force participation over time ('Long-Run Time Substitution Hypothesis') are important explanatory factors for the adoption of washing machines, as these devices can replace the household's input of time into the activity of laundry washing (cf. Chapter 4). The drudgery avoidance hypothesis is associated with a psychologically informed approach toward consumption behavior, i.e. the theory of learning consumers by Ulrich Witt (2001, cf. Chapter 2). It is also consistent with the sociological literature on housework (e.g. Cowan, 1983). The hypothesis postulates that the adoption of washing machines has been motivated by the behavioral disposition to avoid heavy physical effort (Long-Run Drudgery Avoidance Hypothesis) and that, in the absence of drudgery-reducing washing technology, the household tended to display low levels of cleanliness (Short-Run Drudgery Avoidance Hypothesis) (cf. Chapter 4).

With the technology study, we sought to gain first insights into how far one or the other hypothessi is better suited to capture the driving forces underlying the diffusion of washing machines, for the adoption of washing machines for their effort saving or time saving capabilities could not possibly have taken place before such technical achievements were indeed realized and marketed. The technology study revealed that reductions in physical effort were achievable before laundry equipment allowed for substantial time savings with the advent of automation in the 1940s (cf. Chapter 4). We also found that washerwomen, commercial laundries and servants were regularly resorted to in the nineteenth and the beginning of the twentieth century, but gradually disappeared while the technically advanced devices became more widespread – a process which allowed for drudgery avoidance but implied an 'insourcing' of work (Cowan, 1983, p. 98). These findings put the time substitution argument into question. The observation that the earliest adopters of modernized washing machines were the better-off, full-time homemakers without the intention to participate in the labor force casts further doubt on the explanatory value of the time substitution hypothesis. We thus concluded that the diffusion of washing machines until the 1940s – the advent of automation – might have been associated with the drudgery avoidance motive, but not with the time substitution motive. From the time after *circa* 1940, it is plausible, given the technical preconditions, that the time substitution motive triggered the diffusion of washing machines.

In this chapter, we evaluate the explanatory power of the alternative hypotheses by means of an explorative advertisement study. We examine a selection of washing machine advertisements that appeared in the U.S. women's magazine *Ladies' Home Journal* during the time period 1888–1989 and quantify the frequency with which the advertisements appealed to the motives of time substitution (synonymously: time savings) and drudgery avoidance (synonymously: drudgery reduction, effort reduction, [physical] labor savings), respectively.

The advertisement analysis is based on the conjecture that advertisements illustrate long-term changes in technological progress (synonymously: technical change) that stand in close context to shared consumer goals. More precisely, we postulate that shifts in the advertisement content of a consumption good over time reflect changes in shared consumer motivations for purchasing that good ('Advertisement Content Hypothesis', cf. Section 5.2). We thus focus on that part of the motivational basis for adopting washing machines that consumers should have in common. In fact, when consumers are looking for solutions to their jointly experienced problems, advertisements are a way in which they learn about new consumption possibilities (cf. Chapter 2). Hence, we do not consider advertisements in terms of their manipulative potential for changing or creating consumer desires (Galbraith, 1958, Chapter 11) – in fact, the desires are already given – and we leave out differences in consumer perceptions as to the content of advertisements.

By analyzing the underlying motivations and consumers' actual perceptions of the advanced technologies, we seek to gain further insights into how far the aforementioned hypotheses capture the actual forces behind the propagation of washing machines during the twentieth century. The results presented in this chapter are mainly confined to the two motivations of time substitution and drudgery avoidance, which are negative associations with regard to the activity of clothes washing. In addition, we also take a look at the intensity with which the advertisements (synonymously: 'ads') have broached the issue of the cleanliness of clothes, which is a positively defined association related to the output of this domestic activity. When ads refer to the visual or hygienic cleanliness of clothes, they indirectly appeal to the needs for health and social recognition, which have been identified as the ultimate goals behind this activity (cf. Chapter 3). We thus analytically separate the motives associated with doing laundry – corresponding to 'preferences for the use of time' – from those related to the output of the household production process – corresponding to 'commodities' (cf. Chapter 2). Our dataset further lends itself to document which different technical solutions, i.e. washer types, power sources and so on, that have been created to reduce the washday burden – referred to here as the product's 'characteristics' (Lancaster, 1966). It thus allows for a plausibility check of our findings with regard to the preceding technology study (cf. Chapter 4). Note that the advertisement analysis is confined to the United States. The results thus cannot easily be generalized to hold for the Western world.

The chapter is organized as follows. In Section 5.2, we present our hypotheses on the relationship between consumer motivations on the one hand and product advertisements on the other. Section 5.3 describes the method of data collection. We then present some general figures on the development of washing machine advertisements over time (Section 5.4), followed by a description of the variety of washing machine advertisements in terms of technical characteristics and brands (Section 5.5). In Section 5.6, we analyze the advertisements with regard to the relative frequency with which they link technically advanced clothes washers to the motives of time substitution and physical labor savings. We also take a look at the motive of cleanliness of clothes. Section 5.7 concludes this chapter.

5.2 Consumer Motivations and Advertisements

The advertisement content analysis is based on the hypothesis that shared consumer motivations shape the path of technological progress and product diffusion over time and are also reflected in advertisements on technically advanced consumption goods (see below). Let us recall the underlying line of argument introduced in Chapter 2. Given that consumers share certain basic needs for their common genetic endowment (Witt, 2001) and that these commonalities make them experience certain circumstances, activities and living conditions in a similar way, consumers agree in classifying certain situations as pleasant or unpleasant. Let us denote such unpleasant situations more in general as consumer 'problems'. Then, consumers facing the same kinds of problems are united in looking for solutions to these jointly experienced problems. As a consequence, there is a potentially large latent demand for consumption goods addressing these problems and hence a strong incentive for producers to carry out an innovative search in that direction, i.e. toward satisfying consumer needs in a better way (Witt, 1993).

When technological progress is being directed toward problems ranked 'relevant' in society, then, consumers' true problems and producers' creative efforts show a high level of congruity. Naturally, producers might come up with different types of consumption goods, i.e. technological variants of the same basic product. However, all these types of consumption goods should be directed at the same kind of basic problem for which they seek to offer a solution. Note that, with this argument, we do not intend to separate cause and effect, but argue that certain historical conditions can breed rather synchronized activities of producers and consumers.

Product advertisements, then, are one way in which producers inform consumers about the problem solution offered and, vice versa, by which consumers can learn about such options. Advertisements on newly developed consumption goods can thus be expected to contain some reference to the original problem which has given rise to the innovative research and technological progress in the first place. In a given historical context, all advertisements, even when promoting different technological variants of the same basic product, point to the latest technological advances which hold the capability of satisfying consumer needs better than the previous, less advanced product. They address the same kinds of consumer problems and appeal to the same motive for purchase. In other words, washer ads point to the same 'service characteristics' in the sense of Saviotti and Metcalfe (1984), i.e. the usefulness of washing machines in the eyes of consumers.[1]

The acquisition of one of these technically advanced consumption goods is the consumer's problem-solving strategy. Over time, consumers' problems change, when old ones are solved – particularly with the adoption of advanced products – and new ones come into focus. Innovative search is then directed toward these new problems. When, as a consequence, technically even further advanced products are being developed and advertised, the content of product advertisements shifts accordingly (cf. Chapter 2):

> H.5.1: Producers use advertisements to inform consumers about existing problem solutions. Shifts in advertisement content of a product over long time periods reflect changes in shared consumer motivations for consuming that product (Advertisement Content Hypothesis).

Technological progress comes about both gradually and in big leaps (Abernathy and Utterback, 1978; Tushman and Anderson, 1986). Thus, it might take some time until a problem is completely solved and the corresponding motive disappears from advertisements. The hypothesis therefore applies to long-run shifts in shared consumer motivations over time periods of, say, 30–50 years or so. Basic needs, in the sense of Witt (2001), are the most intuitive explanation for commonalities in consumers' perceptions of problems and their search for problem solutions, but commonalities might also stem from other factors, for instance, shared social understandings (cf. Chapter 3). When certain basic needs are no longer appealed to in advertisements, satiation – at least temporary – with regard to the specific consumption activity has occurred.

Although our analysis is confined to one very specific interrelation between consumer motivations, technological progress and product advertisements, we do acknowledge that, in addition to this, many more interdependencies exist. For one thing, product innovation is not only directed toward shared consumer motivations, but to very distinct consumer motives also. Moreover, advertisements are not the only way in which consumers learn about new consumption goods and their potential to solve consumers' problems; naturally, there are further channels by which information about new products is communicated, for instance, by word of mouth.[2] Advertisements need not only pick up existing consumer motivations but might also seek to create new desires, particularly beyond the point that the most urgent consumer motives have been satisfied. These aspects are not relevant here, however, and they do not contradict the line of argument we have developed.

The problem studied here is the unpleasant experience of the washday during the times of 'Blue Monday' in the nineteenth century (cf. Chapter 4). With the prevailing washing technology – tub, scrubboard and soap – clothes washing was not only a time-consuming activity. With the scrubbing of clothes, the lifting of wet textiles, the carrying of water, the handling of irons and so forth, doing laundry demanded a high level of physical exertion over an extended period of time. Given the innate behavioral tendency to avoid such drudgery, nineteenth-century consumers faced a trade-off between wanting to have clean clothes on one side (satisfying the needs of health and social recognition) and wanting to avoid drudgery on the other (cf. Chapter 4). Practically all consumers should have recognized the problems posed by these conflicting motivations. Likewise, it is also plausible that all consumers realized that clothes washing was a very time-intensive activity. That inventors and producers came to know about this situation is not unlikely, given that clothes washing was an issue for each and every person in society. Possibly, the activities of the 'home economics' movement described earlier (cf. Chapter 4) could also have played a role here. Producers recognizing these problems should have directed their innovative searches toward effort-reducing and time saving technological progress. Still, while addressing the same kind of problems, producers need not come up with the same technical solutions. In fact, a large variety of technological variants of clothes washers has been available, at least in the early phases of technological progress (cf. Chapter 4).[3] According to our hypothesis, these washing machines should have been advertised as instruments to save time and physical labor when doing laundry. These aspects can thus be assumed to have shown up to a similar extent in all washer ads – until the point in time that these problems were successfully solved. In what follows, we will analyze whether this conjecture applies to the washer ads appearing in *Ladies' Home Journal*. But let us turn to the database first.

5.3 Data Collection

The analysis is based on a selection of washing machine advertisements that appeared in the U.S. women's magazine *Ladies' Home Journal* between 1888 and 1989. The first issue of *Ladies' Home Journal* dates back to December 1883. It was an extremely popular magazine, already reaching a circulation of about 1 million at the beginning of the twentieth century (Fox, 1990). The actual scope of readers might have been even larger, as such magazines, as rather expensive items, were exchanged between readers (Strasser (2000[1982], preface). For most of its existence, the journal appeared on a monthly basis. It is still issued at present. We have restricted our research to this specific outlet for the reasons that the magazine is already well established as an object of analysis, particularly in the sociological field, and that it is also available in Germany to a large extent. In fact, *Ladies' Home Journal* is often referred to in the sociological literature on housework (cf. Cowan, 1976; Matthews, 1987, p. 168; Fox, 1990; Strasser, 2000[1982], p. 255) as the magazine is an important historical document from which to extract rich descriptions of the living conditions, tools, expectations and aspirations with which housework has been carried out.

Our analysis of washer ads covers three distinct time periods over a whole time span of 100 years (1888–1989), namely 1888–1919, 1940–1960 and 1970–1989 (altogether 70 years) – the issues from the missing time periods not being available in Germany. Two issues per year were selected for analysis, namely the June and the November issues. We based this decision on a pre-analysis of the number of pages and the number of advertisements per issue over the year and chose the aforementioned issues for their salience within the course of one year. The November issue was always at the higher end of the number of pages as well as the number of ads, compared with other months. It was also a prominent issue in that it addressed Thanksgiving and Christmas. The remaining issues were of about equal length. We chose the June issue for the regularly occurring topic 'June brides', assuming that this issue might have received particularly more consumer attention than other issues.

Certainly, by examining this one journal only and merely a few issues of it, we cannot claim to give a representative overview of the market for washing machines in terms of advertisement activities and product variety as some devices might simply not have been advertised in this specific women's magazine. In fact, in view of the overview of technological progress given earlier (cf. Chapter 4) and our results to be discussed below, the actual variety of washer types and brands might have been larger than it appears here. Still, the sample of two issues per year should be sufficient, given that the kind of technological progress we examine does not manifest itself in shorter time periods. Moreover, the details of all sorts of technical solutions are not of interest here. The type of information we are looking for can certainly be extracted from this sample, namely the long-term development of technology successions (cf. Section 5.2). Although at some point in time, many technical variants might have been available – all with more or less different characteristics – they have all been directed toward finding solutions to one and the same basic problem.

For each issue studied (i.e. June and November of all of the selected years), we collected the following pieces of information:

1   number of pages per issue
2   overall number of advertisements per issue (including washing machines)
3   number of advertisements on washing machines per issue
4   size of the washing machine advertisements
5   whether the advertised washers possessed explicitly defined technical characteristics
6   brand and producer (company) of the advertised washing machine
7   whether explicitly defined motives (labor savings, time savings, cleanliness) occurred in a specific washing machine advertisement or not.

Let us take a look at this in some more detail.

Ad 1   As pages, we counted all pages of the journal, including the covers and supplementary material but exclusive of vouchers (e.g. for food).
Ad 2   We counted the overall sum of ads in each issue. All advertisements were registered apart from fashion advertisements (they are not launched by producers themselves, but prepared by the magazine and do not contain specific messages), want ads (e.g. agents for household appliances) and ads to subscribe to the magazine.
Ad 3   Here, only those ads were counted which clearly put the product of interest, i.e. washing machines, at center stage. There were also few advertisements by companies, like *Firestone* or *General Electric*, which included pictures of washing machines among other company products but which did not specifically refer to washing machines. Thus, no motives for the purchase of washing machines could be identified and the ad was not counted as relevant. Advertisements addressing washing machines and another product (usually wringers or detergents) were considered for our analysis when they contained at least one motive for purchasing the washing machine itself. We did not use weights to account for the presence of these other products within the same ad, but counted one ad for washing machines. We specifically excluded laundry stoves, which are complementary equipment rather than washers themselves.[4]
Ad 4   All washing machine ads have been categorized according to their size. The following table lists the categories of size which we distinguished and the weights that were given (cf. Table 5.1). We consider differences in size when we analyze the content in terms of the motives appealed to (cf. Section 5.6).
Ad 5   We did not intend to compile a complete list of the technical characteristics of the advertised washers. Instead, we looked for the presence of very specific characteristics (e.g. power sources, washer types, etc.) based on the technology study (cf. Chapter 4). We then coded '1' if the characteristic

was present and '0' if not. For collecting the technical characteristics, it was necessary – in contrast to the coding of the motives (see below) – to take both the text messages and the pictures into account. For example, while the fact that a washing machine is 'electric' was still mentioned in the text of advertisements until 1919, this information was later left out, when all available machines were electric. With regard to the design of the washers, especially the missing gears, and with the knowledge of the prevalent technical characteristics, washers could still easily be classified as being electricity driven.

Ad 6 For every washing machine advertised, the brand name and, if available, the name of the company was captured.

Ad 7 For coding the motives appearing in the washing machine advertisements, only text messages were paid attention to. Although there were hardly any washer ads without any pictures whatsoever, we excluded potential information from the pictures for the subjective element of their inter-pretation. Note that we did not intend to give a full description of all positive or negative associations related to the advertised clothes washers. Instead, we scanned the ads for the presence of those motives that we have identified as being relevant, based on our previous discussion, namely time savings, physical labor savings and cleanliness. We then coded '1' if the motive was included and '0' if not.

The coding of the ads with regard to the motives of time savings and physical labor savings was an iterative process. Drawing upon our technology study, we started off from a set of plausible expressions that would hint at these motives such as 'end of drudgery', 'reduces effort', 'is a time saver' and so forth. We then modified and extended the set with regard to the expressions that we encountered. An overview of the expressions which actually occurred in the ads is given in the following table (cf. Table 5.2).

For the largest share of ads, it was not difficult to decide if one or both of these motives were appealed to in a given ad, as the text messages were pretty clear (cf. Table 5.2). In cases where very general terms were used such as 'it saves work' or 'you only push a button', we coded the ad as being related to both motives. When an expression like 'it saves work' occurred together with

Table 5.1 Categorization of Washer Ads According to Size

Size	Category	Mean size of ad (in pages)
Less than one-eigth of a page	A	0.0625
One-eighth of a page to less than a quarter page	B	0.1875
A quarter page to less than half a page	C	0.3750
Half a page to less than a whole page	D	0.75
Whole page	E	1.00
One-and-a-half pages	F	1.50
Two pages	G	2.00

Table 5.2 Categorizing Advertisements with Regard to Consumer Motives: Some Examples

Motive of Time Substitution	Motive of Drudgery Avoidance
• will save you time	• will save you labor
• waste not your time	• does away with all the drudgery
• twice as rapidly	• waste not your strength
• does washing of an ordinary family in one hour	• not back straining
• great time saver	• operate without exertion
• washes quicker	• turning slavery of washday into real comfort
• no supervision	• take the hard work out of the washday
• half the time old washers need	• save your muscular effort
• washes in as little as an hour	

another expression clearly indicating time savings, we concluded that the former expression meant a reduction in effort. Also coded as appealing to the motive of drudgery avoidance was reference to domestic servants and washerwomen and the argument that, with the modern devices, those were no longer needed for doing laundry (in Chapter 4, we concluded that the replacement of servants with washing machines was associated with the motive of drudgery avoidance rather than that of time savings, cf. Chapter 4).

One and the same ad could show up in several motive categories if more than one motive was expressed in the ad. As it turned out, there was not one advertisement which appealed to one motive only. Whenever appeals to time or labor savings occurred, at least one other reason for purchasing washers could easily be identified, for example, cleanliness of clothes, durability of the product and so on. Still, the ads could be differentiated with regard to the respective motives of time substitution and physical labor savings. The raw data were categorized as follows:

- We denoted ads that contained a reference to time substitution and further motives, but physical labor savings, as 'TS'.
- Likewise, washer ads appealing to effort reduction and other motives but time substitution were counted as 'LS'.
- Advertisements hinting both at time and labor savings were counted as 'LSTS'.
- All remaining ads, where no reference to either time savings or labor savings was made, were categorized as 'other content'.

For the subsequent analyses, the series 'LSTS' was divided equally (half-and-half) among the series 'TS' and 'LS', yielding the series 'motive time savings' and 'motive labor savings', respectively. Together with the series 'other content', they add up to 100 per cent.

Concerning cleanliness of clothes, three categories were distinguished: hygienic cleanliness (e.g. germ removal), visual cleanliness (e.g. whiteness of clothes) and general cleanliness (e.g. 'cleans more thoroughly'). We also counted whether reference was made to clothing care, i.e. to how far the textiles were secure from being damaged during the washing procedure.

To our knowledge, quantitative information as we have gathered here is very rare. We are aware of only one comparable study, the analysis by Fox (1990), which draws on neither the household production theory nor a needs-based consumption account whatsoever. Fox has also scanned the *Ladies' Home Journal* for ads on household technology and categorized them according to the reasons for purchase given in these ads. Our approach, however, is distinct from her study in terms of the scope of research, the time period analyzed and the categorization. Fox examines all household appliances and analyzes the collected data at the aggregate level without differentiating further into product categories such as washing machines. Moreover, the analysis covers eight consecutive decades (1909–1980), but there is no information on the yearly development. Fox also selected a smaller amount of issues, i.e. in each decade, four issues occurring in two subsequent years (32 issues altogether). Finally, the categorization differs from our approach in that Fox has looked for other characteristics and assigned each ad to only one category.[5] To begin with, let us now take a look at the development of washing machine advertisements over time.

5.4 Trends in Washing Machine Advertisements

Before we analyze the technical characteristics and quantify how the relative importance of the motives of time substitution and reductions in effort has evolved over time in advertisements for washing machines, let us first take a look at the general trends in washer ads.

The following figure illustrates that first ads on washing machines appeared in *Ladies' Home Journal* in 1889, i.e. almost at the very beginning of our dataset. In the following 100 years, washing machines have rather continuously been advertised in this magazine – at least in the 70 years that were studied (cf. Figure 5.1). Altogether, our sample of *Ladies' Home Journal* includes 125 washer ads.

The advertisement intensity shows strong fluctuations over time. For some years, the two chosen issues of the journal contain no such ads at all, while there is a remarkable peak around 1948, i.e. in the postwar period. The same point is illustrated in the subsequent figure (cf. Figure 5.2), where the ads are cumulated over the years (continuing after the breaks with the level reached at the previous observation). A roughly s-shaped curve is the result, including an accelerated period of ads from the middle of the 1940s onward and a flattening during the 1980s.

The postwar years are also prominent with regard to the average number of washer ads per year: while roughly one advertisement per year appears in the first time period from 1888–1919 (i.e. 31 ads over 32 years), on average more than three ads per annum were detected in the second period from 1940–1960

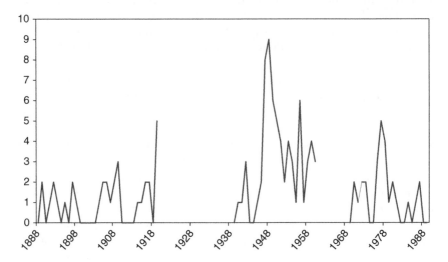

Figure 5.1 Absolute Number of Advertisements for Washing Machines per Year.

Source: *Ladies' Home Journal*, June and November issues.

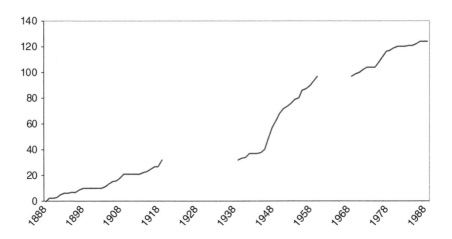

Figure 5.2 Cumulated Number of Advertisements for Washing Machines.

Source: *Ladies' Home Journal*, June and November issues.

(altogether, 67 ads). From 1970 onward, on average at least one advertisement occurred every year (altogether, 27 ads).

In relation to the overall number of advertisements, appearing in one issue of *Ladies' Home Journal*, washer ads make up only a small share. Over five-year periods,

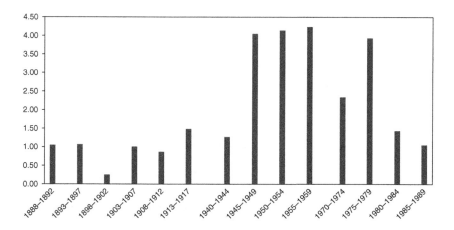

Figure 5.3 Advertisements of Washing Machines as Percentages of All Advertisements (5-Year Periods).

Source: *Ladies' Home Journal*, June and November issues.

washer ads count for about 1–4 per cent of all ads per issue (cf. Figure 5.3). Here again, the postwar years are sticking out, covering in the five-year representation the larger period from 1945–1959. Thus, not only in absolute terms were washing machines advertised more intensively after World War II, but in relative terms also, i.e. these devices gained prominence in comparison with other content.

5.5 Variety of Washing Machines

The following tables contain information on the technical characteristics of the advertised washing machines, disaggregated over the three time periods 1888–1919, 1940–1960 and 1970–1989. The analysis draws upon the technology study (cf. Chapter 4) and captures those characteristics that correspond with the major technical leaps in laundry technology over the past 200 years (i.e. mechanization, electrification and automation). It is confined to the power sources of washing machines, the washer types, the existence of automation and the type of drying mechanisms.

Table 5.3 Power Sources of Washing Machines

	Manual	*Electricity*	*Water*	*Steam*	*Sum*
1888–1919	0.48	0.39	0.10	0.03	1.00
1940–1960	0.00	1.00	0.00	0.00	1.00
1970–1989	0.00	1.00	0.00	0.00	1.00

Source: *Ladies' Home Journal*, June and November issues.
Notes: Share of all washer ads per time period (rounded to two decimals).

Let us turn to the power sources first. While almost half of the washers advertised until 1919 had to be operated by hand, already a large share of electric washers were available (cf. Table 5.3). Devices driven by water power or steam power existed in parallel, but they were advertised to a much smaller extent. From the second time period onward, only electric washing machines appeared in the journal.

Concerning the washer types, advertisements covered a large variety of washers until 1919 (cf. Table 5.4). The cylinder-type washer was most prominent and appeared in about 45 per cent of the washer ads. However, advertisements also depicted the dolly-type washer, the vacuum washer and others. This variety shrank substantially during the second time period, when only cylinder and agitator types appeared in the ads. From the 1970s onward, all the washer models advertised were based on the agitator principle.

With regard to the automation of washers, the three time periods witness remarkable differences. While none of the advertised washing machines were automatic until 1919, during the second time period, already roughly two-thirds of the ads depicted automatic devices (cf. Table 5.5). The very first automatic washer captured with this dataset appeared in 1945 in form of the *Bendix* washer. From the 1970s onward, all advertisements were related to automatic devices.

Advertisements also reflect shifts in the frequency distribution of drying mechanisms over time (cf. Table 5.6). Wringers, as an attachment to washers, appeared in nearly two-thirds of the advertisements in the first time period, shrank substantially in the second and were no longer present in the last. In

Table 5.4 Washer Types

	Dolly	Cylinder	Agitator	Rocker	Vacuum	Steam	Other	Sum
1888–1919	0.26	0.45	0.10	0.10	0.03	0.03	0.03	1.00
1940–1960	0.00	0.27	0.73	0.00	0.00	0.00	0.00	1.00
1970–1989	0.00	0.00	1.00	0.00	0.00	0.00	0.00	1.00

Source: *Ladies' Home Journal*, June and November issues.
Notes: Share of all washer ads per time period (rounded to two decimals).

Table 5.5 Share of Automatic Washers

	Automatic washers
1888–1919	0.00
1940–1960	0.64
1970–1989	1.00

Source: *Ladies' Home Journal*, June and November issues.
Notes: Share of all washer ads per time period (rounded to two decimals).

Table 5.6 Drying Mechanisms Included in Washers

	None	*Attached wringer*	*Attached dryer*	*Combined washer-dryer*	*Sum*
1888–1919	0.39	0.61	0.00	0.00	1.00
1940–1960	0.29	0.23	0.33	0.15	1.00
1970–1989	0.69	0.00	0.31	0.00	1.00

Source: *Ladies' Home Journal*, June and November issues.
Notes: Share of all washer ads per time period (rounded to two decimals).

contrast to that, dryers as an attachment to washers did not appear in the ads until 1919; they were depicted in about one-third of ads both in the second and the third time period. The majority of washers in the last time period were advertised without any reference to drying mechanisms. Our dataset further reveals that washer-dryer combinations were only available from 1940–1960. In view of the insights of the technology study (cf. Chapter 4), this very last finding is rather unlikely, however.

These figures nicely illustrate how washing machines have become stand-ardized products over time: having started from a larger variety of technical variants at the end of the nineteenth century in terms of washer types and power sources, this variety shrank in the middle time period and then con-verged to one prevailing product, namely the agitator-type, electric and auto-matic washing machine. By and large, our dataset mirrors the general phases of technical development described earlier (cf. Chapter 4). For that reason, we expect the dataset to be sufficiently adequate for the subsequent content analy-sis concerning consumer motivations.

Before turning to this issue, let us have a final look at changes in the variety of washer brands over time. When the number of brands is correlated with the number of producers, then differences in the variety of brands could be an indicator – a very rough proxy indeed – for how strongly producers are attracted toward a specific market. We analyzed both the text messages and the pictures and captured – for each washing machine advertisement – the corresponding brand name. In the following table, we explicitly list all brands that occurred at least twice over the whole time span analyzed; the remaining ads were summed up in the category 'All other washers' (cf. Table 5.7). Our dataset reveals significant shifts in the number of advertised washer brands over time. In the period from 1940–1960, there was a higher variety of washer brands advertised than in both the first and the last time span – although the middle time period is the shortest period in terms of years. In fact, in the peak year 1948, seven out of nine ads dealt with different brands (1947: seven out of eight; 1949: six out of six; 1950: four out of five) (not shown in the table). So again, the peak years are clearly prominent. Note that a similar general picture emerges when companies and not brands are depicted (not shown in the table).

Table 5.7 Number of Washer Ads per Brand Name

	1888–1919	1940–1960	1970–1989
Western washer and Horton washer	10	2	
Rocker washer	3		
Peoria washer	3		
Coffield washer	3		
Acme washer	2		
Thor washer	2	2	
Bendix and Philco washer		10	
Whirlpool washer		8	1
Maytag washer		7	5
Dexter washer		5	
Speed queen		4	4
Frigidare washer		4	
Voss washer		3	
Hotpoint washer		1	3
Westinghouse washer		2	1
General Electric washer		2	3
Nordge washer		2	1
Firestone washer		2	
Kelvinator washer		2	
Blackstone washer		2	
Hoover washer			2
Apex washer		2	
Monitor washer		2	
Kenmore washer			4
All other washer	8	5	3
SUM	31	67	27

Source: *Ladies' Home Journal,* June and November issues.

The following section provides insights into the arguments with which these technical advances have been sold. We analyze to which extent advertisements have appealed to the motivations of time savings and drudgery avoidance respectively and if there are changes in the relative importance of these motives over time.

5.6 Motives of Time Substitution, Drudgery Avoidance and Cleanliness

In this section, we gather information with which to confront the time substitution hypothesis and the drudgery avoidance hypothesis derived earlier (cf. Section 5.1). We examine the extent (absolute and relative frequencies) to which the distinct motives of time substitution and physical labor savings have appeared in the advertisements of washing machines from 1888–1989 (cf. the list of keywords, Table 5.2). Certainly, without elaborate statistics, we cannot test the hypotheses in a strict statistical sense. We interpret the data as evidence in support of a hypothesis when a sufficiently large share of ads contains a reference to the respective motive. The motive relatively dominating the advertisement content during a given time period is interpreted as the most important motive for purchasing washing machines in that exact time period.

For assessing the significance of the motives within each of the time periods, differences in the sizes of the advertisements will be taken into account, i.e. the number of ads will be weighted by the size of the respective advertisements. The rationale is simple: fewer but larger ads with a specific message are potentially as important as many smaller ads containing a different motive. For the three time periods analyzed, we obtained the following size distributions (cf. Table 5.8; cf. Table 5.1 for the categories of size that we distinguished and the weights that were given). Table 5.8 shows that advertisements for washing machines grew larger in size over time. While the majority of ads were smaller than one-eighth of a page in the first time period (16 out of 31), almost every ad filled a whole page in the last period (22 out of 27). As we did not collect information on the average size of all ads (including washing machines), we cannot draw conclusions as to the relative importance of washing machines compared with other content. Recall, however, that washing machines became relatively more important in the postwar era in terms of filling a larger share of all ads per issue (cf. Section 5.4).

Table 5.8 lists the distribution of ads by size, without reference to motives. The joint picture of size and motives, yielding weighted motives, is painted in Table 5.9. Recall that the series 'motive labor savings' contains the number of washer ads appealing to effort reduction and other motives, but time savings (LS) plus half of the series LSTS, i.e. the number of advertisements hinting at both time savings and labor savings. The series 'motive time savings' counts the washer ads which contained a reference to time substitution and further motives, but physical labor savings (TS) plus half of the series LSTS. All the remaining ads, where no reference to either time or physical labor savings was made, were categorized as 'other content'. The series add up to 100 per cent. Interestingly, not all washer ads in a given time period address the same motives: some washers are advertised as time-savers while other washer ads emphasize the labor saving capability only. Apparently, producers do not only differ in terms of the problem solutions offered, i.e. in terms of the technical variants invented and marketed (cf. Section 5.5); they also seem to tackle different problems of the washing procedure – at least, when it comes to selling their products.

Table 5.8 Distribution of Washer Ads per Time Period by Size

	A (small)	*B*	*C*	*D*	*E*	*F*	*G (large)*	*SUM*
1888–1919	16	7	7	0	1	0	0	31
1940–1960	6	3	3	18	35	0	2	67
1970–1989	0	0	0	4	22	1	0	27

Notes: Absolute numbers per time period.
Source: *Ladies' Home Journal,* June and November issues.

Table 5.9 Motives in Advertisements of Washing Machines by Time Period and Size

	Number of ads with motive labor savings						Number of ads with motive time savings						Number of ads with other content						Sum of ads		
	I		II		III		I		II		III		I		II		III		I	II	III
	n.w.	w.	n.w.	w.	n.w.	n.	n.w.	w.	n.w.	w.	n.w.	w.	n.w.	w.	n.w.	w.	n.w.	w.			
A	8	0.5	1	0.0625	0	0	6	0.375	3	0.1875	0	0	2	0.125	2	0.125	0	0	16	6	0
B	4	0.75	1	0.1875	0	0	3	0.5675	2	0.375	0	0	0	0	0	0	0	0	7	3	0
C	4	1.5	0	0	0	0	2	0.75	2	0.75	0	0	1	0.375	1	0.375	0	0	7	3	0
D	0	0	6.25	4.875	0	0	0	0	10.5	7.875	3	2.25	0	0	1	0.75	1	0.75	0	18	4
E	1	0.5	14	14	0	0	0	0	14	14	1	1.0	0	0	7	7	21	21	1	35	22
F	0	0	0	0	0.5	0.5	0	0	0	0	0.5	0.75	0	0	0	0	0	0	0	0	1
G	0	0	0.5	1	0	0	0	0	0.5	1	0	0	0	0	1	2	0	0	0	2	0
SUM		3.25		20.125	0.5	0.5		2.1875		24.1875		4		0.5		10.25		21.75	5.9375	54.5625	26.25

Notes: I: 1888–1919; II: 1940–1960; III: 1970–1989; n.w.: absolute numbers not weighted; w.: weighted numbers
Source: Ladies' Home Journal, June and November issues.

Table 5.9 depicts how the motives are distributed over the size categories in each of the three time periods. The numbers in column 'w' are of interest, i.e. the mean page volumes or number of ads weighted by size. When adding up the mean page volumes of a specific motive per period, we obtain an indicator of the temporal significance of this exact motive that can be compared with that of the other motive and used to evaluate the plausibility of the hypotheses of time substitution and drudgery avoidance.

The core results of the advertisement analysis are summarized in Table 5.10. We find that both motives of time substitution and physical labor savings have indeed shown up in washing machine advertisements appearing in the two chosen issues of *Ladies' Home Journal* from 1888–1989. We further find that the relative importance of these motives compared with other content has decreased over time, witnessing a sharp decline from the second to the third time period. Although time savings were already the subject of a large share of advertisements in the first 30 years of our dataset, the motive of physical labor savings, covering a share of *circa* 55 per cent, dominated the content of washer ads in that time period. In contrast to that, the motive of time savings showed up in about 44 per cent of the ads and thus stood at center stage in the second time period. Note that the gap between the relative frequencies of these motives is substantially larger in the first than in the second period (18 versus 7 percentage points). From 1970–1989, physical labor savings were hardly mentioned in the ads anymore. The time substitution motive, however, was still found in 15 per cent of the ads; 83 per cent of washer ads were classified as 'of other content'.

The advertisement analysis lends support to both the time substitution hypothesis and the drudgery avoidance hypothesis: both relevant motives were addressed in a significant share of the washer ads over an extended period of time before they practically disappeared from the ads from the 1970s onward. When we assume that these motives have also occurred in the missing time period 1920–1939, then producers have referred to these motivations for roughly seven consecutive decades. With regard to the individual time periods, the explanatory power of the hypotheses differs, however. The motive of labor savings dominated the advertisement content until 1919 and was thus, according to our argument, a more important motive for the purchase of washing

Table 5.10 Motives of Time Savings and Labor Savings in Advertisements for Washing Machines

	1888–1919 (I)	*1940–1960 (II)*	*1970–1989 (III)*
Motive labor savings	0.55	0.37	0.02
Motive time savings	0.37	0.44	0.15
Other content	0.08	0.19	0.83
	1.00	1.00	1.00

Notes: Share of washer ads per time period by motive (weighted; rounded to two decimals).
Source: *Ladies' Home Journal*, June and November issues.

machines than the time substitution motive; for the middle period, starting in 1940, it is exactly the other way round.

These general trends match the findings gathered in the previous chapter on technological progress in washing machines from the middle of the nineteenth century onward: compared with the conditions of 'Blue Monday', technically advanced washing machines have, since 1937, been able to eliminate the lion's share of time and physical labor inputs into the activity of clothes washing (cf. Chapter 4).

Still, the advertisement data also point to a slightly different picture than our inquiry into the history of technology. Most strikingly, labor savings and time substitution have been advertised in parallel, already in the period from 1888–1919, although the engineering-oriented description of technological progress would suggest otherwise. The aggregate figures presented so far, however, obscure whether the time saving motive had appeared only by the end of that time period, possibly with the market introduction of electric washing machines. In order to better assess this issue, we split up the dataset into five-year periods and examined again the relative shares of weighted washer ads.[6] We obtained a figure which indicates smaller shifts in advertisement content over time. The figure reveals that the motive of time substitution in doing laundry had already occurred in washing machine advertisements from the very beginning of our dataset, i.e. 1888 onward (cf. Figure 5.4). Note also that reductions in effort were still alluded to in the period 1970–1974.

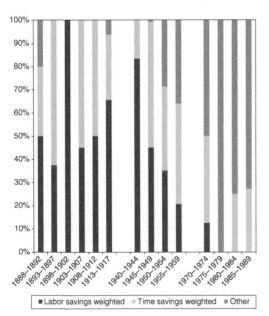

Figure 5.4 Motives of Labor Savings and Time Savings in Washing Machine Advertisements.

Notes: Relative shares, based on 5-year sums of washer advertisements by motive (weighted).
Source: *Ladies' Home Journal*, June and November issues.

Before we discuss these findings, let us take a look at the peak years, i.e. 1945–1959. Particularly from 1945–1949, all washer ads referred to either labor savings or time savings, or even to both motives. From 1950 onward, both motives still occurred in the larger share of washer ads, but more than a quarter of the ads appealed to 'other content' only. Overall, the time saving motive slightly dominates the advertisement content in the peak year period.

How can we interpret this discrepancy between the advertisement data and our study into the history of washing technology? Consider first the finding that reductions in effort were still alluded to after 1970. It clearly stands in contrast to our earlier argument that the major achievements in drudgery reduction have been realized with electrification and the propagation of running hot and cold water in the home, namely from the 1920s until after World War II. Certainly, it took until the 1960s before the majority of U.S. households could actually enjoy these improved living conditions and possessed a modernized device – but not until after 1970. We would thus not expect washer ads beyond that point in time to refer to labor savings. Taking a closer look at these ads reveals that technical changes, which have been rather minor compared with the aforementioned big leaps, have also been mentioned as saving labor, particularly improvements in spin drying (which reduces the weight of the clothes) or modifications in the construction of washing machines (for ergonomic reasons). Ads in the first decades of the dataset pertain to physical labor savings, however. It could be a general pattern that, as soon as the more serious issues have been dealt with, minor issues become emphasized more strongly and are still linked to the original consumer problem. As we lack further information, we cannot scrutinize this conjecture in more detail. We can easily make sense of the observation that time savings were already advertised from the beginning onward. From the perspective of producers, the simultaneous appeal to both motives is not surprising because, next to the effort of clothes washing, the mere length of the washday will also have been a subject of complaints. By claiming that modernized washers would be able to both reduce time and effort, although this might technically not have been feasible, producers would appeal to two problems at the same time, thus making their product potentially more attractive. This finding could thus indicate that producers had already recognized in advance that the prospect of time savings would motivate the purchase of washing machines – long before the devices could actually offer appropriate solutions to that problem. This finding could be interpreted as an indicator of shared social understandings between producers and consumers, having triggered innovative efforts toward labor saving and time saving solutions.

How can we interpret the finding that, according to our dataset, washing machines have been advertised most intensively in the postwar years? Consider the following line of argument. According to Witt (1993), both the intensity of the innovative search and the rate of innovations are historically contingent and vary with the urgency of problems to which these innovations shall bring a solution. Drawing upon this idea, fluctuations in advertisement intensity might also be traced back to the urgency of the problems which the respective product addresses, for producers might want to make their products visible in times of potentially high demand, i.e. when there is a high propensity for consumers to look for solutions. In a longitudinal perspective, time periods of relatively high advertisement activities could then point to a relatively high awareness of consumers and producers in looking for and offering problem solutions, respectively. From a cross-sectional perspective, a higher advertisement intensity of a product compared with other advertisement content could indicate that the problems addressed by this product might be relatively more urgent than the problems other products seek to solve. Particular prominence, in terms of the advertisement intensity of washing machines, is shown in the postwar years, both in absolute and in relative terms. The postwar years could thus be time periods in which the motives mentioned in the washer ads were rather pressing issues from the consumers' perspective, possibly even more important than other issues. We found that both motives of labor savings and time savings made up a significant share of the washer ads in the peak year period. Washing machines enabling physical labor savings should become more important when the conflict between drudgery avoidance on one side and health and social recognition on the other has intensified, particularly by an increase in cleanliness standards (cf. Chapters 3–4). In contrast to that, the achievement of time savings in doing laundry can be expected to become more important in times of rising opportunity costs of time and higher female labor force participation rates (cf. Short-Run Time Substitution Hypothesis and Long-Run Time Substitution Hypothesis, Chapter 2). However, there might be several other reasons behind the higher advertisement intensity, for instance, a higher purchasing power of consumers, a stronger competition between producers and so forth. Based on the information gathered here, we thus cannot assess whether this conjecture applies to our case.

Note that there was not one advertisement which appealed to one motive only. Whenever appeals to time substitution or physical labor savings occurred, at least one other reason for purchasing washers could easily be identified. Those other motives have not been coded, apart from that of the cleanliness of clothes. To this issue, we now turn. Recall that cleanliness of clothes is a positively defined association pertaining to the output of the household production process of clothes washing. Three categories were distinguished: hygienic cleanliness, visual cleanliness and general cleanliness. In addition, we captured whether a reference was made to clothing care. We calculated relative shares of the respective motives in relation to the number of ads per time period. The results are summarized in Table 5.11. Note that the columns do not add up to 100 per cent because every single ad can contain all three motives.

We found that some reference to the cleanliness of textiles appeared in all three time periods. Cleanliness motives have been emphasized most strongly

Table 5.11 Motives of Cleanliness and Clothing Care in Advertisements of Washing Machines

Time period	Some reference to cleanliness	General cleanliness	Visual cleanliness	Hygienic cleanliness	Clothing care
1888–1919	53.7	48.4	1.1	4.2	53.6
1940–1960	74.6	56.7	28.4	7.3	42.6
1970–1989	28.6	28.6	0.0	0.0	20.9

Notes: Percentage of all ads per time period (rounded to one decimal).
Source: *Ladies' Home Journal*, June and November issues.

in the middle time period – which includes the postwar period and the peak years – when roughly three out of four washer ads mentioned this aspect. Most frequently, the reference to cleanliness was of the general kind. Visual and hygienic aspects have also been referred to, yet only in the first and second time periods, and also to a much lesser extent. Particularly in the middle period, nearly 3 out of 10 washer ads related the purchase of washing machines to visible cleanliness. In all time periods, advertisements made some reference to clothing care. However, this motive strongly lost importance over time, from being mentioned in more than every second ad in the first time period to only every fifth in the last decades of our dataset.

That washing machines have indeed been associated with hygienic and visual cleanliness for several decades underlines the close relationship between the activity of clothes washing and the need for health and social recognition. The drop in the mentioning of cleanliness, as well as clothing care, toward the end of our dataset is consistent with the historical development presented earlier. At the turn of the century, the damage done to clothes was the subject of debate (cf. Chapter 4) and producers certainly had to address clothing care in a proactive manner, particularly in view of the competition from power laundries. Reference to cleanliness, particularly hygienic cleanliness, was important with regard to the emerging social norm of cleanliness (cf. Chapter 3). These issues disappeared from the agenda after the problems were successfully solved, such that producers no longer had to allude to these issues in washing machine advertisements.

5.7 Conclusions

In this chapter, the driving forces underlying the diffusion of washing machines in the United States during the twentieth century were examined by means of an advertisement analysis. We investigated a selection of advertisements on clothes washers appearing in the U.S. women magazine *Ladies' Home Journal* between 1888 and 1989 with regard to the reasons given for purchasing these products. Two hypotheses were scrutinized, the time substitution hypothesis and the drudgery avoidance hypothesis, which are associated with the household production function approach (Becker, 1965; Michael and Becker, 1973) and a needs-based approach toward consumption behavior (Witt, 2001), respectively (cf. Chapter 2).

The analysis was based on the hypothesis that shifts in advertisement content over time reflect changes in joint consumer motivations for consuming certain products (Advertisement Content Hypothesis). We interpreted the data as evidence in support of a hypothesis when a sufficiently large share of ads contained a reference to the motive of drudgery avoidance (synonymously: effort reduction, [physical] labor savings) or time substitution (synonymously: time savings). The motive relatively dominating the advertisement content during a given time period was interpreted as the most important motive for purchasing washing machines in that exact time period.

The analysis revealed that washing machine advertisements have indeed appealed to both motives for several decades. Reductions in effort dominated the content of advertisements from 1888–1919, while time substitution was the prevailing motive of ads from 1940–1960. From 1970 onward, labor savings and time savings hardly occurred anymore as motives in the ads. The analysis further revealed that washing machines have been linked to the hygienic and visual cleanliness of clothes for several decades and thus underlined the close relationship between the activity of clothes washing on one side and the needs for health and social recognition on the other (cf. Chapter 3).

With regard to the hypotheses, we interpret the findings as follows. Both the time saving concern and the labor saving concern have been recognized by producers as fundamental consumer motives for the adoption of washing machines. Therefore, these motives have been alluded to in advertisements for decades. The desire to reduce the drudgery of the washday was the consumers' most urgent problem. In the beginning, advertisements thus appealed to the labor saving motive more strongly. When this motive was satisfied by technically advanced washing machines, advertisements shifted and emphasized more strongly the next fundamental problem, the consumers' time saving concern. In the 1970s, both problems were successfully solved and practically disappeared from the agenda. In other words, by 1970, consumers came to associate physical labor savings and time savings with the electric, automatic washing machine, rendering it obsolete for producers to refer to these motives in the ads. Note, however, that although need satisfaction or problem solution was feasible by the adoption of technically advanced clothes washers, and although reference to these motives no longer had to be made to trigger the purchase of these devices, this does not mean that the motives, as such, have 'vanished'. Concerning replacement purchases, time savings and labor savings will have remained as underlying motives, only that these motives could not stimulate further growth in consumption. In order for that to happen, washing machines would have to become associated with further motives, for example, needs that are hard to satiate (Witt, 2001).

Recall that the big leap in terms of effort reduction was achieved with electrification in the 1920s and, in terms of time savings, with automation in the 1940s (cf. Chapter 4). The essential results of the advertisement analysis are hence consistent with the technology study. However, we also found some discrepancies between the results of the advertisement analysis and the actual phases of technological progress described earlier. First, motives for purchase were already mentioned in the washer ads before products could actually cater to these desires from a technical point of view. Second, some motives were still mentioned for quite some time in the washer ads after the respective problem appeared to have been solved. We suggested interpreting these observations in the way that producers showed some ability to anticipate consumer desires and that advertisement content shifted to minor issues once the biggest problems had been solved. This finding implies that, based on the advertisement content analysis alone, we cannot sharply discriminate between problem recognition and problem solution. At a more general level, our analysis reveals that advertisement content alone is not sufficient to assess changes in the material conditions of doing the laundry over time. If we think in general trends over some decades, as we have suggested, the joint information from the technology study and the advertisement analysis is consistent, however.

In the following chapter, we will investigate whether washing machines have indeed been employed for time substitution purposes. To that end, we will present some quantitative information on the implications of technical change in the domestic production of cleanliness for cleanliness consumption patterns and time allocation patterns.

Notes

1 Note that the service characteristics of a certain product need not be perceived similarly by all consumers. Similarities, however, might stem from shared social understandings that come about by means of public discourse or general social and economic trends affecting all consumers alike.
2 Lavin (1995), for example, argues that radio soap operas have played an important role in the 1930s in the United States for spreading information about new products.
3 Technical advances in washing technology after 'Blue Monday' can be divided into the phases of mechanization, electrification and automation (cf. Chapter 4).
4 Naturally, we cannot guarantee to have not overlooked an advertisement when scanning the journal. By double checking, however, we sought to minimize this problem.
5 To be precise, the assignment of advertisements to the characteristics categories is not made fully transparent in the paper by Fox (1990). The shares of ads per category add up to 100 per cent in each time period. Fox (1990) does not appear to have applied any kind of weighting scheme. However, she mentions that '[v]ery occasionally, an ad was double-coded' (Fox, 1990, p. 36). Moreover, although this is also not made explicit, the categorization is probably not exhaustive in that all motives occurring are included. Finally, Fox does not list technical characteristics.
6 The dataset cannot be divided completely into five-year periods. In Figure 5.4, we therefore left out the 'boundary years' 1918–1919 and 1960.

References

Abernathy W. J., Utterback, James M. (1978): 'Patterns of industrial innovation', *Technology Review* 80 (7), pp. 40–47.

Becker, G. S. (1965): 'A theory of the allocation of time', *The Economic Journal*, 75 (299), pp. 49–517.

Cowan, R. S. (1976): 'The "industrial revolution" in the home: Household technology and social change in the 20th century', *Technology and Culture*, 17 (1), pp. 1–23.

Cowan, R. S. (1983): *More Work for Mother*, Basic Books, New York.

Fox, B. J. (1990): 'Selling the mechanized household: 70 years of ads in *Ladies' Home Journal*', *Gender & Society*, 4 (1), pp. 25–40.

Galbraith, J. K. (1958): *The Affluent Society*, The Riverside Press, Cambridge, MA.

Lancaster, K. (1966): 'A new approach to consumer theory', *Journal of Political Economy*, 74, pp. 132–157.

Lavin, M. (1995): Creating consumers in the 1930s: Irna Phillips and the radio soap opera, *Journal of Consumer Research*, 22, pp. 75–99.

Matthews, G. (1987): *Just a Housewife: The Rise and Fall of Domesticity in America*, Oxford University Press, New York.

Michael, R. T., Becker G. S. (1973): 'On the new theory of consumer behavior', *Swedish Journal of Economics*, 75 (4), pp. 378–396.

Saviotti, P. P., Metcalfe, J. S. (1984): 'A theoretical approach to the construction of technological output indicators', *Research Policy*, 13, pp. 141–151.

Strasser, S. (2000) [1982]: *Never Done: A History of American Housework*, Henry Holt and Company, New York.

Tushman, M. L., Anderson, P. (1986): 'Technological discontinuties and organizational environments', *Administrative Science Quarterly*, 31, pp. 439–465.

Witt, U. (1993): 'Emergence and dissemination of innovations: Some principles of evolutionary economics', in Day, R. H., Chen, P. (eds.): *Nonlinear Dynamics Evolutionary Economics*, Oxford University Press, Oxford, United Kingdom.

Witt, U. (2001): 'Learning to consume: A theory of wants and the growth of demand', *Journal of Evolutionary Economics*, 11, pp. 23–36.

6 Patterns of Cleanliness Consumption and Time Use

6.1 Introduction

In the previous two chapters, we have examined the driving forces behind the diffusion of washing machines in the United States during the twentieth century by tracing the progress in laundry technology (cf. Chapter 4) and analyzing shifts in advertisement content for clothes washers (cf. Chapter 5). Two alternative hypotheses have structured the analyses: the time substitution hypothesis of the household production function approach (Becker, 1965; Michael and Becker, 1973) and the drudgery avoidance hypothesis associated with the theory of learning consumers (Witt, 2001).

The household production function approach by Gary Becker (Becker, 1965; Michael and Becker, 1973) asserts that there are strong structural interdependencies between the wage rate, female labor force participation, expenditures on goods and services and time use patterns (cf. Chapter 2). In fact, women participating in the labor force should face higher opportunity costs of time than do nonworking women, inducing the former to outsource a larger share of domestic tasks and use more goods and less of their own time in unpaid domestic production activities. Given a certain wage rate, households with women participating in the labor force thus have a stronger incentive to adopt washing machines compared with households with nonworking women (Short-Run Time Substitution Hypothesis, cf. Chapter 4). In addition, an increase in female labor force participation over time is a sufficient condition for the purchase of time saving washing machines which replace the household's input of time into the domestic activity of laundry washing (Long-Run Time Substitution Hypothesis, cf. Chapter 4). In fact, Michael and Becker (1973) suggest that the time substitution hypothesis is applicable to analyze the adoption decision of domestic appliances which are 'time savers'.

The drudgery avoidance hypothesis can be derived from the theory of learning consumers by Ulrich Witt (2001), which is a needs-based account of consumption behavior (cf. Chapter 2). The hypothesis relates the adoption of washing machines to the behavioral disposition to avoid heavy physical effort (Long-Run Drudgery Avoidance Hypothesis) and argues that, in the absence of drudgery-reducing washing technology, the household tends to display low levels of cleanliness (Short-Run Drudgery Avoidance Hypothesis, cf. Chapter 4). In that interpretation, the adoption of washing machines is the consumer's strategy to cope with the trade-off between cleanliness (i.e. the basic needs of health and social recognition) on one side and drudgery avoidance on the other.

We found support for both hypotheses by showing that physical labor savings and time savings indeed became feasible with technically advanced washing machines during the twentieth century (cf. Chapter 4) and that these motives were apparently of such importance that they were mentioned in washing machine advertisements for roughly seven decades (cf. Chapter 5). In historical terms, the motive to avoid the drudgery of doing the laundry appears to have preceded time saving concerns, which might have triggered the proliferation of laundry technology only from the 1940s onward.

With the advertisement analysis and the technology study, we gathered some initial valuable findings with which to confront the alternative hypotheses. While these approaches were already quite insightful for better understanding the factors behind the proliferation of modern laundry technology, they do not allow testing of the hypotheses in a strict statistical sense. In addition, with regard to the Becker hypothesis of time substitution, we have thus far examined only one very specific aspect, namely the motive of time saving. We did not pay attention to further, yet decisive, elements of the hypothesis – opportunity costs of time and employment status of the wife. To these issues, we turn in this chapter.

More precisely, we investigate whether washing machines have indeed been employed for time substitution purposes by addressing the following questions:

1 Are there systematic differences between employed and nonemployed women in terms of expenditures on and ownership of washing machines?
2 Are there systematic differences between employed and nonemployed women in terms of the use of laundry services?
3 Does the time spent doing the laundry vary with the employment status of the wife and/or ownership of a washing machine?

Quite some empirical material has been accumulated so far, including cross-sectional studies and time-series data, which can be applied to provide answers to these questions and thus put the time substitution hypothesis to a test. This body of literature will be reviewed to find out if higher opportunity costs of time increase the likelihood of possessing a washing machine or making use of laundry services and whether employed women spend less time doing the laundry than nonemployed women.

By studying the demand for washing machines and laundry services as well as the time allocated for washing clothes, we widen the scope taken so far and analyze patterns of cleanliness consumption as a whole. Recall that cleanliness in the form of clean clothes has been conceptualized as the outcome of the household production process of laundry washing and that clean clothes have been assumed to have instrumental value for the household's ultimate goals – referred to as 'commodities' by Gary Becker and conceptualized here as basic consumer needs (cf. Chapter 2). With the term 'cleanliness consumption', we depict the inputs into this household production process, i.e. expenditures on consumer goods and services as well as the utilization of the respective goods.

We proceed as follows. In Section 6.2, we briefly introduce the hypotheses and concepts beyond the household production function approach on which the reviewed empirical work on the interdependency between female employment and the demand for washing machines has been based. In Section 6.3, we turn to the body of literature which has examined the interdependencies between wives' employment status on one side and cleanliness consumption on the other. Both longitudinal and cross-sectional evidence will be presented in order to put both the Long-Run Time Substitution Hypothesis and the Short-Run Time Substitution Hypothesis to the test. Changes in the household's time allocation patterns will be addressed afterward, again from a longitudinal and a cross-sectional perspective (Section 6.4). Driving forces beyond female employment will be discussed afterward (Section 6.5). Section 6.6 concludes this chapter.

6.2 Wives' Employment and the Demand for Goods and Services

The increasing technological endowment of the home, the transformation of housework, shifts in the labor division between the market and the home and the corresponding demand for goods and services has received much scholarly attention, not only in the economics discipline but even more so in the sociological literature and by historians of technology (e.g. cf. Becker, 1965; Cowan, 1983; Lebergott, 1993; Matthews, 1987; Strasser, 2000 [1982]; Mokyr, 2000; de Vries, 1994). Particularly, the activity of clothes washing has been examined from various angles, including technological progress in washing machines from the middle of the nineteenth century onward (e.g. Giedion, 1948; Cowan, 1983; Hartmann, 1974; Hardyment, 1988; Mohun, 1999; Strasser, 2000 [1982]), the widespread diffusion of these devices in the twentieth century and changes in the material conditions of doing laundry (e.g. Matthews, 1987; Preece, 1990; Bowden and Offer, 1994), furthermore the ideology of housework, standards of cleanliness and the increase in laundry amounts (e.g. Cowan, 1976; Cowan, 1983; Matthews, 1987; Shove, 2003a; Ruedenauer and Griesshammer, 2004). In addition, a multitude of studies has dealt with the implications of the homemaker's entry into the labor force on the demand for washing machines and laundry services, on labor division at home and on time spent doing the laundry.

The rich collection of stylized facts on the subject gathered by sociologists and historians of technology has not yet given rise to an encompassing theoretical account in these disciplines. In contrast to that, with the household production function approach, Gary Becker has put forth an overarching economic framework with which the aforementioned diverse phenomena and their interdependencies can be studied (Becker, 1965; Michael and Becker, 1973) (for a critical discussion of this account, particularly concerning the treatment of preferences, cf. Chapter 2). Interestingly, the majority of the studies reviewed in Section 6.3 base the hypothesis that wives' employment status and the demand for durables and services are related, not on the opportunity cost argument of Gary Becker but on hypotheses by Mincer (1960) and Galbraith (1973), referred to as the 'Mincer Hypothesis' or the 'Galbraith Hypothesis', respectively (e.g. Strober, 1977; Nichols and Fox, 1983; Bryant, 1988). These hypotheses also address the context between female labor force participation and expenditures on durable goods. Galbraith (1973, p. 239) expects these variables to be negatively related (holding income constant), as domestic appliances require some input of time for their maintenance, i.e. to make use of them at all. Hence, he expects the use of durables and the housewives' time to be complementary.[1] Galbraith's hypothesis seems to be quite narrow, however, given that many appliances do bear the potential to save time, apart from maintenance time (Strober, 1977). The opposite effect is hypothesized by Mincer (1960), who draws upon the 'permanent income hypothesis' by Friedman (1957). According to Mincer, wives' income is a transitory source of income only. It will go into savings and, eventually, into the purchase of durable goods as the latter ones are assumed to correspond to savings. Mincer thus postulates a positive interrelationship between wives' employment on one side and durable goods expenditures on the other – which is the same prediction as Becker's, yet based on different arguments.

The point of departure of Becker's account, that housework is a time-intensive, unpaid form of work which women might cut down when they enter the labor force, has also attracted much attention in the sociological literature (e.g. Nichols and Fox, 1983; Bellante and Foster, 1984; Weagley and Norum, 1989). Besides reference to the aforementioned hypotheses, one also finds a relation to the more general notion of 'time pressure' or 'time availability' on the part of the wife (e.g. Cohen, 1988; Foster *et al.*, 1981; Spitze, 1999) to explain the strategies of 'domestic outsourcing' (cf. Strasser, 2000 [1982]). The rationale behind these strategies of domestic outsourcing goes as follows: usually, women do the lion's share of the housework. Once they take up an occupation outside the home or increase the time they spend in their current occupation, it is usually up to them to reorganize their schedules because other family members do not compensate for women's market work (e.g. Preece, 1990, p. 336). Therefore, women participating in the labor force face a trade-off between market work and housework. As they simply have less time available for domestic tasks, they are urged to make use of outsourcing options to a larger extent. To rely on goods and services more strongly for getting the housework done (domestic outsourcing) is one way to harmonize housework and market work. In this strand of literature, three further options have been identified: a reduction of leisure time, a reduction of the quantity and/or quality of domestic output and a more egalitarian division of house-work duties (Strober and Weinberg, 1977).[2]

The argument of domestic outsourcing is compatible with the household production function approach according to which the – ex post – time pressure which women face after having entered the labor force has been anticipated and taken into account – ex ante – when deciding about such entry in the first place. Yet, the two approaches put an emphasis on slightly different aspects of wives' labor force participation: while Becker views it as a rational opportunity cost calculus, driven by efficiency considerations (cf. Chapter 2), the sociological approach points to gender-related aspects of the division of housework.

There are a couple of empirical findings which suggest that the demand for washing machines and wives' employment might indeed be closely related. First, women indeed do most of the housework (e.g. Shelton, 1990; Shelton, 1996). Clothes washing, especially, is mainly a women's job in many countries (e.g. Bianchi *et al.*, 2000; Bittman *et al.*, 2004; Egerton *et al.*, 2006, p. 58). And even when wives' salaries are higher than their husbands' incomes, women keep the responsibility for clothes washing – which does not hold for many other activities, for example cooking (Stafford and Duncan, 1977). In fact, the gender gap concerning time spent in this housework activity is largest (van der Lippe *et al.*, 2004). Second, when women enter the labor force, other house-hold members usually do not help with the adjustment by taking up a larger share of housework (Walker and Woods, 1976; Nichols and Metzen, 1978; Vickery, 1979; Preece, 1990, p. 336). It appears that the use of time of home-maker and spouse are substitutes only for a small share of housework activities (Key, 1990).[3]

Whether wives' employment is the decisive factor behind the demand for washing machines will be scrutinized in the following literature review (cf. Section 6.3). We turn to longitudinal evidence first before we summa-rize the findings of empirical work comparing dual-earner with single-earner households in terms of their cleanliness consumption patterns.

6.3 Evidence: Wives' Employment and Cleanliness Consumption

6.3.1 Longitudinal Evidence

In this section, we summarize the material with which both aspects of the time substitution hypothesis can be put to the test. We begin by taking a look at the development of the rate of female labor force participation on one side and the ownership level of clothes washers on the other. That way, we gain some insights to evaluate the explanatory power of the Long-Run Time Substitution Hypothesis for cleanliness consumption patterns. We compile statistics for the United States.

Let us turn to the diffusion of clothes washers first (cf. Table 6.1). In 1922, clothes washers were still very rare and could be found in about one-fifth of

Table 6.1 Ownership of a Clothes Washers and Female Labor Force Participation in the United States

	Diffusion degree of clothes washers	Female labor force participation	Gap
1920	20.2 [1922]	23.7	–3.5
1930	35.2	24.8	10.4
1940	61.1	25.8	35.3
1950	75.2	29	46.2
1960	85.4	34.5	50.9
1970	92.1	42.6	49.5

Notes: Diffusion degree in percent of wired households; female labor force participation in percent of the population (total); gap in percentage points.
Source: For diffusion degree of clothes washer, cf. Bowden and Offer (1994). For female labor force participation, cf. Goldin (1986).

wired U.S. households only. By 1940, this number had tripled. By 1970, the larger share of the U.S. population had acquired a washing machine, reaching a circulation of more than 90 per cent. When clothes washers became more widespread, female labor force participation also increased, yet to a much smaller extent, from roughly 24 per cent in 1920 to about 43 per cent in 1970. These simple figures convey a clear message: at a given point in time, more households possessed washing machines than there were employed wives, the exception being the 1920s. Moreover, the gap between ownership of washers and female employment has widened with time, when many more households had purchased washing machines than additional women had entered the labor force.

Note that this finding should hold even if we replace the series by Bowden and Offer (1994) with a series that takes into account the whole American population and not wired U.S. households only.[4] Certainly, when taking as a basis all American households, the figures for 1920 and 1930 would be smaller than the depicted numbers, given that only small parts of the population had electricity in the home (cf. Chapter 4). Also, at the end of the series, the ownership level of washers might be overestimated, given that the U.S. Residential Energy Consumption Survey has found that, currently, four out of five U.S. households possess this device (EIA, 2011). However, the figures do not have to be taken at face value to detect the general long-term trend of a widening gap between these two time series.

The two series depicted here correspond to the population level and do not indicate whether the respective owners of washing machines are families with a working wife. In other words, it cannot be assessed whether the series 'diffusion degree' on one side and 'female labor force participation' on the other show any sort of correlation whatsoever. However, we know for a fact that, at the beginning of the proliferation process of modern laundry technology, wives' employment was not a triggering factor. Recall the finding by Cowan (1976), according to which the first adopters of washing machines in the 1920s and 1930s were middle-class housewives who had no intention of joining the labor force (cf. Chapter 4). What becomes clear, in addition, is that nearly every household has had an incentive to purchase a clothes washer – at least by the end of the time period studied (and possibly even earlier). This observation might be interpreted in the way that another underlying principle has been at work, such that households – as soon as they could afford these devices – have purchased clothes washers, independent of whether the wife stayed at home or not. These simple figures suggest that rising female labor force participation has not been the decisive factor behind the diffusion of washing machines. Thus, the Long-Run Time Substitution Hypothesis must be rejected.

6.3.2 Cross-Sectional Evidence

In this subsection, we present studies with which the Short-Run Time Substitution Hypothesis can be scrutinized. We turn to the body of literature, which has analyzed – on a cross-sectional basis – the interdependencies between the employment status of the wife on one side and cleanliness consumption on the other. We seek to find out whether there are systematic differences between employed and nonemployed women in terms of expenditures on and ownership of washing machines and expenditures on and the use of laundry services. The overview is mainly confined to the United States and includes studies related to other countries only to a minor extent. For completeness, the results for clothes dryers are enumerated as well.

There is a multitude of studies on the demand for household appliances such as dishwashers, refrigerators, microwaves and so forth (cf. Strober and Weinberg, 1980; Foster *et al.*, 1981, Preece, 1990).[5] For this literature survey, only studies analyzing the consumption of cleanliness have been taken into account. Studies which examine durable goods as an aggregate were also considered as far as they include clothes washers in this aggregate. Although not all studies make this explicit, it appears that all reviewed studies focus on wives as additional earners for a family, i.e. dual-earner households. Moreover, many studies do not appear to draw upon the household production function approach and the concept of opportunity costs of time, but relate the demand for household appliances to the increased time pressure of working women, i.e. a reduced availability of time for doing housework once the woman increases her labor market commitments. They are nevertheless suited to put the time substitution hypothesis to the test (cf. Section 6.2).

By no means can we claim to present a complete literature survey here. Instead, the most prominent studies will be paid attention to. Table 6.2 summarizes the results relevant to our research questions. Note that we do not list all the control variables that have been included in the respective analyses (for instance, if and how many children are in the home, the age of household members, home ownership and so forth). The studies are presented in chronological order to detect more easily if the relationships

Table 6.2 Summary of Studies on the Relationship Between Wives' Employment Status and the Demand for Goods and Services (Focus: Clothes Washing)

Author	Region, time period	Dependent variables: demand for goods and services	Independent variables: wive's employment status	Major findings: which effect does wives employment status have on demand for goods and services	
Douglas 1976	United States and France, n.a.	Purchase of laundry services (yes, no)	Employed, nonemployed	• WE and purchase of laundry services	0
Walker and Woods 1976	United States, 1968	Paid outside help (yes, no)	Employed, nonemployed	• Families with employed wives are more likely to use paid help both occasionally (26% vs. 21%) and regularly (9% vs. 4%)	+
Strober 1977	United States, 1968	Exp. share of durable goods (incl. washing machines)	Employed, nonemployed	• WE and exp. share of durable goods, when controlling for income	0
				• Income and exp. share of durable goods	+
Strober and Weinberg 1977	United States, 1968	Purchase of clothes washer (yes, no); if purchase: exp. level of clothes washer	Employed, nonemployed; if employed: recent entry into labor force or not	• WE and likelihood of washer purchase (yes, no), controlling for income	0
				• WE and level of expenditures, controlling for income	0
				• Income and purchase of washers	+
				• Income and level of expenditures	+
Stafford and Duncan 1977	United States, 1975–1976	Ownership: clothes washer (yes, no); clothes dryer (yes, no)	Working wives hourly wage rate	• WE and ownership clothes washer, holding income constant	−
				• WE and ownership clothes dryer, holding income constant	+
				• Income and ownership clothes washer	+
				• Income and ownership clothes dryer	+
Vickery 1979	United States, 1972–1973	Exp. on dry cleaning and clothing care	Employed (full-time, part-time), nonemployed	• WE and exp. on dry cleaning and clothing care	+

Study	Country, Year	Variables	Employment categories	Findings	Sign
Strober and Weinberg 1980	United States, 1977	Purchase (yes, no): clothes washer, clothes dryer; Ownership (yes, no): clothes washer; clothes dryer	Employed, nonemployed; if employed: recent entry into labor force or not	• WE and purchase of washer or dryer, controlling for income	0
				• WE and ownership of washer or dryer, controlling for income	0
				• Income and purchase	+
				• income and ownership	+
Foster et al. 1981	United States, 1972–1973	Exp.: clothes washer, clothes dryer	Employed, nonemployed	• WE and exp. on washer or dryer, controlling for income (income not significant)	0
Schaninger and Allen 1981	Canada, 1977	Ownership (yes, no): clothes washer, clothes dryer	Non-working, low-occupational status working, high occupational status working	• Income and exp. on washer or dryer	0
				• WE and ownership clothes washer and dryer	+
Ketkar and Cho 1982	United States, 1972–1973	Exp. on household furnishings and equipment (appliances, furniture, linen, toys, antiques)	Nonemployed, full-time employed, part-time employed	• Full-time employed wife and exp. on household furnishings etc.	0
				• Part-time employed wife and exp. on household furnishings etc.	−
				• Total exp. and exp. on household furnishings etc.	+
Weinberg and Winer 1983	United States, 1977	Purchase: clothes washer, clothes dryer (yes, no); if yes: level of exp. on washer or dryer	Employed, nonemployed	• WE and purchase of washers or dryers (yes, no)	0
				• WE and exp. level on washers or dryers	0
				• Income and purchase of washers or dryers (yes, no)	0
				• Income and exp. level on washers or dryers	0

(Continued)

Table 6.2 (Continued)

Author	Region, time period	Dependent variables: demand for goods and services	Independent variables: wive's employment status	Major findings: which effect does wives employment status have on demand for goods and services	
Nickols and Fox 1983	United States, 1977–1979	Ownership clothes washer, clothes dryer (yes, no) Purchase of dry cleaning and laundry services Number of loads washed past seven days	Employed, nonemployed (based on hours worked per week the week before the interview)	• WE and ownership washers or dryers • Income and ownership washers or dryers • WE and purchase of dry cleaning and laundry services • Income and purchase of dry cleaning and laundry services • WE and number of wash loads	0 + 0 + 0
Bellante and Foster 1984	United States, 1972–1973	Exp. services: clothing care (dry cleaning and laundry sent out, clothing repair and alterations); domestic services (cleaning, laundering, cooking, other)	Nonemployed, full time employed, part-time employed; weeks worked	• Family income and exp. on both service categories • Weeks worked and exp. on both service categories • Part-time employment and exp. on clothing care • Full-time employment and exp. on clothing care • WE and exp. on both service categories	+ 0 + 0 0
Lovingood and McCullough 1986	United States, n.a.	Ownership: automatic washer, clothes dryer	hours in paid employment	• WE and ownership clothes washer • WE and ownership clothes dryer • Income and ownership clothes washer • Income and ownership clothes dryer	0 + + +
Bryant 1988	United States, 1977–1978	Exp.: durable goods (aggregate)	Hours of market work per year	• WE and exp. on durables are complements (i.e. demand for durables falls the more hours worked) • Financial resources (i.e. income minus earnings of wife): not significant	− 0

Study	Country, period	Dependent variable	Labor force variable	Findings	Effect
Kim 1989	Canada, 1982–1983	Ownership (yes, no): automatic clothes washer; electric clothes dryer	Employed, nonemployed	WE and ownership clothes washer	+
				Income and ownership clothes washer	0
Weagley and Norum 1989	United States, n.a.	Purchase of clothes laundering service (yes, no)	Wage rate; average hours of work per week	Wage rate and purchase laundry services	0
				Hours of work and purchase laundry services	0
Yang and Magrabi 1989	United States, 1984	Exp.: clothing care services (laundry and dry cleaning apparel, minus coin-operated laundry and dry cleaning, plus repair and alteration of clothing and accessories); domestic services (housekeeping services, misc. home services, laundry and dry cleaning of items other than clothing)	Nonemployed, full-time employed, part-time employed; number of hours worked; WED: dummy	No control ownership appliances	0
				WE and exp. on clothing care and dom. services	0
				Hours per week and exp. on clothing care and dom. services	0
				WED and exp. clothing care services and dom. services	+
				Income and exp. on clothing care services	+
				Income and exp. on domestic services	+
Rubin et al. 1990	United States, 1972–1973 vs. 1984	Exp.: household furnishings and equipment, apparel and services	Nonemployed, part-time employed, full-time employed	Among groups of equal income level, WE and exp. on household furnishings and equipment	0
				Among groups of equal income level, WE and exp. on apparel and services: only 1972, lowest income group (other: no effect)	+
				Income and exp. on apparel and services	+
				Income and exp. on household furnishings and equipment	0

(Continued)

Table 6.2 (Continued)

Author	Region, time period	Dependent variables: demand for goods and services	Independent variables: wive's employment status	Major findings: which effect does wives employment status have on demand for goods and services
Soberon-Ferrer and Dardis 1991	United States, 1984–1985	Exp. services: clothes washing (dry cleaning and laundry sent out, clothing repair and alterations); domestic services (cleaning, laundering, cooking, other)	Hours worked	• Hours worked by husband and wife and exp. on clothing care + • Wage rate wife and exp. on domestic services + • Unearned income and exp. on domestic services + • Higher education and exp. on clothing care + • No difference between part time and full time employed wives on domestic services and clothing care 0
Van der Lippe *et al.* 2004	Netherlands, 1995	Ownership clothes dryer (yes, no)	Wife in double earner household (yes, no) *vs.* single earner household WED: dummies for highest education attainment *vs.* basic vocational or less	• WE and ownership clothes dryer 0 • Income and ownership dryer + • WED and ownership dryer 0

Notes: Exp.: expenditure; WE: wives employment; WED: wives education. +: positive effect; –: negative effect; 0: no effect.
Endnote to table: Ketcar and Cho (1982) use the terminology of 'head of the household' and 'spouse.' In the table, we replaced 'spouse' by 'wife' so to grasp more easily what is meant: the potential influence of an additional earner in dual-earner households, which in most of the cases is indeed the wife

examined have undergone systematic changes over time. All studies are of a cross-sectional nature but the method of data collection might have exceeded one calendar year.

Let us turn first to those studies which analyze ownership of and expenditures on washing machines Although the picture is somewhat mixed, the majority of studies do not find a significant statistical relationship between the employment status of the homemaker and the presence of clothes washers in the home, the exception being the studies by Schaninger and Allen (1981) and Kim (1989), which do not apply to the United States. A further rather robust finding is the significant positive impact of household income on the demand for washing machines, i.e. the higher the household's income, the more likely that the family will own a washing machine. The analyses which measure the purchase of durable goods, including washing machines, as an aggregate yield similar results, namely that income has a positive effect on such outlays while the employment status of the wife does not unfold any impact. Only the analysis by Bryant (1988) features the exceptional finding that expenditures on durable goods are lower for families with working wives than nonworking wives. Concerning the use of and expenditures on laundry services for instance, making use of dry-cleaning, a similar picture emerges. While two studies find that the expenditures on laundry services increase with higher labor force participation of the wife (i.e. Vickery, 1979; Soberon-Ferrer and Dardis, 1991), most studies do not detect such a relationship whatsoever. Concerning the impact of income on the demand for services, the findings are inconclusive.

Overall, it is found that – once income is controlled for, i.e. the fact that earnings by the wife increase family income – households with working wives are not more likely than those with nonworking wives to possess a washing machine and they do not systematically spend more on such tools or on laundry services. This is a stable finding over time. Taking the empirical results at face value, there are no significant differences between households with nonworking wives versus households with working wives in terms of their cleanliness consumption patterns.

Many arguments have been brought forth as to why the postulated relationship between the employment status of the wife and household cleanliness consumption does not exist. A couple of arguments are related to the statistical approaches taken in these analyses. To begin with, there might simply be statistical shortcomings in terms of the estimation technique (Yang and Magrabi, 1989; Oropesa, 1993). In addition, when almost every household possesses a washing machine or hardly anyone makes use of services, the variance in the dependent variable might be too small to possibly affect the econometric results (Weagley and Norum, 1989). Furthermore, potentially relevant control variables might have been neglected. In fact, sometimes the ownership of a clothes washer is not being controlled for when examining the demand for laundry services (cf. Weagley and Norum, 1989). Beyond that, informal help is often not included as a control variable but might very well explain why employed wives do not make use of laundry services to a larger extent

(Spitze, 1999).[6] If these objections were legitimate, the results of the reviewed studies could not be taken as evidence against the time substitution hypothesis. However, one should bear in mind that, in principle, any econometric analysis can be criticized for one or the other reason, making it difficult to gather any findings with which to put the hypothesis to the test.

Taking the empirical findings seriously, many arguments have been put forth to make sense of the missing link between the employment status of the wife and household cleanliness consumption. Some arguments emphasize the impact of consumer preferences on the demand for household appliances. In that regard, the value of time will have no effect on the demand for market alternatives when home-produced and market-produced goods are not considered substitutes in the eyes of consumers (Weagley and Norum, 1989). Such limits to substitutability can have technical as well as preference-based origins and are fixed in the short run (e.g. Jara-Díaz, 2003). We have already alluded to this point when discussing the demand for laundry services from a historical perspective (cf. Chapter 4). Moreover, similarities in cleanliness consumption patterns might result from time saving appliances being considered 'necessities'; they are purchased by all households alike as soon as they become affordable, making family income and not opportunity costs of time the decisive variable (Strober and Weinberg, 1977). Note that it is yet to be explained why all households alike might consider washing machines as a 'necessity'.

Several authors have argued that structural factors were more decisive in explaining the ownership of time saving durable goods than differences in female labor force participation. The conjecture put forth most frequently concerns the presence, number and age of children at home. In that regard, families with nonworking wives (rather than working wives) are more likely to buy appliances to cope with the growing workload when young children are part of the home.[7] This is one way to explain what, if not female employment, triggers the demand for household appliances. The conjecture implies that one could find families, both with working and with nonworking wives, equally equipped with washing machines when they show the same family structure. Note that statistical analyses, when including the presence of children among the control variables, should be able to detect whether an independent effect of the employment status of the wife remains or not. As a further structural factor, the availability of washing machines in home dwellings might play a role (Strober and Weinberg, 1977). Certainly, this factor could also be controlled for. Finally, the price of using dry-cleaning services might exceed the price of doing the laundry at home (including the costs of equipment, energy, etc.) (Weagley and Norum, 1989), such that the use of services need not pay off for employed wives (Yang and Magrabi, 1989). To examine this conjecture, it has to be controlled for ownership of clothes washers.

Further but somewhat weaker arguments have been put forth. With regard to the use of laundry services, one argument says that the time input for doing the laundry at home is practically negligible today so that this activity does not put particular time pressure on employed wives, especially as it can be carried out in parallel with other activities. Hence, there might be no need for working wives to opt for services more strongly. In order to draw such a conclusion, the ownership of washing machines has to be controlled for in the analysis, which has not always been the case. Moreover, the argument is not consistent with the prediction of the household production function approach: by assuming that the price of time is higher for employed than for nonemployed women, unpaid time uses are always more costly for the former group of households – no matter how small. Elsewhere it is argued that the Beckerian account deals with the demand for services of durable goods, while empirical studies examine the ownership of these tools instead and are thus not suited to put its core hypothesis to the test (Weagley and Norum, 1989). This argument draws upon Pollak's (1969) short-run maximization model where not only labor force commitments are fixed, but the household technology is given as well. However, we see no reason why cross-sectional studies should not be able to capture this situation: they measure the adjustment in household technology that households have made up to that point, including a recent entry of the wife into the labor force and a simultaneous acquisition of new appliances. Another argument criticizes the conclusion that, once it is controlled for income, wives' employment does not affect the demand for services, as an indirect effect of wives' employment might nevertheless be present (Oropesa, 1993). The time substitution hypothesis, however, links opportunity costs of time to outsourcing patterns – a relationship that should persist even after controlling for the growth in family income.

To sum this up, the reviewed studies yield a clear result in total: differences in opportunity costs of time appear to not be the central explanatory factor behind cleanliness consumption patterns in the United States during the twentieth century. Household income, in contrast, was shown to have an effect in almost all studies. As it is quite unlikely that all of these studies suffer from severe statistical shortcomings, we interpret the findings as evidence against the time substitution hypothesis (Short-Run Time Substitution Hypothesis). In the following section, we examine whether washing machines have indeed been employed to save time when doing laundry.

6.4 Evidence: Wives' Employment and Time Use Patterns

6.4.1 Longitudinal Evidence

Hitherto, we have reviewed time series data and empirical studies on the context between wives' employment status on one side and outsourcing patterns of the household on the other. We interpreted the findings as evidence against both the Short-Run Time Substitution Hypothesis and the Long-Run Time Substitution Hypothesis.

Next, we turn to changes in the households' time allocation patterns. Although working wives do not appear to have had a stronger incentive to purchase washing machines than did nonworking women, from a technical perspective, time savings in clothes washing would indeed have been feasible from the 1940s onward (cf. Chapter 4). Particularly from that point in time onward, washing machines might have been acquired in order to reduce the time spent doing the laundry and to better harmonize market work and domestic duties. In this section, we analyze whether the time allocated toward washing clothes has decreased over the twentieth century, and if the time spent on this household chore varies with the employment status of the wife and/or ownership of a washing machine. Time savings might have been a relevant motive for the adoption of washing machines, if households had indeed substantially reduced the time devoted to washing clothes. If employment status or changes therein had an impact on time allocation patterns, this would be consistent with the time substitution hypothesis. Note that this interpretation goes beyond the scope of the two elements of the hypothesis which pertain to employment status and washing machine ownership only, and do not make statements about time use patterns (cf. Chapter 4). The material shall be presented, however, as it connects with the findings of the technology study and the advertisement analysis and deepens our understanding of the subject. We turn to longitudinal evidence first before we review cross-sectional studies.[8]

Information on household use of time can be obtained from various studies and household surveys which measure time allocation among distinct activity categories such as shopping, food preparation or laundry washing. In the United States, the large-scale 'American Time Use Survey' has been carried out once every decade since the 1960s (cf. Robinson and Godbey, 1997; for the method of time use surveys, cf. Juster, 1985; Juster and Stafford, 1991).[9] Recently, the isolated findings have been connected and have been corrected for changes in the demographic composition of the panel so as to trace the development for households with the same sociodemographic characteristics (e.g. Egerton *et al.*, 2006; Aguiar and Hurst, 2007; Ramey and Francis, 2009). As a result, long-term shifts in time allocation patterns over the past four decades of the twentieth century can now be analyzed. Before the 1960s, a couple of unrelated studies have collected information on housework activities and time allocation in the United States.

Let us have a look at the aggregate patterns first, i.e. the general trends in time allocation between housework and market work. Information on time use patterns in the United States dating back to the 1920s has been compiled by Vanek (1974) and by Preece (1990). Vanek finds that from 1926–1927 until 1965–1966, housework time for full-time homemakers, i.e. nonemployed women, has been rather constant. Preece (1990), analyzing several distinct housework categories, finds a similar pattern. According to Preece (1990, p. 446), between 1926 and 1952, the housework norm was based on the pattern of the full-time homemaker. It required that wives personally cared for the family members by doing housework. Thus, there was no particular incentive to save time. For the few employed wives, it was difficult to ask for support in household maintenance tasks as they deviated from the norm. Over time, although not before 1952, housework patterns of employed women and full-time homemakers became more similar, including similar time use patterns.

In the 1960s and afterward, data on these very broad time use categories have been collected by the large-scale U.S. time use survey. The findings are depicted in Table 6.3.[10] They show that from 1965–2003, a remarkable decline in the average housework hours (referred to as 'non-market work') took place, namely a reduction by circa 4 hours per week. Opposite developments were observed for men and women. While men's contribution to household mainte-nance activities slightly rose, women substantially reduced the time spent doing housework by about 10 hours per week.[11] In parallel, women increased market work time, yet to a smaller extent.[12] The figures do not reveal whether a dif-ferent development took place for families with employed wives as opposed to families with nonemployed wives, or if a similar reduction in housework time occurred in these groups.[13]

Time allocation data have also been compiled for the activity of clothes washing. According to Vanek (1974), full-time homemakers in 1965–1966 spent about the same amount of time doing the laundry than 40 years earlier, in 1926–1927, while in the meantime, some shifts upward and downward have taken place (Vanek, 1974, p. 116). In 1925, when electric clothes washers were available, full-time homemakers spent more than 5 hours per week washing clothes, whereas in 1964, slightly more than 6 hours per week were devoted to this activity. Interestingly, in the period from 1949–1953, when washing machines became automatic, full-time homemakers spent more time on the weekly laundry than in the period before and afterward, namely nearly 7 hours more. Also, Preece (1990, Chapter 8) finds an almost stable pattern, with only a slight increase in time spent doing the laundry between 1925 and 1953. She draws upon the 1926 Oregon Study by Wilson (1929) and the 1952 New York Study by Wiegand (1953) and Walker (1955) (Preece, 1990, Chapter 3), and provides figures for washing and ironing taken together as well as for clothes washing alone.[14] The figures for clothes washing alone are roughly of the same magnitude as those mentioned by Vanek.[15] Preece estimates that, in the 1920s, farm households and urban households respectively spent *circa* 6.5 and 7 hours per week washing and ironing, whereas both farm and urban households spent *circa* 4 hours per week on clothes washing alone (excluding

Table 6.3 Changes in Time Use Patterns in the United States, 1965–2003

	Market work, core	*Market work, total*	*Nonmarket work, core*	*Non-market work, total*
Average	−1.0	−4.3	−4.4	−3.8
Men	−6.6	−12.1	+1.4	+3.8
Women	+3.8	+2.5	−9.4	−10.3

Source: Aguiar and Hurst (2007).

Notes: Hours per week, age group 21–65, figures adjusted for demographic changes (rounded to one decimal).

ironing, sewing, fancywork and the like) (Preece, 1990, p. 311). For the year 1952, Preece (1990, p. 311) estimates that all women spent *circa* 7.5 hours per week doing laundry and related tasks, whereas urban homemakers and farm families devoted 4–4.5 hours each week to clothes washing alone. For 1952, Preece (1990) also compiled figures for urban households with employed wives.[16] She found those households to have spent less time with that activity than their nonemployed counterparts, i.e. *circa* 3 hours per week on washing and ironing together and about 2.5 hours per week on clothes washing alone. According to Preece (1990, p. 315), this pattern is not to be explained by washing machine ownership; instead, employed wives' homes were slightly less well equipped, and fewer had washing machines and, particularly, automatic washers than urban homemakers.

According to Preece (1990, Chapter 8, p. 88) and Vanek (1974), the major reductions in time spent washing and ironing appeared only after the 1950s or the 1960s, respectively, particularly until the 1970s. More precisely, Preece (1990, p. 311) identifies a decline between 1952 and 1978. The figures compiled elsewhere (Bianchi *et al.*, 2000; Egerton *et al.* 2006, p. 58) support this statement.[17] Again, these figures do not make reference to the employment status of the wife. Preece (1990, Chapter 8), however, finds that the gap between employed women and nonemployed women concerning the time spent on clothes maintenance has become smaller over time, i.e. from the 1960s onward (clothes maintenance being more broadly defined than clothes washing). Table 6.4 once again summarizes the findings in the literature. As it is a compilation from different sources, the figures for the respective years can be put in relation to one another but do not represent a consistent time series dataset.

Although the material compiled here has to be interpreted with caution, a clear trend both for housework in general and for clothes washing in particular can be detected: housework hours and time spent doing laundry have not changed much between the 1920s and the 1960s, but declined remarkably from the 1960s onward. In other words, from the 1960s onward, when many potentially time saving household appliances had been invented, marketed and diffused in the American population (exemplarily depicted here for washing machines, cf. Table 6.1), households cut down the overall housework hours

Table 6.4 Changes in Average Weekly Hours of Laundry Washing in the United States

	1900	1925–1927	1952	1965	1975	1985	1995
All women	7	5 to 6	7.5	5.8	3.2	2.4	1.9
Married women	n.a.	n.a.	n.a.	6.6	3.8	2.7	2.4

Source: The figures for 1900 and 1925–1927 are taken from Lebergott (1993, p. 51). For 1925–1927, two figures are given for urban and rural women (5 or 6 hours per week respectively). The figure for 1952 is taken from Preece and covers farm families and urban homemakers (1990, p. 311). The figures of 1965–1995 are taken from Bianchi *et al.* (2000) and pertain to the age group 25–64 years.

and the time they spent washing clothes. The motive to save time in doing laundry thus might have triggered the diffusion of washing machines in the second half of the twentieth century, while it was not relevant in the first half. In parallel, women have increased the weekly hours committed to market work. If market work hours were correlated with the rate of female labor force participation (cf. Table 6.1), these observations could be interpreted as evidence in favor of the Long-Run Time Substitution Hypothesis and would also be consistent with the idea of domestic outsourcing. In that regard, after the 1960s, washing machines would have been acquired in order to fulfill labor market commitments and to harmonize duties both at home and at work. Such a correlation is not unlikely, given the rising participation of women in the workforce throughout the twentieth century. Because of a lack of data on market work time, we cannot assess the Long-Run Time Substitution Hypothesis for the period before the 1960s. The observation by Vanek (1974) pertains to full-time homemakers, i.e. the group of nonemployed women. The same holds for the figures cited by Preece (1990) for the time period before 1952.

Although at first sight, the time saving motive in general and the opportunity costs argument in particular appear to capture what has driven the diffusion of washing machines in the second half of the twentieth century, the findings collected here also raise some doubts. To begin with, recall that many more households had adopted washing machines than additional women had entered the labor force (cf. Section 6.3). Consider also the finding by Preece (1990) that the gap between households with employed wives and nonemployed wives concerning the time spent doing laundry declined and converged toward fairly similar time use patterns. Note also that the gap was not associated with washing machine ownership.[18] These observations cannot be explained by labor market commitments and speak against an impact of opportunity costs of time so that we would stick to our earlier interpretation and reject the Long-Run Time Substitution Hypothesis.

Another observation casts further doubt on the Beckerian interpretation. By and large, the depicted time use trends are in line with our earlier findings that, from a technical perspective, time savings in clothes washing were hardly feasible before the widespread diffusion of automatic washers from the 1940s onward (cf. Chapter 4).[19] Thus, with given standards of cleanliness, one would not have expected to observe time savings before that point in time – yet possibly earlier than in the 1960s, given the technical preconditions and the appeal to time saving concerns in washing machine advertisements (cf. Chapter 5). Partly, this might have been the result of a time lag in the diffusion of automatic washing machines. In addition, behavioral reactions might have produced this outcome. In that regard, washing machines adopted between the 1940s and the 1960s might not have been employed to reduce the hours spent washing clothes but to cope with an increase in laundry amounts, resulting in constant time use patterns. In fact, Preece (1990, Chapter 8, p. 316, p. 338) argues that the slight increase in time spent washing and ironing between 1926 and 1952 is the result of an increase in standards of clothing care as well as an increase in the amount of clothes owned and washed (she presents detailed figures for farm and urban households, respectively).[20] According to Klepp (2003), consumers have also started to launder textiles which previously had not been part of the 'laundry basket' in the nineteenth century. Changes in social norms made the old standards of cleaning unacceptable (Preece, 1990, p. 303).[21] Also, after the 1950s, laundry quantities continued to increase (Shove, 2003b; Shove, 2003a). We come back to these issues in Section 6.5.

6.4.2 Cross-Sectional Evidence

We now briefly turn to the question of whether differences in employment status and ownership of washing machines are reflected in time use patterns. The studies listed below might contribute to a better understanding of the empirical insights gathered so far: if we find that working women, in comparison with nonworking women, have not employed washing machines to reduce the time spent doing the laundry, labor force commitments and the price of time are most likely not the decisive factors for the acquisition of washing machines. In that regard, the findings would confirm the interpretation given earlier.

Table 6.5 summarizes the main findings from U.S. studies dealing with the activity of clothes washing and the determinants of time use. We have not found nearly as many studies on this issue as there are on the relationship between female employment and ownership of washing machines (cf. Section 6.3). For illustrative purposes, we also include findings gathered for other countries and clothes dryers.[22] Left out of this overview are further studies from the 1920s and 1930s, in which farm owners and inhabitants of villages or towns are compared in terms of the time spent doing housework in general (cf. Reid, 1934).

Concerning the relationship between the employment status of the wife and time spent doing the laundry, the results are inconclusive. Among the reviewed studies, nearly as many studies found a negative relationship between these variables (studies using data from 1965–1968) as there were studies that did not detect any relationship whatsoever (studies examining data for 1968–1985). Some of these studies appear not to have controlled for the household's income, which might have affected the statistical results. With regard to the correlation between ownership of washing machines and time use patterns, the findings also do not yield a clear picture, as all possible outcomes have been found, i.e. a negative, a positive and no relationship. Likewise, for clothes dryers, no consistent picture emerges.

Summing up the evidence collected in this section, it remains questionable whether opportunity costs of time do capture what is driving time use patterns in clothes washing. Longitudinal evidence suggests that the time saving motive might have contributed to the proliferation of clothes washers in the second half of the twentieth century. However, one cannot exclude that time savings have occurred only as a side effect for all households alike, while the adoption of clothes washers has truly happened for other reasons.[23]

Table 6.5 Summary of Studies on the Relationship Between Wives' Employment Status, Ownership of a Washing Machine and/or Clothes Dryer and Time Spent Doing the Laundry

Author	Region, time period	Dependent variable	Independent variable	Major findings	
Robinson and Converse 1972	United States, 1965–1966	Time spent doing laundry	WE: employed, nonemployed	• WE and time use	−
Stafford 1983	United States, 1967–1968	Time spent clothing care	Length of the workday of employed wife	• WE and time use • No control for income	−
Bryant 1996 on Walker and Woods (1976)	United States, 1958	Time spent in activity "care of clothing and linen" (hours per day)	WE: employed, nonemployed	• WE and time use	0
Gramm 1974	United States, 1970	Time spent doing laundry	Wage rate of the wife	• WE and time use • No control for income	0
Robinson and Godbey 1997	United States, 1985	Time spent doing laundry (percentage of hours per week)	WE: employed, nonemployed	• WE and time use	0
Wilson 1929	United States, 1926	Time spent clothes washing	Presence of electricity and modern plumbing (probably also clothes washer)	• Better equipment and time use (savings of 40 minutes per week)	−
Robinson 1980	United States, 1975	Time spent doing laundry (change in minutes per day compared to average)	Ownership: washing machine; clothes dryer	• Ownership washer: +4 minutes • Ownership of dryer: −5 minutes	+ −
Lovingood and McCullough 1986	United States, n.a.	Time spent with care and construction of clothing and household linen	Ownership: automatic washing machine, clothes dryer	• Ownership washer and time use • Ownership dryer and time use	0 0
Bitman et al. 2004	Australia, 1997	Time spent doing laundry (minutes per day)	Ownership clothes dryer (yes, no)	• When family owns dryer woman spends 3 minutes more per day doing the laundry • Income and time spent doing the laundry	+ 0
Van der Lippe et al. 2004	Nether-lands, 1995	Time spent doing laundry	Ownership clothes dryer (yes, no) WE: wife in double earner household (yes, no) vs. single earner household	• Ownership dryer and time spent doing the laundry • Income and time spent doing the laundry • WE and time spent doing the laundry	0 0 −

Notes: Exp.: expenditure; WE: wives employment; WED: wives education. +: positive effect; −: negative effect; 0: no effect.

6.5 Beyond Time Substitution

Let us now come to an overall assessment of the explanatory value of the time substitution hypothesis and the drudgery avoidance hypothesis, respectively, for the evolution of cleanliness consumption patterns in the United States. In the past three chapters, we have analyzed several aspects of washing machine diffusion: technological progress in laundry technology (cf. Chapter 4), product advertisements and consumer learning processes (cf. Chapter 5), washing machine ownership and utilization (cf. Chapter 6).

From the technology study, we learned that – in comparison with the days of 'Blue Monday' – washing machines allowed for time savings from the 1940s onward, when washers became automatic, while technical achievements in physical labor savings had already been realized by the 1920s (cf. Chapter 4). The motive to save time was most frequently referred to in washing machine advertisements between 1940 and 1960, after a period in which the drudgery avoidance motive had dominated the content from *circa* 1890–1920 (cf. Chapter 5). In this chapter, we additionally compiled data on the time households spent doing the laundry and found it to have been more or less stable in the first decades of the twentieth century before it dropped substantially from about the 1960s onward (cf. Section 6.4). In view of these results, one can conclude that both motives of time savings and physical labor savings are likely to have driven the demand for washing machines during the twentieth century, while each motive unfolded its major impact in a different time period. Leaving aside small discrepancies in terms of the exact time periods identified in each analysis, it appears that the drudgery avoidance motive has shaped cleanliness consumption patterns in the first half and the time saving motive in the second half of the twentieth century.

The concrete underlying hypotheses have been more complex, however (cf. Chapter 4). Let us turn first to the time substitution hypothesis associated with the household production function approach. The Short-Run Time Substitution Hypothesis postulates that, given a certain wage rate, households with women participating in the labor force have a stronger incentive to purchase a washing machine than households with nonworking women, as the former should value time higher than the latter. The Long-Run Time Substitution Hypothesis argues that an increase in female labor force participation is a sufficient condition for the purchase of time saving washing machines which replace the household's input of time into the domestic activity of laundry washing. Without reference to the relative price of time, market wages or the employment status of the wife, the analyses hitherto – albeit consistent with Gary Becker's household production function approach as regards the motive of time savings – show no original connection to the central variable, opportunity costs of time, and to the time substitution hypothesis in the specific forms derived here. For that reason, we have analyzed in this chapter the time substitution hypothesis as such by reviewing studies that paid particular attention to the effects of the employment status of the wife on cleanliness consumption patterns. The evidence collected here casts a doubt on the opportunity cost argument. Differences and changes in female employment appear not to capture what has driven the demand for washing machines and laundry services in the twentieth century.

As the relative price of time does not appear to matter, alternative arguments have to be found. The drudgery avoidance hypothesis has been derived from the theory of learning consumers (cf. Chapter 2). It argues that the adoption of washing machines has been motivated by the behavioral disposition to avoid heavy physical effort (Long-Run Drudgery Avoidance Hypothesis) (cf. Chapter 4). It further postulates that, in the absence of drudgery-reducing washing technology, the household tended to display low levels of cleanliness (Short-Run Drudgery Avoidance Hypothesis). In this chapter, we have not added further material to directly scrutinize the drudgery avoidance hypothesis. The data compiled here allow the drawing of some conclusions, however, based on the following findings: first, given the high diffusion degree of washing machines in the American population, practically every household has had an incentive to acquire a modern clothes washer. Thus, there appears to be a motivation for the adoption of washing machines that all consumers – independent of wives' employment – have in common. Secondly, households did not immediately save time with the appearance of the fully automatic washing machine in the 1940s, but employed the modern tools to cope with increasing laundry quantities, which (partly) offset the otherwise achievable time savings.[24]

It appears that driving forces have been at work that made the acquisition of washing machines equally desirable for practically all American households. Certainly, the 'common motivation' could be the time saving motive. With the electric automatic washing machine, a given amount of laundry could be cleansed with a smaller input of the household's time compared with doing laundry by hand or utilizing less modern technological forerunners. To find these devices being adopted for their time saving abilities is thus plausible and also consistent with Gary Becker's household production function approach, in whose reading washing machines reduce the 'shadow price' of doing laundry at home and make the 'commodity' cleanliness cheaper (cf. Chapter 2). The productivity gains in domestic production processes enable higher cleanliness levels at no additional cost (constant time use patterns in clothes washing). Alternatively, some resources of time can be freed up to be used in other activities (time savings in clothes washing). From the perspective of productivity considerations, time savings have the same effect as declining relative prices of clothes washers. Interestingly, real prices of washing machines have indeed declined from the 1950s onward, which also might have contributed to their propagation.[25] Productivity gains yield the same incentive for both families with working wives and those with nonworking wives to purchase modern clothes washers. Note, however, that in this interpretation, time savings are not in themselves a motive for adoption, but rather the 'vehicle' for achieving other underlying goals, for instance, coping with higher laundry amounts or spending time in other, more valuable activities. In order to identify these other goals and understand which behavioral reactions will coincide with washing machine ownership, the 'black box' of consumer motivations has to be opened.

Given our knowledge of the basic needs associated with cleanliness (cf. Chapter 3), the development of the material conditions of doing laundry (cf. Chapter 4) and the impact of the broader social environment on cleanliness standards (cf. Chapter 3), washing machine ownership can be explained without taking recourse to aspects of time allocation, once the disutility arising from drudgery is accounted for as an additional factor in the household's choice.

Psychological insights show that the avoidance of heavy physical effort is an innate behavioral disposition (cf. Chapter 2) which stood in conflict with doing the laundry in the nineteenth century, when exactly such drudgery was required to cope with the weekly wash. In contrast to that, it is no longer challenged by doing laundry nowadays, thanks to the modern equipment and the achievements in the wider technological system (cf. Chapter 4). Clothes washing is ultimately directed toward satisfying the basic needs for health and social recognition. While health and social recognition are positively defined associations related to the 'household production output' of cleanliness, drudgery is a negatively defined association pertaining to the 'production process' of laundry washing itself. During the twentieth century, these motivations shaped the evolution of cleanliness consumption patterns in the United States. The drudgery avoidance motive has driven consumers to acquire technically advanced washing machines as soon as they enabled physical labor savings (recall that the major achievements in physical labor savings had already been realized in the 1920s) (Long-Run Drudgery Avoidance Hypothesis). With the emerging social norm of cleanliness and increasing cleanliness standards, which have affected all consumers alike (irrespective of the employment status of wives), the trade-off between cleanliness on one side and drudgery avoidance on the other became intensified. In the absence of the possibility to keep cleanliness standards low and laundry amounts small, washing machines have been adopted as the household's problem-solving strategy (Short-Run Drudgery Avoidance Hypothesis). These factors finally resulted in a homogenization of cleanliness consumption patterns.

An overall assessment of the relative importance of each of these factors is very difficult. However, we would go so far as to attribute the larger explanatory power to the drudgery avoidance hypothesis in the following sense: the drudgery avoidance motive alone would have been sufficient for the proliferation of washing machines to have taken place. Consider the following thought experiment. What would have happened if women had not entered the labor force in such great numbers in the twentieth century? We assert that washing machines would still have been purchased to a similar extent: first, ownership is independent of female employment; second, the diffusion of clothes washers had already started before significant time savings became technically feasible; and third, washing machines were not immediately employed to save time in some absolute amount. In reverse, if more women withdrew again from the labor market, would households go back to the conditions of domestic production in the nineteenth century? Certainly not, as it would imply reviving the trade-off formerly solved. Proponents of the household production function approach might argue that, simply for reasons of productivity, such a switch back would not be rational. But then again, opportunity costs of time are only relevant to the extent that other uses of time are forgone when a relatively inefficient household technology is used. Hence, differences or changes in the value of time do not appear to lie at the core of this process. The household's outsourcing decision, resulting in the adoption of washing machines, thus appears in a new light.

We shall not forget to mention that the proliferation process was contingent upon the long-term growth in personal income (cf. Burwell and Swezey, 1990), which made feasible this acquisition for practically every U.S. household. So when these appliances became affordable, every household acquired a washing machine, resulting in the present situation whereby the majority of U.S. consumers are owners of washing machines – we can speak of a saturated market here – and rate this device as a 'necessity' item (Taylor *et al.*, 2009).

6.6 Conclusions

In this chapter, we compiled statistical material that is suited to put Becker's time substitution hypothesis to the test. In order to find out whether opportunity costs of time have had an effect on cleanliness consumption patterns in the United States in the twentieth century, we reviewed cross-sectional evidence pertaining to differences in employment status of wives (Short-Run Time Substitution Hypothesis) and discussed some simple time series on changes in female labor force participation over time (Long-Run Time Substitution Hypothesis). In addition, we gathered figures on time use patterns pertaining to housework in general and the activity of clothes washing in particular. By examining an aspect of the hypothesis that has been neglected so far, namely the impact of the employment status of wives, we complemented the insights derived from the technology study (cf. Chapter 4) and advertisement analysis (cf. Chapter 5), which focused on time savings more in general.

The cross-sectional analyses reviewed in this chapter cast doubt on the explanatory potential of the Short-Run Time Substitution Hypothesis: households with employed wives are not more likely to own washing machines or to make use of laundry services than those with nonemployed wives. The household's income, however, positively correlated with the demand for clothes washers. Long-term trends in female labor force participation and washing machine ownership corroborate this finding: the widening gap between these time series speaks against the Long-Run Time Substitution Hypothesis. Apparently, every U.S. household who could afford the technically advanced equipment has acquired this product throughout the twentieth century, independent of the employment status of the wife.

Time use figures underline the conclusions drawn earlier: that the demand for washing machines was connected with a motive to save time in the second half of the twentieth century. In this very general specification, the time substitution hypothesis cannot be rejected. However, the absolute time savings in clothes washing appear not to be associated with opportunity costs of time, as cross-sectional findings regarding the interdependency between female employment and time spent doing the laundry are inconclusive.

As the employment status of wives appears not to be the decisive factor in the purchase of washing machines, a different explanation has to be given. We interpreted the findings gathered as evidence in favor of the drudgery avoidance hypothesis. The shared human motivation to avoid heavy physical effort has driven all consumers, independent of wives' employment status, to acquire modern laundry technology as it offered a solution to the conflict in motivations between cleanliness (i.e. health and social recognition) on one side and drudgery avoidance on the other. The growth in household income and not the value of time was decisive for households to make the switch to the technically advanced products. In the time period until the 1940s, this interpretation stems directly from the collected facts (cf. Chapters 4 and 5), as the relevance of the time saving motive had already been excluded for that time period. For the time period afterward, i.e. roughly the second half of the twentieth century, this conclusion is not so straightforward and thus contains an interpretative element. We would go so far, however, as to attribute the larger explanatory power to the drudgery avoidance hypothesis: even if households had endless amounts of time, they still would have had an incentive to purchase advanced washing machines because of the possibility to eliminate the drudgery of clothes washing that more simple laundry equipment would imply.

The arguments laid out here point to the fact that the time substitution hypothesis, in its original form, is not sufficient to fully understand the changes in the domestic production of cleanliness over the past 200 years. Although, at a general level, time saving capital goods were substituted for human time and physical labor and went hand in hand with an increase in female labor force participation, the actual processes producing this outcome have been much more complex than the household production function approach suggests. Technical progress in washing machines, the emerging social norm of cleanliness, growth in income and consumer learning processes have converged toward a homogenization of cleanliness consumption patterns and the mass market for washing machines in the twentieth century.

In the following chapter, we draw upon the theory of learning consumers (cf. Chapter 2) and the insights collected here in order to venture an outlook on future patterns of cleanliness consumption and the implications for household energy consumption (cf. Chapter 7).

Notes

1 Note that a similar argument has been put forth by Linder (1970), saying that consumption goods absorb maintenance time.
2 Note that Becker (1965) does not treat leisure time as a distinct time use category but defines it as one of the household's ultimate goals. In his approach, a reduction in

leisure time thus corresponds to a decline in domestic output. Moreover, according to the household production function approach, a redistribution of housework duties is not a plausible strategy; under the assumption that rising female labor force participation in dual-earner households is incentivized by increasing market wages, men have in principle the same incentive to cut down on housework, not to expand it.

3 Based on these observations, it is often argued that laundry washing is still closely intertwined with gender ideologies, much more like other housework activities where men are willing to step in. As a consequence, doing the laundry, like hardly any other domestic task, still attracts the attention of feminist scholars (e.g. Hartmann, 1974; Cowan, 1983; Strasser, 2000 [1982]).

4 We use the series by Bowden and Offer (1994) for lack of an alternative.

5 A large body of literature focuses on food consumption, i.e. the purchase of convenience products or 'meals away from home' (e.g. Reilly, 1982; Kinsey, 1983; Cohen, 1988; Oropesa, 1993).

6 Spitze (1999) does not find evidence in that regard, however. Recall also that such informal help would not include the spouse as clothes washing usually remains the woman's duty and spouses do not participate in this activity (e.g. Bianchi *et al.*, 2000).

7 In a study of the United States, focusing on housework in general, Morgan *et al.* (1966) found that appliances tend to be purchased when families are growing.

8 In these analyses, we have focused on time savings in general without taking female employment into account.

9 There are many ways to obtain information on households' time use patterns (Juster, 1985, p. 25). For example, employers collect data on their employees' working time. Inferences can also be drawn from sales of tickets for the theater, sports events or the movie theater. When the households themselves are addressed for obtaining time use information, there are three options: direct observation of household behavior, duration surveys (week, month, year) based on a stylized list of activities and time use diaries. The diary method is said to have comparatively the most advantages.

10 Core Market Work includes the time spent working for pay, both in the main job and in other jobs (including time spent working at home). Total Market Work includes Core Market Work plus any time spent on other work-related activities (including commuting time, formal breaks at work, time spent searching for jobs, etc.). Core nonmarket work covers food preparation, food presentation, kitchen/food cleanup, washing/drying clothes, ironing, dusting, vacuuming, indoor cleaning, indoor painting and so on. Total nonmarket work includes core housework plus shopping/obtaining goods and services, plus all other home production (including vehicle repair, outdoor repair, outdoor painting, etc.) (cf. Aguiar and Hurst, 2007).

11 The observation that men's contribution to housework has increased deserves a proper explanation, given that rising wages do not only imply an incentive for women to increase market work. The general causal relationships, as established by the household production function approach, should hold for both family members alike, unless further arguments like bargaining power or efficiency gains from specialization are taken into account (cf. Becker, 1991).

12 Aguiar and Hurst (2007) do present figures differentiated with regard to educational status and find that higher-educated women have increased market work more strongly than women with lower educational level; at the same time, higher educated women have reduced housework hours to a smaller extent than their less educated counterparts. If educational status were a proxy for employment status, this would be a surprising finding regarding the prediction of the time substitution hypothesis. This 'inconsistency' stems from the fact that the time use survey defines a further time use category, namely leisure time, which corresponds to a 'commodity' in the household production function approach (Becker, 1965).

13 This argument implies that, next to housework time and market work time (the time use categories depicted here), there is at least one further time use category which

nonemployed wives expand when cutting down on housework time. This is indeed the case (leisure time) (Aguiar and Hurst, 2007).

14 For data for the year 1978, Preece (1990, Chapter 3) draws upon the Eleven-State Study. For the specific questions addressed, she also makes use of further studies (cf. Preece, 1990, p. 483).

15 Preece (1990, p. 325) refers to Vanek only once and not in the context of time use patterns. We thus conclude that she has not drawn from the same database as Vanek.

16 Homemakers were categorized as employed wives when they spent more than 15 hours per week in the paid labor force (Preece, 1990, p. 9).

17 The figures presented by Egerton and coauthors are a little bit lower than the ones by Bianchi *et al.*, but show the same basic trends with the major reduction in time use occurring from the 1960s to the 1970s (Egerton *et al.*, 2006, p. 58).

18 Employed wives might have used laundry services to a larger extent, however.

19 According to Lebergott (1993, p. 60), not only technical progress in washing machines enabled time savings in laundry washing. He posits that an important factor was simply the lower amounts of diapers to be cleaned with a decline in the number of children and the use of disposable diapers from 1900–1990 (for a similar argument, cf. Preece, 1990, p. 302). From the 1970s onward, the introduction and widespread use of permanent press fabric also played a role by substantially reducing the time spent ironing (Preece, 1990, p. 317).

20 The number of pieces washed per person per week doubled, both for farm households and urban households (Preece, 1990, p. 307).

21 Preece (1990, p. 303) points out that wearing a limited wardrobe is noticeable and that an increased number of activities may require different types of outfits.

22 These studies often treat time and labor input of the household as if they were the same thing, arguing that time input is a proxy for the input of human resources into housework activities (cf. Lovingood and McCullough, 1986). We have critically discussed this issue in Chapter 4.

23 In addition, based on the data collected here, we cannot exclude that the observed decline in time spent doing housework during the second half of the twentieth century has similarly taken place in households with employed wives and with full-time homemakers, as no information on employment status is given. If a similar development were the case, it would also require a proper explanation besides labor market commitments. Recall, however, the findings with regard to women's educational status, according to which higher education is correlated with a smaller reduction in housework hours (Aguiar and Hurst, 2007).

24 Certainly, a time lag in the diffusion of clothes washers might also have played a role but would not weaken the argument made here, as cleanliness standards have definitely and durably shifted upward (cf. Chapter 7).

25 Not only prices for washing machines show a long-term decline in real prices. The same trend holds for practically all household appliances since 1955 in the United States, i.e. dishwashers, refrigerators and entertainment appliances also (Burwell and Swezey, 1990).

References

Aguiar M., Hurst E. (2007): 'Measuring trends in leisure: The allocation of time over five decades', *Quarterly Journal of Economics*, 122 (3), pp. 969–1006.

Becker, G. S. (1965): 'A theory of the allocation of time', *The Economic Journal*, 75 (299), pp. 49–517.

Becker, G. S. (1991): *A Treatise on the Family*, Harvard University Press, Cambridge, MA.

Bellante, D., Foster, A. C. (1984): 'Working wives and expenditure on services', *Journal of Consumer Research*, 11, pp. 700–707.

Bianchi, S. M., Milkie, M. A., Sayer, L. C., Robinson, J. P. (2000): 'Is anyone doing the housework? Trends in the gender division of household labor', *Social Forces*, 79 (1), pp. 191–228.

Bittman, M., Mahmud, J., Wajcman, J. (2004): 'Appliances and their impact: The ownership of domestic technology and time spent on household work', *The British Journal of Sociology*, 55 (3), pp. 401–423.

Bowden, S., Offer, A. (1994): 'Household appliances and the use of time: The United States and Britain since the 1920s', *Economic History Review*, 47 (4), pp. 725–748.

Bryant, K. (1988): 'Durables and wives' employment yet again', *Journal of Consumer Research*, 15 (1), pp. 37–47.

Bryant, W. K. (1996): 'A comparison of the household work of married females; the mid 1920s and the late 1960s', *Family and Consumer Sciences Research Journal*, 24 (4), pp. 358–384.

Burwell, C. C., Swezey, B. G. (1990): 'The home: Evolving technologies for satisfying human wants', in Schur, S. H., Burwell, C. C., Devine, W. D. Jr., Sonenblum, S. (eds): *Electricity in the American Economy: Agent of Technological Progress, Contributions in Economics and Economic History*, Greenwood Press, New York.

Cohen, P. N. (1988): 'Replacing housework in the service economy: Gender, class and race-ethnicity in service spending', *Gender and Society*, 12 (2), pp. 219–231.

Cowan, R. S. (1976): 'The "industrial revolution" in the home: Household technology and social change in the 20th century', *Technology and Culture*, 17 (1), pp. 1–23.

Cowan, R. S. (1983): *More Work for Mother*, Basic Books, New York.

de Vries, J. (1994): 'The industrial revolution and the industrious revolution', *Journal of Economic History*, 54 (2), pp. 249–270.

Douglas, S. P. (1976): 'Cross-national comparisons and consumer stereo types: A case of working and non-working wives in the U.S. and France', *Journal of Consumer Research*, 3, pp. 12–20.

Egerton, M., Fisher, K., Gershuny, J. (2006): 'American time use 1965–2003: The construction of a historical comparative file, and consideration of its usefulness in the construction of extended national accounts for the USA', *Institute for Social and Economic Research Working Paper*, pp. 5–28.

EIA (2011): Annual Energy Review 2011, Energy Information Administration, Table 2.6 Household End Uses: Fuel Types, Appliances, and Electronics, Selected Years, 1978–2009; (http://www.eia.gov/totalenergy/data/annual/pdf/sec2_21.pdf, retrieved: 30.08.2016)

Foster, A. C., Abdel-Ghany, M., Ferguson, C. E. (1981): 'Wife's employment: Its influence on major family expenditures', *Journal of Consumer Studies and Home Economics*, 5, pp. 115–124.

Friedman, M. (1957): *A Theory of the Consumption Function*, Princeton University Press, Princeton, NJ.

Galbraith, J. K. (1973): *Economics and the Public Purpose*, Houghton Mifflin Co., Boston.

Giedion, S. (1948): *Mechanization Takes Command: A Contribution to Anonymous History*, Norton, New York.

Goldin, C. (1986): 'The Female Labor Force and American Economic Growth, 1890–1980', in Engerman, S. L., Gallman, R. E. (eds): *Long-Term Factors in American Economic Growth, Studies in Income and Wealth, No. 51*, University of Chicago Press, Chicago and London.

Gramm, W. L. (1974): 'The Demand for the Wife's Non-Market Time', *Southern Economic Journal*, 41 (1), pp. 124–133.

Hardyment, C. (1988): *From Mangle to Microwave: The Mechanization of Household Work*, Polity Press, Cambridge, United Kingdom.

Hartmann, H. I. (1974): *Capitalism and Women's Work in the Home, 1900–1930*, Dissertation, Yale University, CT.

Jara-Díaz, S. R. (2003): 'On the goods-activities technical relations in the time allocation theory', *Transportation*, 30, pp. 245–260.

Juster, F. T. (1985): 'A note on recent changes in time use', in Juster, F. T., Stafford, F. P. (eds.): *Time, Goods, and Well-Being*, University of Michigan, Ann Arbor, MI.

Juster, F. T., Stafford, F. P. (1991): 'The allocation of time: Empirical findings, behavioral models, and problems of measurement', *Journal of Economic Literature*, 29 (2), pp. 471–522.

Ketkar, S. L., Cho, W. (1982): 'Demographic Factors and the Pattern of Household Expenditures in the United States', *Atlantic Economic Journal*, pp. 16–27.

Key, R. (1990): 'Complementary and substitutability in family members' time allocated to household production activities', *Lifestyles: Family and Economic Issues*, 11 (3), pp. 225–256.

Kim, C. (1989): 'Working wives' time saving tendencies: Durable ownership, convenience food consumption, and meal purchases', *Journal of Economic Psychology*, 10, pp. 391–409.

Kinsey, J. (1983): 'Working wives and the marginal propensity to consume food away from home', *American Journal of Agricultural Economics*, 65 (1), pp. 10–19.

Klepp, I. G. (2003): 'Clothes and cleanliness', *Ethnologia Scandinavia*, 33, pp. 61–73.

Lebergott, S. (1993): *Pursuing Happiness: American Consumers in the Twentieth Century*, Princeton University Press, Princeton, NJ.

Linder, S. B. (1970): *The Harried Leisure Class*, Columbia University Press, New York and London.

Lovingood, R. P., McCullough, J. L. (1986): 'Appliance ownership and household work time', *Home Economics Research Journal*, 14 (3), pp. 326–335.

Matthews, G. (1987): *Just a Housewife, The Rise and Fall of Domesticity in America*, Oxford University Press, New York.

Michael, R. T., Becker G. S. (1973): 'On the new theory of consumer behavior', *Swedish Journal of Economics*, 75 (4), pp. 378–396.

Mincer, J. (1960): 'Employment and consumption', *Review of Economics and Statistics*, 42, pp. 20–26.

Mohun, A. P. (1999): *Steam Laundries: Gender, Technology, and Work in the United States and Great Britain, 1880–1940*, The Johns Hopkins University Press, Baltimore and London.

Mokyr, J. (2000), *The Gifts of Athena: Historical Origins of the Knowledge Economy*, Princeton University Press, Princeton, NJ.

Morgan, J., Baerwalt, N., Sirageldin, I. (1966): *Productive Americans*, Survey Research Center, University of Michigan, Ann Arbor, MI.

Nichols, S. Y., Fox, K. D. (1983): 'Buying time and saving time: Strategies for managing household production', *Journal of Consumer Research*, 10, pp. 197–208.

Nichols, S., Metzen, E. (1978): 'Housework time of husband and wife', *Home Economics Research Journal*, 7, pp. 85–97.

Oropesa, R. S. (1993): 'Female labor force participation and time saving household technology: A case study of the microwave from 1978 to 1989', *The Journal of Consumer Research*, 19 (4), pp. 567–579.

Pollak, R. A. (1969): 'Conditional demand functions and consumption theories', *Quarterly Journal of Economics*, 83, pp. 60–78.

Preece, A. G. (1990): Housework and American Standards of Living, 1920–1980, Ph.D. Dissertation, University of Berkeley, California.

Ramey V. A., Francis N. (2009): 'A century of work and leisure', *American Economic Journal Macroeconomics*, 1 (2), pp. 189–224.

Reid, M. G. (1934): *The Economics of Household Production*, John Wiley & Sons, Inc., New York.

Reilly, M. D. (1982): 'Working wives and convenience consumption', *Journal of Consumer Research*, 8 (4), pp. 407–418.

Robinson, J. P. (1980): 'Housework technology and household work', in Berk, S. F. (ed.): *Women and Household Labor*, Sage, Beverly Hills.

Robinson, J. P., Converse, P. E. (1972): 'Social change reflected in the use of time', in Campbell, A., Converse, P. E. (eds.): *The Human Meaning of Social Change*, Russell Sage Foundation, New York.

Robinson, J. P., Godbey, G. (1997): *Time for Life: The Surprising Ways Americans Use Their Time*, second edition, The Pennsylvania State University Press, University Park, PA.

Rubin, R. M., Riney, B. J., Molina, D. J. (1990): 'Expenditure Pattern Differentials Between One-Earner and Dual-Earner Households: 1972–1973 and 1984', *Journal of Consumer Research*, 17 (1), pp. 43–52.

Ruedenauer, I., Griesshammer, R. (2004): *Produkt-Nachhaltigkeitsanalyse von Waschmaschinen und Waschprozessen*, Oeko-Institut e.V., Freiburg, Germany.

Schaninger, C. M., Allen, C. T. (1981): 'Wife's occupational status as a consumer behavior construct', *The Journal of Consumer Research*, 8 (2), pp. 189–196.

Shelton, B. A. (1990): 'The distribution of household tasks: Does wife's employment status make a difference', *Journal of Family Issues*, 11, pp. 115–153.

Shelton, B. A. (1996): 'The division of household labor', *Annual Review of Sociology*, 22, pp. 299–322.

Shove, E. (2003a): 'Converging conventions of comfort, cleanliness and convenience', *Journal of Consumer Policy*, 26, pp. 395–418.

Shove, E. (2003b): *Comfort, Cleanliness and Convenience: The Social Organization of Normality*, Berg, Oxford and New York.

Soberon-Ferrer, H., Dardis, R. (1991): 'Determinants of household expenditures for services', *Journal of Consumer Research*, 17, pp. 385–397.

Spitze, G., Loscocco, K. (1999): 'Women's position in the household', *The Quarterly Review of Economics and Finance*, 39, pp. 647–666.

Stafford, F, Duncan, G. (1977): 'The use of time and technology by households in the United States' University of Michigan, Department of Economics.

Stafford, K. (1983): 'The Effects of Wife's Employment Time on Her Household Work Time', *Home Economics Research Journal*, 11 (3), pp. 257–266.

Strasser, S. (2000) [1982]: *Never Done: A History of American Housework*, Henry Holt and Company, New York.

Strober, M. H. (1977): 'Wives' labor force behavior and family consumption patterns', *American Economic Review*, 67 (1), pp. 410–417.

Strober, M. H., Weinberg, C. B. (1977): 'Working wives and major family expenditures', *The Journal of Consumer Research*, 4 (3), pp. 141–147.

Strober, M. H., Weinberg, C. B. (1980): 'Strategies used by working and nonworking wives to reduce time pressures', *The Journal of Consumer Research*, 6 (4), pp. 338–348.

Taylor, P., Funk, C., Clark, A. (2009): 'Luxury or necessity? Things we can't live without: the list has grown in the past decade', Working Paper, Pew Research Center, Washington D.C.

van der Lippe, T., Tijdens, K., De Ruijter, E. (2004): 'Outsourcing of domestic tasks and time saving effects', *Journal of Family Issues*, 25, pp. 216–240.

Vanek, J. (1974): 'Time spent in housework', *Scientific American*, 231, pp. 116–120.

Vickery, C. (1979): 'Women's economic contribution to the family', in Smith, R. E. (ed.): *The Subtle Revolution*, Urban Institute, Washington, DC.

Walker, K. (1955): *Homemaking Work Units of New York State Households*, Ph.D. Dissertation, Cornell University.

Walker, K. E., Woods, M. E. (1976): *Time Use: A Measure of Household Production of Family Goods and Services*, American Home Economics Ass., Washington, DC.

Weagley, R. O, Norum P.S. (1989): 'Household demand for market, purchased home producible commodities', *Family and Consumer Sciences Research Journal*, 18 (6), pp. 6–18.

Weinberg, C. B., Winer, R. S. (1983): 'Working Wives and Major Family Expenditures: Replication and Extension', *Journal of Consumer Research*, 10 (2), pp. 259–263.

Wiegand, E. (1953): Comparative Use of Time of Farm and City Full-Time Homemakers and Homemakers in the Labor Force in Relation to Home Management, Ph.D. Dissertation, Cornell University, NY.

Wilson, M. (1929): 'Time use by Oregon farm homemakers', *Oregon Agriculture Experiment Station Bulletin No. 256*, Oregon State Agricultural College, Corvallis, OR.

Witt, U. (2001): 'Learning to consume: A theory of wants and the growth of demand', *Journal of Evolutionary Economics*, 11, pp. 23–36.

Yang, S., Magrabi, F. M. (1989): 'Expenditures for services, wife's employment, and other household characteristics', *Home Economics Research Journal*, 18, pp. 133–147.

7 Cleanliness Consumption and the Rebound Effect of Energy Efficiency

7.1 Introduction

The technological means of doing the laundry have been substantially transformed over the past 200 years (cf. Giedion, 1948; Hardyment, 1988; Strasser, 2000[1982]; cf. Chapter 4). At the beginning of the twentieth century, not even one out of ten U.S. families possessed a washing machine, while practically all households had to deal with scrubboards and tubs, which made clothes washing a highly detested, time- and physical labor-consuming task (e.g. Cowan, 1983; Giedion, 1948; Hardyment, 1988). Given that hardly any tools were available for doing the laundry back then except a simple washboard and homemade soap, and that all water had to be carried into and out of the house, it is no surprise to learn that clean clothes were not paid much attention to by the majority of consumers (cf. Chapter 3). In fact, consumers possessed few clothes and changed them regularly only for the Sunday visit to the church (Strasser, 2000[1982], p. 106). At the same time, there were also wealthy middle-class households who outperformed the majority of consumers in terms of financial resources and cleanliness of appearance (Ashenburg, 2007, p. 169). These levels of cleanliness, however, were not the result of their own labor; instead, well-to-do households usually outsourced this task to domestic servants or washerwomen (cf. Chapter 4).

Over the course of time, laundry equipment became more advanced, going through four distinct phases of technological progress, beginning with 'Blue Monday' (nineteenth century) to mechanization (end of the nineteenth century), electrification (around 1915) and automation (around 1940) (cf. Chapter 4). At present, four out of five U.S. households own an electric, automatic washing machine (EIA, 2011), which, in comparison with the nineteenth-century conditions, makes not only time savings, but more importantly, substantial reductions in physical effort feasible ('drudgery'). Hence, laundry washing can no longer be called 'backbreaking labor' today (Buehr, 1965, p. 61). While nineteenth-century consumers did face a trade-off between wanting clean clothes on one side but having to take into account drudgery on the other, due to modern laundry equipment, no such trade-off exists at present.[1]

With the proliferation of technically advanced washing machines during the twentieth century, households' levels of cleanliness have changed substantially and consumers have increased the amount of clothes washed (e.g. Cowan, 1983; Klepp, 2003; Shove, 2003a; Silberzahn-Jandt, 1991; Strasser, 2000[1982]; Preece, 1990). Already, with the advent of the electricity-driven washing machine in the 1920s, clothes were changed more often (Hewes, 1930; Strasser, 2000 [1982], p. 268; Wilson, 1929) – a trend that has continued for quite some time in the twentieth century. U.S. consumers nowadays wash about three times the amount that was common in the 1950s (Shove, 2003b). Similar developments have taken place in other industrialized countries.[2] That the mechanization of the home went hand in hand with rising household standards is by now commonplace in the sociological literature (e.g. Fine, 1999; Robinson, 1980; Schor, 1991, p. 89; Strasser, 2000 [1982]). It was through the influential book by Ruth Schwartz Cowan (1983) that the increase in household standards in general, including standards of cleanliness, came to attention – referred to as the 'Cowan paradox'.[3] In addition, consumers nowadays display fairly similar standards of cleanliness. This assimilation of cleanliness standards between consumer groups of different financial strengths was contingent upon technological progress: not only did less well-to-do consumers lack the financial means to pay servants for their support in housekeeping, but even with growing income there would not have been sufficient human labor (i.e. workers) to achieve these higher standards for everyone.[4]

This past co-development of technological progress in washing machines and rising laundry quantities can be interpreted as a 'rebound effect'. In most general terms, rebound effects can be defined as the consumption of a resource (e.g. fuel) or the use of a technology in response to technological progress. In a more narrow sense, the term has been coined in energy economics to depict the response of consumer behavior to energy-efficiency progress, by which technically feasible energy savings are partly being offset. The possibility of the rebound effect has triggered a debate in energy economics concerning the usefulness of the promotion of energy-efficiency progress for lowering energy consumption. In view of this debate, rebound effects have primarily been treated as an empirical question. In contrast to that, progress in theoretical research has been rather modest. The neoclassical model of consumer behavior is the frame of reference for micro-level analyses. It views efficiency progress as a decrease in a product's utilization costs and analyzes behavioral responses through the lens of the price elasticity of demand. However, although utilization patterns for more efficient domestic appliances are likely to reflect consumer price sensitivity to a certain extent, focusing on relative prices alone, i.e. decreasing product utilization costs, might be too limited a perspective.

In view of energy requirements and the widespread diffusion of washing machines, these devices have also come into focus of policy attention, including the use of energy-efficiency labels. Promoting the diffusion of more energy-efficient washing machines need not be an effective energy-saving policy, however, when consumers come to utilize washing machines more often. As washing machines are an example of continuous technological progress throughout the twentieth century, having coincided with a growth in laundry amounts, the occurrence of rebound effects as a consequence of further efficiency improvements is a plausible scenario.

In this chapter, we seek to evaluate whether further energy-efficiency improvements in washing machines are likely to be accompanied by take-back effects. We analyze this issue from a theoretical perspective, not within the established frame of reference but from the perspective of a needs-based account of consumption behavior, namely the theory of learning consumers (Witt, 2001; cf. Chapter 2). More precisely, while analyzing the case of washing machines in particular, we also argue for a broadening of the theoretical basis of rebound analysis in general. We posit that consumption theories dealing with consumer needs and consumer learning processes can fruitfully add to the insights derived from the neoclassical model. To that end, we integrate the concepts of consumer needs and their satiation properties into the body of literature on rebound effects. In fact, we view the rebound effect on energy-efficiency progress as a special case of behavioral reactions to technological progress more in general, which are contingent on consumer needs that are not yet satiated with regard to a specific consumption activity.

This chapter contains six sections. The theoretical background of – and empirical evidence on – rebound effects are presented in more detail in the next section (Section 7.2). Therein, we also identify the research gap in the literature, i.e. the neglect of saturation effects in demand. In Section 7.3, we show how the concepts of consumer needs and their satiation properties can be integrated into an analysis of the rebound effect, and we derive the core hypotheses of this analysis. Section 7.4 repeats some core background information on the case study of clothes washing. Afterward, we study the satiation properties of the needs associated with laundry washing and discuss whether the future occurrence of rebound effects is a plausible scenario (Section 7.5). Section 7.6 concludes this chapter.

7.2 The Rebound Effect of Energy Efficiency

7.2.1 Theory and Evidence

In this section, we describe how rebound effects have been defined and analyzed from the perspective of neoclassical consumer theory, which is the conventional approach in the literature. Moreover, we identify which questions are left open in that approach.

In most general terms, rebound effects could be defined as the consumption of a resource or the use of a technology in response to technological progress, namely efficiency improvements. In the literature, the term rebound has been coined to describe the case that energy savings, as predicted by engineering analysis, do not occur, as energy-efficiency improvements are accompanied by a more intensive use of fuel or the respective energy-using technology (e.g. Brookes, 1978; Khazzoom, 1980; Khazzoom, 1987). In short, rebound describes the discrepancy between potential and actual energy savings, which stems from behavioral reactions in contrast to keeping the status quo. It is usually measured as a percentage of the savings predicted by engineering (Madlener and Alcott, 2009, p. 370).

Different types of rebound effects are distinguished, depending on the scope of research, i.e. micro- or macro-level analyses (see, for example, Herring and Roy, 2007). Economy-wide effects are also termed the 'Jevons' paradox' (e.g. Polimeni and Polimeni, 2006). Direct and indirect rebound effects are micro-level phenomena (e.g. Madlener and Alcott, 2009), which have been discussed in the context of production processes (Birol and Keppler, 2000) and consumption behavior (Berkhout *et al.*, 2000). Let us focus on the consumption side. Direct effects concern one consumption activity, such as laundry washing, in isolation. Indirect effects denote growth in the use of energy services in other consumption contexts, hence changes in the demand for other goods. To study indirect effects, more than one consumption activity has to be taken into account. Whether indirect effects occur depends on the relative resource intensity of the respective consumption activities and the direction of change (Berkhout *et al.*, 2000). Our case study analysis is confined to direct micro-level effects in consumer behavior (synonymously: household behavior).[5]

The engineering definition of the direct rebound effect is an efficiency elasticity of demand, whereas the economic literature usually conceptualizes it as a price elasticity of demand, i.e. a change in the price of energy services followed by a change in behavior (Sorrel and Dimitropoulos, 2008). We are interested in the economic interpretation. Two kinds of price elasticities of demand have to be distinguished: a) with regard to a unit of energy input, and b) with regard to energy services, i.e. 'useful work' obtained from one unit of energy input. Note that the concept of 'energy services' is central to the arguments. Several scholars have pointed out that energy is not wanted for itself but for the 'useful' services it can provide when consumed jointly with other equipment (cf. Berkhout *et al.*, 2000; Binswanger, 2004; Buenstorf, 2004; Davis, 2008; Shove, 2003c).

The theoretical frame of reference for rebound analysis is the neoclassical model of consumer behavior with its assumptions of complete information, optimization and nonsatiation. From this perspective, rebound effects look as follows. Consider efficiency improvements in washing machines, leaving capital costs aside for now. Through efficiency improvements, the effective price of the particular energy service offered by this equipment – namely cleaning a given amount of clothes – is reduced. Or, to use the terminology of the household production function approach (Becker, 1965; cf. Chapter 2), the 'shadow price' of clean clothes is lowered. When the costs of energy services – and hence the total costs of production – fall, more energy-using outputs, i.e. clean clothes, can be afforded at no additional costs (direct effect). Alternatively, the realized savings can be employed to raise the consumption of other (energy-using) goods (indirect effect). Depending on the shapes of the indifference curves, a rational consumer would adjust his or her consumption patterns in one way or another.

But let us focus on direct effects. From the perspective of neoclassical consumer theory, the actual occurrence of the direct rebound effect is not a surprising event, be it with regard to more energy-efficient washing machines, the example depicted here, or any other electricity-driven household appliance. This change of behavior might be reflected in aggregate demand also (Khazzoom, 1980, p. 22):

[A]s long as the price elasticity of demand [...] is not zero, we may reasonably expect the impact of improved efficiency to be an upward pressure on demand.

At the same time, it is also plausible that a direct effect fails to appear. Regarding the interrelation between the efficiency of a household appliance and its utilization rate, Khazzoom (1980) has put forth the following conjecture. He maintains that the elasticity of the utilization rate with respect to the own appliance efficiency is positively correlated with the given intensity of utilization and will 'approach zero as the utilization rate approaches 100 per cent'. This relationship can be represented in the form of a sigmoid curve, depicting the utilization intensity of a durable good as a function of its efficiency. In other words, when household appliances become more (energy) efficient, they will be used more intensively – however, only up to the specific point where the utilization rate reaches it maximum.

The possibility of the rebound effect has triggered a debate in energy economics concerning the usefulness of the promotion of efficiency progress. Birol and Keppler (2000, p. 462), for example, articulate the positive side of the rebound effect as a driver of economic growth. Other scholars raise skepticism against technological progress and 'technological optimism', as such (cf. Postman, 1993; Salmon, 1977). They argue, partly without recourse to the rebound literature, that it makes much more sense to change consumer expectations concerning 'normal' standards of living (e.g. Chappells and Shove, 2005; Rudin, 2000; Shove, 2003a) and that efficiency programs are a waste of resources (Rudin, 2000). Shove (2003c, p. 195) even claims that consumer expectations are contingent on technological possibilities and that consumers tend to take for granted the standards of living made possible with technological advances. In view of this debate, it is not surprising that, up to now, rebound effects have primarily been treated as an empirical question so to assess the magnitude of the problem in the first place. In simple terms, if it could be shown that such effects do not occur, one might come to a positive assessment of technological progress as a strategy to cope with depleting natural resources.

Quite a few studies from the 1980s onward deal with an empirical assessment of the rebound effect. Microeconomic studies are probably more common than macroeconomic analyses.[6] Estimates of the direct effect have primarily taken historical and cross-sectional data to study the price elasticity of demand to changing energy prices (e.g. Berkhout *et al.*, 2000; Roy, 2000). The magnitudes of estimated take-back effects vary significantly depending on the definition, i.e. the boundaries of the phenomenon studied. The classical example is efficiency progress regarding cars, a case for which rebound effects have indeed been detected (e.g. de Haan *et al.*, 2006; Greene, 1992; Khazzoom, 1980). Only a few studies deal with household appliances, and if they do, they usually analyze space heating or cooling systems and refrigerators, finding medium size direct effects, i.e. estimates from 10–30 per cent for space heating and in the range of 10–50 per cent for cooling appliances (Greening *et al.*, 2000; Khazzoom, 1987). Some scholars evaluate the magnitude of rebound effects as rather moderate, anyway (e.g. Berkhout *et al.*, 2000; Schipper and Grubb, 2000).

In order to explain why rebound effects are likely to occur in one case but not in another, some arguments have been put forth. It has been pointed out that, for an assessment of the rebound, capital costs of durable goods have to be taken into account (e.g. Madlener and Alcott, 2009; Sorrell and Dimitropoulos, 2008). When more efficient technology is more expensive than devices with comparable product characteristics but a lower efficiency level, the actual reduction in the effective price of energy services turns out to be much smaller than would otherwise calculate. Thus, estimates for the rebound effect – neglecting capital costs – might be biased in terms of overestimating the effect (Sorrell and Dimitropoulos, 2008). In addition to that, the consumer's purpose might play a role. Consumers might buy more efficient products in an anticipatory manner because they plan to use them more (endogeneity problem). In such a situation, the decline in the price of energy services does not 'induce' the consumer to utilize the device more intensively – the demand is already there. Moreover, that the more efficient product might be more expensive is not 'an obstacle' to a higher utilization rate. A similar argument has been brought forth in the context of time saving appliances, where households have been shown to purchase such products, particularly when the family is expanding (e.g. Morgan *et al.*, 1966).

These arguments are certainly relevant and provide some insights into the occurrence of rebound effects. As they remain within the neoclassical framework they are valid irrespective of the consumption activity studied. They might not be sufficient, however, to come to a deeper understanding of what is driving the consumption of specific goods and services.

7.2.2 Limitations

Per definition, the rebound effect describes the case whereby consumers utilize energy-driven products more intensively when those become more energy efficient. Within the neoclassical model, this behavioral response is explained as a reaction to a drop in the product's utilization costs (when taking higher capital costs into account, this might only hold over the entire lifespan of a product). That consumers do realize this decrease in the effective price of energy services is quite plausible in view of the use of energy-efficiency labels for many products. Still, a few general points can be criticized about the treatment of rebound effects within a neoclassical frame of analysis, beginning with the assumptions of optimization and complete information. Optimal responses to changes in the effective price of energy services imply that the consumer can assess the energy savings resulting from efficiency progress in a product, *a*, as well as the additional costs of consuming more of product *a* or of another product, *b*. Certainly, the more 'intelligent' household appliances become, particularly by including feedback and sensor devices (e.g. Abrahamse *et al.*, 2005; McCalley, 2006), the closer consumers might come to understanding such technical aspects and taking optimal actions.[7] However, the energy costs of utilizing certain products cannot easily be identified; from the perspective of the consumer they are usually hidden as a part of the monthly energy bill. Likewise, the price of energy services offered by a specific product cannot easily be assessed (Berkhout *et al.*, 2000). As a more realistic assumption, energy-efficiency improvements might induce some sort of behavioral responses but those need not be the result of a detailed calculus.

A further substantial shortcoming of the neoclassical framework is its narrow focus in the context of changing relative prices and changes in behavior. The neoclassical analysis of rebound effects remains purely at the technological level and analyzes consumption goods in their ability to enhance the efficiency of consumption processes: according to this rationale, consumers should always appreciate and purchase more efficient energy-using products, as those allow expanding product utilization at no additional cost (nonsatiation assumption). But correlation should not be confounded with causality. Despite a certain 'co-movement' of effective prices and consumption patterns in the past (which empirical studies might detect), observable changes in consumption patterns might truly have to be attributed to driving forces other than consumers recognizing a drop in product utilization costs. Given that the rebound effect is measured as the gap between potential and actual energy savings, it can in principle include other effects as well, which happen *in parallel* with technological advances.

More importantly, the theoretical model lacks the treatment of saturation levels of demand. Recall the aforementioned postulate by Khazzoom (1980), according to which the occurrence of rebound effects is contingent upon the utilization rate of a respective appliance prior to efficiency progress. What is the possible upper limit of the utilization rate of a given appliance? Is this merely a technical question or do other factors have to be taken into account? How can the gap between the present and the maximum utilization rate be determined? Certainly, the relative utilization rate could be measured as a technical feature of the domestic appliance in question. Let, for example, the maximum utilization rate of a heating system correspond to its use at maximum temperature throughout the winter. A relative utilization rate of 50 per cent would hence mean that the heating is switched on only every second day during winter. Such an approach is not very helpful, however, given that many household appliances will probably be used at levels way below their technical maximum, even if utilization became practically free of costs. Our central point is that the study of rebound effects would gain substantially when saturation levels of demand were taken into account, i.e. the intensity of product utilization where the own price elasticity becomes zero. The issue of saturation has been neglected in research up to now, although several scholars have emphasized its relevance (e.g. Greening *et al.* 2000; Madlener and Alcott, 2009). Madlener and Alcott (2009, p. 374) point out, nearly thirty years after Khazzoom's seminal contribution:

> Energy efficiency enables (but does not always implicate) greater energy consumption; hence our analyses must include 'the consumer'. That is, saturation or any deliberate decision to abstain from additional consumption (sufficiency strategy) does lower rebound, rendering large rebound effects [...] by no means an unavoidable consequence.

By taking saturation effects into account, a better assessment of direction and scope of behavioral responses to an effective price change would be feasible. The neoclassical framework does not allow statements to be made about whether the direct rebound effect might or might not occur, as consumer motivations remain a 'black box' (for a more detailed discussion, cf. Chapter 2) Scholarly research on rebound effects has not yet extended the theoretical underpinnings of consumer behavior beyond neoclassical theory.[8] We make a modest attempt here to fill this lacuna. In order to come to terms with the concept of demand saturation, we suggest turning to a needs–based account of consumption behavior, the theory of learning consumers (Witt, 2001) introduced in Chapter 2. With the concepts of consumer needs and their satiation properties, this account opens up a conceptual and theoretical path toward the analysis of demand saturation. In addition to that, it deals with changes in consumer behavior for causes other than changing relative prices. To these issues, we turn in the next section.

7.3 Consumption Behavior from a Needs–Based Perspective

7.3.1 Needs and Their Satiation Properties as Basic Concepts

The consideration of saturation effects in the analysis of the rebound has been identified as one of the core issues of research. Khazzoom (1980) already pointed out that the relative utilization rate of a device previous to technological improvement will affect the behavioral response to efficiency progress. However, he did not define the central concept of the relative utilization rate further. Drawing upon the theory of learning consumers by Witt (2001), we suggest tackling the phenomenon of demand saturation with the concepts of basic consumer needs and their levels of satiation. We hypothesize that the *direct rebound effect* will only occur when the needs appealed to by a specific consumption activity are not yet satiated. The approach we suggest is twofold: first, the consumer needs which have driven the past development of a specific consumption activity are to be identified. In a second step, the future dynamics of these needs have to be assessed, while considering potential moments of satiation. We exemplarily depict how to tackle this issue for the case study of cleanliness consumption, i.e. more energy-efficient washing machines. Note that the approach put forth here to study the occurrence of take-back effects is not confined to this context. It can be applied to analyze more in general whether changes in the material conditions of specific consumption activities are followed by consumption growth in that exact activity. In this reading, the rebound effect on energy-efficiency progress is a special case of behavioral responses to technological progress in consumption activities more in general.

The theory of learning consumers has been presented in much detail in Chapter 2. Let us summarize only the most relevant points here. Witt's account differs from neoclassical consumer theory – to date, the theoretical benchmark of rebound analysis – in two decisive points. First, Witt puts forth a framework with which the role of consumer motivations for changing consumption patterns can be analyzed in a systematic manner. It is the feedback between the evolution of products on one side and the evolution of motivations for consuming certain products on the other that is examined in order to understand consumption growth. Second, the theory deviates from the nonsatiation assumption. It acknowledges that consumers might be temporarily satiated with regard to certain needs in a specific consumption activity and analyzes the conditions under which such satiation levels would shift.

More precisely, the theory of learning consumers assumes consumer behavior to be directed toward the satisfaction of basic needs. Through their basic needs, individuals are motivated to engage in consumptive activities. Need satisfaction is achieved by the consumption of specific goods and services of appropriate quality and quantity. This means that, in principle, a specific – yet temporary – satiation level exists for each need, which can be reached by appropriate consumption activities. Subsequent acts of consumption for that exact activity are motivated when deviations of inner physiological or psychological states from that temporary satiation level (re)occur.[9] The important point is that consumers are not assumed to have a priori knowledge about the suitability of consumption activities for need satisfaction (i.e. about their usefulness). On the contrary, associations between consumption activities on one side and the removal of deprivation states on the other have to be learned over the course of a consumer's life. The theory of learning consumers differentiates between several types of learning processes, namely noncognitive versus cognitive forms of learning and individual as opposed to social learning processes (Witt, 2001; cf. Chapter 2). Although the need satisfaction property is, in principle, an objective attribute of a product, it still has to be explored by the consumer first. In addition to that, consumers develop beliefs concerning appropriate consumption levels of certain goods and services.

For several reasons, the need satisfaction capacity to be discovered is not an entirely subjective matter. First, the common genetic basis which humans share makes some products more suitable for need satisfaction than others, which will hold for all consumers alike. Second, similarities in learning processes emerge whenever consumers encounter similar sources of information – including a certain homogenization of beliefs in intensively interacting consumer groups. And finally, the satisfaction of the need for social recognition depends upon carrying out particular, socially agreed-upon forms of consumption behavior. While levels of need satisfaction, which can be achieved by consuming a given product quantity and quality, can in principle differ between consumers, despite their common genetic background – namely for different individual experiences – there exists homogeneity with respect to the need for social recognition as it is based on socially agreed-upon signals or standards, implying specific consumption patterns. In other words, in order to receive social recognition, for example, by complying with social norms, consumers have to consume a 'prescribed' product quality and quantity (cf. Chapter 3). Because of these regularities and objective properties of consumer behavior, the needs-based account lends itself to making some general statements about the occurrence of rebound effects.

7.3.2 Drivers behind Changing Consumption Patterns

Consumption activities are motivated by deprivation states of basic needs and are directed toward satisfying the needs appealed to. At a given point in time, consumption patterns reflect the individual and social learning processes that have taken place up to that point. Given the continuous appearance of new or qualitatively modified (i.e. technically advanced) products on the market, consumer exploration processes as to the usefulness of specific consumption activities do not come to a halt. Instead, they are constantly taking place and alter the means-ends-relationships between basic needs on one side and consumption activities on the other. As a result of such consumer-side learning processes, the patterns of consumption are malleable in the long run. While some products might disappear from the market, other products might witness consumption growth. Witt's account identifies three major types of causes that lead to upward shifts in specific consumption activities (Witt, 2001):

1   Consumption activities become newly associated with a not yet satiated need (condition [1]).
2   By product innovation, i.e. technological progress, the satiating component of a consumption activity is reduced or eliminated (condition [2]).
3   The consumption level required for receiving social recognition increases as a result of social learning processes (condition [3]).

Let us take a closer look at these driving forces. Condition [1] describes the case of a changing means-end-relationship as a result of a learning process. To be precise, the consumer discovers that a specific consumption activity appeals to an additional consumer need. Such a new association might come about by more 'bottom-up' consumer-side exploration processes, for example, individual, noncognitive learning processes. In addition, the new association might be established 'top-down' as a supply side strategy, coming about by advertising or other forms of social-cognitive learning processes. By relating a consumption activity to a further not yet satiated consumer need, a 'combination good' will emerge which might give rise to an increase in consumption. Witt (2001) depicts this interrelation as follows (Witt 2001, p. 32):

> Product innovations are brought to the market [...] intended to appeal to several wants [i.e. needs; *the author*] at the same time. Products serving a combination of wants have the following property. When approaching the level of satiation the motivation to consume a direct input vanishes unless the act of consumption is simultaneously serving other, not yet satiated, innate wants. If a combination good c appeals to several wants, and if some of them are not yet satiated at a certain consumption level, or cannot so easily be satiated, a sufficient motivation for continuing to consume good c may therefore [...] be maintained.

As a further supply-side strategy, the 'satiating component' of a product might be reduced or eliminated by technical modification (condition [2]). For food-stuff, for example, this means diminishing the caloric content of the product, thus reducing the feeling of satiety and allowing for an increase in consumption (Manig and Moneta, 2014; Ruprecht, 2005). In a very general perspective, this case might include the modification of aspects of a consumption activity that would otherwise effectively hinder consumption beyond a certain level as it goes against a basic behavioral tendency.

Finally, social learning can alter consumption patterns as consumption activities appealing to social recognition are intertwined with the behavior of other consumers (condition [3]): whenever a sufficient number of consumers and/or a few – but influential – consumers change their behavior in socially relevant activities, other consumers will also have to modify their actions in order to continue satisfying the need for social recognition (cf. Chapter 3). Possibly higher consumption levels or more sophisticated forms of consumption behavior have to be demonstrated to be a socially respected person. According to Witt (2001), social recognition in particular is a need that is 'hard to satiate'.

To sum this up, the level of consumption of a certain product at which specific consumer needs will be satisfied can undergo changes over time. Satiation levels might shift upward as well as downward as a consequence of product innovation (including technological progress) and consumer learning processes. Applying the arguments laid out here to the analysis of rebound effects, it has to be examined, first, which needs relate to the energy-using product in question, and second, what the basic satiation properties of these needs are. Naturally, the satiation level of a need is, in most cases, a nonobservable theoretical construct. However, the motivations that are related to a specific consumption activity can be learned from surveys (for the case analyzed here, clothes washing, both the inputs in their physical form as well as the output of this consumption activity are measurable entities). Based on this, some tentative conclusions can be drawn on how far energy-efficiency progress is likely to translate into consumption growth. The following hypotheses sum up these ideas:

> H.7.1: Technological progress in consumption activities being followed by upward shifts in consumption patterns can result from consumer learning processes concerning the usefulness of the consumption activity for need satisfaction (Shift Hypothesis).

> H.7.2: Direct rebound effects as a reaction to technological progress in a consumption activity will only occur when the consumer needs appealed to by this consumption activity are not yet satiated (Satiation Hypothesis).

We come back to these hypotheses in Section 7.5 when analyzing the satiation properties of the needs with which the consumption activity of clothes washing is associated. In the following section, we briefly summarize some basic information about the case study of cleanliness consumption.

7.4 The Case Study of Cleanliness Consumption

In this section, we summarize some background information and key figures about the consumption of cleanliness. Recall that we defined cleanliness consumption in the form of clean clothes as the outcome of the household production process of laundry washing, assuming that clean clothes have instrumental value for the household's ultimate goals – referred to as 'commodities' by Gary Becker and conceptualized here as basic consumer needs (cf. Chapter 2). With the term 'cleanliness consumption', we depicted the inputs into this household production process, i.e. expenditures on both consumer goods and services as well as the utilization of the respective goods. As such, it contains the acquisition of washing machines, expenditures on soap or detergents and the utilization of the respective products, particularly the utilization of washing machines as reflected in laundry quantities and time use patterns.

At present, the majority of households in industrialized countries use washing machines to ensure cleanliness. In the United States, the diffusion degree of this device amounts to about 83 per cent, pointing to a saturated market (EIA, 2011). Even higher ownership levels hold for the United Kingdom and Germany, for instance.[10] Replacement purchases are rarely made. With a potential of about 1,840 washing cycles per machine and three to four washes per week, a washing machine will last around 10 years, 15 years at most. In contrast to the situation at the beginning of the twentieth century, the market for washing machines shows a high standardization of products at present (cf. Chapter 4). By and large, washing machines are nowadays electric and automatic devices, allowing for substantial reductions in physical effort and time as opposed to washing clothes by hand or with less modern equipment. Still, some variety of washer models is available, i.e. top- and front-loaders, electric versus gas-driven washers, smaller and larger devices and so on. Countries differ in terms of the most common type of washing machine. Top-loaders, for example, are rarely purchased in Germany, while they are very common in the United States (EIA, 2011). Despite permanent technological progress in this complex product, prices of washing machines show a downward trend (Dale *et al.*, 2009; Ellis *et al.*, 2007). Interestingly, washing machines have been characterized as a 'necessity' in U.S. consumer polls since 1972, meaning that this good has become essential to consumers (Taylor *et al.*, 2009).

With washing machines becoming more widespread among the U.S. population, the time spent doing the laundry has substantially decreased from *circa* 7 hours in 1900 to *circa* 2 hours in 1995 (cf. Chapter 6). In parallel, consumers have increased the amount of clothes washed (cf. Chapter 6). These increasing laundry amounts are reflected in a significant growth in the consumption of soap and detergents in the United States. In 1960, the per capita consumption of soap, detergents and cleaning compounds amounted to about 12.8 kg, while 20.2 kg and 30.1 kg were consumed in 1970 and 1980, respectively (Henkel Survey, 1984).[11] Similar trends hold for Europe (Henkel Survey, 1984).

Over the last decades of the twentieth century, consumption growth has decelerated. More recent figures from the U.S. Consumer Expenditure Survey show that expenditures on laundry and cleaning supplies have been rather constant from the year 2000 onward (cf. Figure 7.1). In addition, the time U.S. households spend doing the laundry ('clothes maintenance') did not change

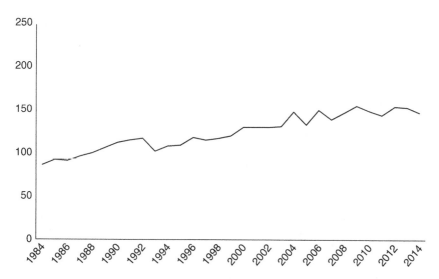

Figure 7.1 Expenditures on Laundry and Cleaning Supplies.

Source: Bureau of Labor Statistics (cf. http://www.bls.gov/cex/csxstnd.htm; retrieved 25.09.2016).

Notes: Average annual expenditures in U.S. dollars (Consumer Expenditure Survey).

much between 1970 and 2003 (Egerton *et al.*, 2006). Similar trends hold for other industrialized countries.[12] Recent replacements of washing machines by U.S. consumers, particularly top-loaders by front-loaders, have been motivated by achievable savings of water and energy, while improvements in cleanliness play only a minor role (Hustvedt *et al.*, 2013).

The largest share of available washing machines is electricity-driven. During the process of laundering itself, energy is used for water heating and agitating the clothes. The higher the temperature chosen, the more energy is required (Ruedenauer and Griesshammer, 2004). For washing machines, the utilization phase is attributed with the major environmental impact by life-cycle assessments, i.e. neither the production phase nor the phase of waste disposal (Sammer and Wuestenhagen, 2006). Over the years, the energy requirements of washing machines have been substantially reduced, but not all devices have reached the same degree of energy efficiency. By and large, more efficient clothes washers are more expensive than comparable, but less efficient, machines (Faberi, 2007; Mebane, 2007). Because of the achievable energy savings, these higher investment costs pay off during the life span of a product (Jaffe and Stavins, 1994).

Current sustainability policies and legislation show a strong emphasis on efficiency progress in energy-using consumer products, i.e. product differentiation along the characteristics of environment friendliness. Also, washing machines have been at the center of policy attention (for an overview, cf. Hustvedt, 2011). A labeling scheme indicating the relative efficiency of these devices has already been introduced in the United States and the European Union.[13] By highlighting the energy requirements of particular clothes washers, consumers are informed about this technical characteristic and enabled to take it into account more easily when deciding about the purchase of a new device.

In view of the energy requirements of clothes washing, the widespread diffusion of these devices and the policy objective of energy savings, it is not surprising that public policies regulate this consumption activity. However, the promotion of efficiency improvements in washing machines need not be an effective policy. With these devices becoming more energy efficient, consumers might use them more intensively, thus producing rebound effects which lower the energy savings made feasible by technological progress. We are aware of only one study that examined the rebound effect with regard to washing machines (Davis, 2008). In a field experiment, a group of households became (exogenously) equipped with more efficient devices, i.e. washing machines were replaced free of charge with more efficient variants. With his approach, Davis (2008) could control for the endogeneity problem in appliance adoption and extract the price effect only.[14] As a result of this replacement, washing machines were not used more intensively. More precisely, Davis (2008) estimated a very small price elasticity of demand, arguing that the price sensitivity of consumers is apparently not that strong.[15] This finding could hint to the fact that a direct rebound effect in the narrow sense might not occur.

We might come to a different conclusion, however, when taking into consideration the past historical development of cleanliness consumption. In fact, when interpreting the time and physical labor savings made feasible with technological progress as a reduction in the relative utilization costs of washing machines (or as a decline in the shadow price of clean clothes), the past co-development of technological progress in washing machines and rising laundry quantities could be interpreted as a rebound effect in a more general sense.[16] In view of this interpretation, the promotion of efficiency progress in washing machines might not be an adequate policy tool for actually achieving energy savings, as consumers appear to react to declining (shadow) prices.

However, this perspective neglects an important point. Although technological progress reducing the input of time and labor into the household production of cleanliness has coincided with an upward shift in cleanliness consumption, it still has to be explained why consumers also *wanted to increase* the levels of cleanliness. The arguments laid out so far leave aside this very central issue as they do not contain a reference to the consumer motivations for carrying out the activity of clothes washing in the first place. We argued that an improved understanding of the historical processes and the future occurrence of rebound effects is achieved when taking into account the consumer needs underlying cleanliness consumption as such. As these motivations will not necessarily trigger further consumption growth, the satiation properties of these needs also have to be studied. The next section deals with the basic needs involved in clothes washing and shows that, in the past, conditions favorable to an increase in cleanliness consumption have existed.

7.5 Basic Needs as Drivers behind Cleanliness Consumption Patterns

7.5.1 Past Evolution of Cleanliness Consumption Patterns

We have argued that the description and interpretation of past consumption developments is an important element of the analysis of the rebound effect as it provides a deeper understanding of the respective consumption activity. In Section 7.1, we gave a stylized overview of the evolution of cleanliness consumption in the United States over the past 150 years. Let us now trace back the evolution of the demand for cleanliness to the innate motives that have been associated with cleanliness consumption. In the previous chapters, we have identified three basic needs as being associated with doing laundry (cf. Chapters 3–6): the need for a healthy, pain-free body, the need for social recognition and the behavioral tendency to avoid heavy physical effort. Note that we leave aside here the motive of time substitution, which did play a role in the development of cleanliness consumption (cf. Chapters 4–6) but is not a basic human need (cf. Chapter 2). Let us briefly summarize the insights gathered so far, beginning with the disposition of drudgery avoidance.

In the nineteenth century, the then-prevailing technique of laundry washing with only the simplest equipment of washboard and tub and the accompanying physical strain made consumers associate cleanliness with painful physical effort (cf. Chapter 4). As the avoidance of such physical pain is an innate behavioral tendency, doing laundry put consumers in a situation of conflict between wanting a clean appearance on the one hand and experiencing drudgery on the other. The drudgery involved in clothes washing clearly was a limiting factor which held cleanliness levels low for the majority of consumers who could not outsource this task. With technological progress, i.e. modern washing machines allowing for physical labor savings, the factor that inhibited the consumption of cleanliness has been eliminated, enabling an increase in consumption, particularly higher laundry amounts (condition [2]). As no such limiting factor exists at present, the trade-off between clean clothes on one side and drudgery avoidance on the other has also been eliminated. Thus, consumers learned to associate the use of washing machines with drudgery avoidance. In more recent times, the drudgery avoidance tendency no longer functions as a motivation for purchasing washing machines; washing machine advertisements no longer appeal to this motive (cf. Chapter 5).

Let us now turn to the need for health. That the washing of clothes and other textiles is a means for achieving hygiene via disinfection is common knowledge today, not only in the medical field but among the general public also. However, what is self-evident today was not that clear 150 or 200 years ago. In fact, the connection between cleanliness of clothes on one side and the avoidance of illness on the other emerged only in the nineteenth century as a consequence of an enhanced understanding of the causes and transmission channels of infectious diseases (cf. Chapter 3). This was a breakthrough in scientific knowledge that became known to the public via social-cognitive learning processes. More precisely, social reformers and home economists carried out educational campaigns, starting around the end of the nineteenth century. The story of how cleanliness became associated with hygiene and health is an example of a consumer learning process about how specific consumption activities can contribute to the satisfaction of basic needs. This learning process has put an upward pressure on cleanliness consumption. Put differently, cleanliness consumption increased when this consumption activity became associated with an additional, not yet satiated need (condition [1]).

Current patterns of cleanliness consumption are not only linked to the need for health but also to the need for social recognition, i.e. to a social norm of cleanliness, to be precise. In concrete terms, consumers nowadays expect one another to be clean and there appears to exist a mutual understanding of what cleanliness means – namely the absence of stains and body odor, as can be ensured by clothes washing. The social norm also has its origin in the historical context of the mid-nineteenth century, when scientific knowledge on the causes of infectious diseases progressed substantially (cf. Chapter 3). At the time of its emergence, the social norm and the social standard of cleanliness was contingent upon changes in health information: when consumers understood that each other's cleanliness translated into each other's health status, they took measures not only to inform the wider public about this fact but also to convince them by pairing objective information and moral appeals. As social recognition is always defined in relation to the behavior of others, changes in the behavior of others also induce the consumer to adjust his or her consumption patterns. When the social standard of cleanliness increased, it put an upward pressure on cleanliness consumption (condition [3]). To be precise, the rising cleanliness standard demanded all consumers to be clean according to an understanding of cleanliness, which clearly exceeded the cleanliness levels of the majority of the population.

Note the interdependencies between the basic needs associated with clothes washing and cleanliness: the social norm has its origin in the context of the Hygienic Movement of the nineteenth century but unfolded its strong impact on consumption patterns only when technological progress in washing machines made this feasible by reducing the drudgery component in this activity. Two historical processes are thus intimately linked: on the one hand, technical advances in clothes washers eliminated the tendency of households to avoid the task of laundry washing. On the other, consumers also had an interest in making use of this improved technology when the social norm of cleanliness came into being.

Based on these insights, we assume the activity of clothes washing still to be directed toward the satisfaction of the basic needs for health and social recognition, which are stable elements in consumer behavior, accounting for a structural component in laundry washing. Drawing upon Witt (2001), we further assume that, at a given point in time, a temporary satiation level of these consumer needs exists – as appealed to by the activity of clothes washing.[17] After having discussed which effects these needs have unfolded on cleanliness consumption in the past, we now turn to the question of which further dynamics are to be expected in the future.

7.5.2 Outlook on Future Patterns of Cleanliness Consumption

As we have just shown, the significance of the identified basic needs in terms of influencing laundry patterns has been contingent upon historical and regional circumstances. The consumer's awareness of the hygienic effects of clean clothing as well as the relevant peer-group standard of cleanliness might also be malleable in the future. In order to venture an outlook on the future development of cleanliness consumption, we thus have to control for systematic changes in the importance of these motivations in the form of a rising hygienic awareness and changing social normative expectations. This short discussion shall yield an understanding of how far the needs related to clothes washing have already been satiated or if further increases in cleanliness consumption are to be expected in the future – thus potentially triggering rebound effects.

Concerning the behavioral disposition of drudgery avoidance, a factor that limits cleanliness consumption does not exist at present. From this perspective, a further upward tendency in consumption is generally feasible. However, the drudgery avoidance disposition alone would not go in favor of a higher utilization rate of washing machines – and thus potentially in favor of the rebound effect. Quite the opposite, yet higher savings in physical effort are only achievable by not washing clothes at all. In other words, it cannot be achieved by purchasing more modernized washing machines and certainly not by increasing laundry amounts. In that regard, a further upward pressure stemming from this motivation is not to be expected.

Likewise, concerning the need for health, we would not expect to see upward shifts in consumption. Certainly, given that cleanliness consumption has increased over the course of a social learning process, an upward tendency in cleanliness consumption as a result of new health knowledge might be possible. However, recent debates in the medical sciences instead point to the fact that current cleanliness levels might actually be too high and not too low from the perspective of consumer health (Hannuksela and Hannuksela, 1996; Matthies, 2003). The current scientific debate thus does not go in favor of a further increase in consumption levels.

Not such a simple answer can be found with regard to the need for social recognition. To begin with, the social standard of cleanliness might change in the future with changes in the beliefs of how clothes washing and health are intertwined. As we have just argued, from the perspective of scientific knowledge, an upward shift in cleanliness is not to be expected such that the social norm, if it is still connected to the cleanliness level justified from a hygienic perspective, should not show further upward tendencies. However, the social norm of cleanliness does not necessarily show such an intimate connection to the hygienic standard any longer, for what is considered appropriate cleanliness from the perspective of society need not correspond with the level actually necessary to meet health concerns from an objective perspective.

When leaving aside the interactions between the social and the hygienic standards, there is still room for changes in the social standard, stemming from the social significance of this particular consumption activity itself. In fact, cleanliness has been said to represent a sociocultural construct (Douglas, 1984; Shove, 2003a), i.e. a concept 'laden with cultural significance and meaning' (Shove, 2003b, p. 195). When clothes are considered 'clean' in terms of meeting social requirements, this is not self-explanatory and hence deserves a definition that is socially shared and agreed upon.[18] In other words, social constructs are historically and technologically shaped evolved beliefs and expectations (Chappells and Shove, 2005). The socially contingent standard of cleanliness can thus differ from – and will most likely exceed – the hygienic standard, for consumption activities which are relevant for the social standing of a person have an immanent tendency to increase (e.g. Frank, 1999; Leibenstein, 1950). The need for health, in turn, represents the minimum level of cleanliness consumption as the physiological origin.

Can we also define an upper limit for the social standard of cleanliness? As a necessary condition for changes in the social standard to affect consumer behavior, changes must either be directly observable and/or consumers must obtain the information that changes in the standard have taken place. We find it plausible to assume that the social standard does not exceed that level of consumption, up to which additional consumption can actually be demonstrated toward others. We refer to this as the 'boundary of visibility' in social standards. The need for social recognition would not motivate consumers to exceed the consumption level which corresponds to the boundary of visibility, as this will not be granted social recognition.

Such a boundary can be expected to hold for the case of cleanliness consumption via clothes washing: beyond a certain cleanliness level, consumers cannot differentiate between different levels of cleanliness – neither in terms of smell nor vision. This boundary of visibility corresponds to a satiation level for the need for social recognition as pertaining to the activity of clothes washing. Can we find indicators that current laundry practices have reached the boundary of visibility, which would let us expect that further increases in efficiency will not lead to rebound effects? Although it is not possible to get direct evidence for such a boundary, some indirect evidence can be found in the figures on cleanliness consumption cited in Section 7.4. Despite the fact that washing machines have become more energy efficient over the past decades, the utilization intensity of washing machines appears not to have changed much recently, at least with regard to the expenditures on laundry and cleaning supplies and with regard to time use patterns. In a long-term perspective, recent patterns of cleanliness consumption thus appear rather stable. These findings might be interpreted in the way that the boundary of visibility has already been reached. Naturally, the same argument would apply for future cleanliness consumption. Thus, consumers are not to be expected to produce yet higher cleanliness levels because those can no longer be demonstrated to other consumers. We are aware, however, that this point is short of hard evidence; in order to sufficiently substantiate our claim, more detailed empirical evidence will have to be gathered.

To sum up, technological progress and consumer learning processes have been closely intertwined in the past and produced a growth in laundry quantities. The trend appears to have come to a halt now as the needs involved in clothes washing have reached their level of satiation. Thus, based on the framework of driving forces considered here, a direct rebound effect on further energy-efficiency progress in washing machines is not likely to occur in the future (cf. Satiation Hypothesis). At a more general level, we have illustrated how changes in cleanliness consumption patterns happening in parallel with progress in technology can be traced back to innate consumer needs and learning processes on the usefulness of cleanliness for the satisfaction of consumers' basic needs (cf. Shift Hypothesis).

7.6 Conclusions

In this chapter, we discussed the occurrence of rebound effects with regard to more energy-efficient washing machines from a theoretical perspective. While we also scrutinized the neoclassical explanation, the goal was to demonstrate that additional insights into the phenomenon of rebound effects will depend upon widening the theoretical basis beyond neoclassical accounts. With the arguments laid out here, we made a first modest step forward in that direction. More precisely, this chapter sought to demonstrate how the analysis would benefit from taking into account the consumer motivations underlying changing consumption patterns. In addition, the description and interpretation of past consumption trends are shown to be an important element of the analysis of rebound effects as it provides a basic understanding of a specific consumption activity. In our view, the rebound effect on energy-efficiency progress is a special case of the more general phenomenon of consumption patterns evolving with technological progress, as long as the consumer needs appealed to by a specific consumption activity are not yet satiated. Thus, a deeper theoretical analysis of the interrelation of technical change and consumer behavior is essential for evaluating the occurrence of rebound effects.

In more concrete terms, it has been shown how the present residential patterns of laundry washing reflect consumers' past learning processes in terms of linking clean clothes to the consumer needs for health and social recognition and associating washing machines with a decline in drudgery. Although further improvements in washing machines in terms of energy efficiency do imply a reduction in their utilization costs (or the shadow price of clean clothes), consumers' reaction to technological progress will depend on the satiation properties of the underlying needs. We found that a further upward tendency in cleanliness consumption is not to be expected, such that a direct rebound effect as a reaction to further technological progress is unlikely – at least from the perspective of the basic needs involved in clothes washing.

Our research has made the following modest contributions. First, we integrated the concepts of consumer needs and their satiation properties and consumer learning processes into the body of literature on rebound effects. Second, we tackled a rather novel case study by analyzing washing machines, while scholarly research has primarily been directed toward studying rebound effects in the context of transportation. Washing machines are an interesting case, as we have shown. They have become more energy efficient in the past, they serve several consumer needs and they are an example of the co-development of technological progress on one side and consumption growth, particularly an increase in laundry quantities, on the other.

Notes

1 The wealthy middle class circumvented this trade-off by resorting to domestic servants (cf. Chapter 4).
2 For the year 2000, the average German household washed about 525 kg of clothes, which was about double the laundry quantity of 1960 (277 kg) (Ruedenauer and Griesshammer, 2004, p. 38).
3 The observation that, despite the big leaps in technical advances, women are still doing so much housework has been referred to as the 'Cowan paradox' (Mokyr, 2000).

4 Cowan (1983) maintains that without technological progress in laundry equipment the current levels of cleanliness would have been out of reach.

5 Taxonomies also mention 'transformational effects' in consumer preferences (e.g. Greening *et al.*, 2000; Madlener and Alcott, 2009) albeit without discussing this further.

6 Polimeni and Polimeni (2006), for instance, find empirical evidence for economy-wide rebound effects.

7 For example, a more recent innovation in washing machines enables the device to 'recognize' and 'react' to suboptimal loading of the tub using sensor technologies. Washing machines then react by either using less water and energy or, alternatively, by 'giving advice' on the dosage of detergent (Ruedenauer and Griesshammer, 2004, pp. 18–22).

8 In the sociological literature, one also finds mechanistic explanations for the rising household standards (e.g. Robinson, 1980). In simple terms, when the housewife is at home 'anyway' and when the adoption of a time saving product reduces the time that is needed for carrying out a certain task, the housewife might simply produce more commodities in the exact same time. Other explanations point to gender roles and fairness of division of labor between the homemaker and the spouse (Bianchi *et al.*, 2000; Cowan, 1976; Fox, 1990; Robinson and Milkie, 1998; Vanek, 1978).

9 Note that the activity of laundry washing is not contingent upon actual states of deprivation occurring. Consumers do not wait until they are ill or until others let them know their disapproval with their appearance, but rather act in an anticipatory manner. By this anticipatory behavior, consumers reinforce certain 'normal' patterns of behavior in society.

10 In the United Kingdom, 92 per cent of all households are equipped with a clothes washer (Rickards *et al.*, 2004) while in Germany, 95 per cent of households own a washing machine (Statistisches Bundesamt, 2007).

11 Cf. also http://www.chemistry.co.nz/deterghistorypart3.htm (retrieved 24.07.2016).

12 The laundry amounts that German consumers handle today have almost stagnated since 1990–2000 (Ruedenauer and Griesshammer, 2004, p. 38). In the year 2000, German households washed an average of 525 kg of clothes, compared with 503 kg per annum in 1990 and only 277 kg in 1970.

13 The energy-efficiency label in the United States is the Energy Star. It is a voluntary endorsement labeling program, initiated in 1992 by the Environmental Protection Agency (EPA) (for more information, cf., e.g. http://energy.gov/sites/prod/files/2013/12/f5/naewg_report.pdf; retrieved 24.07.2016). The EU 'Eco-Design Directive' on energy-using products and their labeling (*EuP Directive 2005/32/EC; Directive 92/75/ECC*) was launched in 2005 and fosters improvements in the energy efficiency of electrical appliances. In addition, a couple of market analyses and consumer surveys on laundry patterns have been initiated and financially supported by EU governments (e.g. Ruedenauer and Griesshammer, 2004; Sammer and Wuestenhagen, 2006; SIFO, 2003).

14 Exactly because of endogeneity problems, Sorrell and Dimitropoulos (2008) criticize the common econometric approach to studying rebound effects and opt for the use of simultaneous equation models. The standard approach for addressing this endogeneity issue in consumer choice is by using a discrete choice model of the adoption of durable goods (Deaton and Muellbauer, 1980, Chapter 13). Dubin and McFadden (1984) suggested a two-step approach in which to include the utilization decision.

15 Recall that the definition of the rebound effect is the price elasticity of demand, i.e. a change in the price of energy services followed by a change in behavior. The case that consumers acquire more efficient appliances in order to use them more is not captured by the definition of the rebound effect – an interpretation upon which the analysis by Davis (2008) draws.

16 In fact, for this phenomenon, a proper concept has been coined: changes in the utilization of a product as a result of time saving innovations in that exact product are referred to as the 'rebound effect with respect to time' (Binswanger, 2004; Jalas, 2002).

17 Note that satiation levels, as studied here, always hold for a specific consumption activity. In other words, although social motives might play a role in many more consumption acts, only the extent to which social recognition is appealed to by clean clothing will be examined here.

18 The understanding (definition) of cleanliness has thus been malleable over the historical course of time (e.g. Cowan, 1983; Tomes, 1998; Vigarello, 1998).

References

Abrahamse, W., Steg, L., Vlek, C., Rothengatter, T. (2005): 'A review of intervention studies aimed at household energy conservation', *Journal of Environmental Psychology*, 25 (3), pp. 273–291.

Ashenburg, K. (2007): *The Dirt on Clean: An Unsanitized History*, North Point Press, New York.

Becker, G. S. (1965): 'A theory of the allocation of time', *The Economic Journal*, 75 (299), pp. 49–517.

Berkhout, P. H. G., Muskens, J. C., Velthuijsen, J. W. (2000): 'Defining the rebound effect', *Energy Policy*, 28 (6–7), pp. 425–432.

Bianchi, S. M., Milkie, M. A., Sayer, L. C., Robinson, J. P. (2000): 'Is anyone doing the housework? Trends in the gender division of household labor', *Social Forces*, 79 (1), pp. 191–228.

Binswanger, M. (2004): 'Time saving innovations and their impact on energy use: Some lessons from a household-production-function approach', *International Journal of Energy Technology and Policy*, 2(3), pp. 209–218.

Birol, F., Keppler, J. H. (2000): 'Prices, technology development and the rebound effect', *Energy Policy*, 28, pp. 457–469.

Brookes, L. (1978): 'Energy policy, the energy price fallacy and the role of nuclear energy in the UK', *Energy Policy*, 6 (2), pp. 94–106.

Buehr, W. (1965): *Home Sweet Home in the Nineteenth Century*, Thomas Y. Crowell Company, New York.

Buenstorf, G. (2004): *The Economics of Energy and the Production Process: An Evolutionary Approach*, Edward Elgar, Cheltenham.

Bureau of Labor Statistics: Consumer Expenditure Survey, Average annual expenditures and characteristics of all consumer units, Series 'Laundry and cleaning supplies' (http://www.bls.gov/cex/csxstnd.htm; retrieved 30.09.2016)

Chappells, H., Shove, E. (2005): 'Debating the future of comfort: Environmental sustainability, energy consumption and the indoor environment,' *Building Research and Information*, 33 (1), pp. 32–40.

Cowan, R. S. (1976): 'The "industrial revolution" in the home: Household technology and social change in the 20th century', *Technology and Culture*, 17 (1), pp. 1–23.

Cowan, R. S. (1983): *More Work for Mother*, Basic Books, New York.

Dale, L., Antinori, C., McNeil, M., McMahon, J. E., Fujita, K. S. (2009): 'Retrospective evaluation of appliance price trends', *Energy Policy*, 37 (2), pp. 597–605.

Davis, L. W. (2008): 'Durable goods and residential demand for energy and water: Evidence from a field trial', *RAND Journal of Economics*, 39 (2), pp. 530–546.

de Haan, P., Mueller, M. G., Peters, A. (2006): 'Does the hybrid Toyota Prius lead to rebound effects? Analysis of size and number of cars previously owned by Swiss Prius buyers', *Ecological Economics*, 58 (3), pp. 592–605.

Deaton, A., Muellbauer, J. (1980): *Economics and Consumer Behavior*, Cambridge University Press, Cambridge, MA.

Douglas, M. (1984): *Purity and Danger: An Analysis of the Concepts of Pollution and Taboo*, Ark Paperbacks, London.

Dubin, J. A., McFadden, D. L. (1984): 'An econometric analysis of residential electric appliance holdings and consumption', *Econometrica*, 52 (2), pp. 345–362.

Egerton, M., Fisher, K., Gershuny, J. (2006): 'American time use 1965–2003: The construction of a historical comparative file, and consideration of its usefulness in the construction of extended national accounts for the USA', *Institute for Social and Economic Research Working Paper*, pp. 5–28.

EIA (2011): Annual Energy Review 2011, Energy Information Administration, Table 2.6 Household End Uses: Fuel Types, Appliances, and Electronics, Selected Years, 1978–2009 (http://www.eia.gov/totalenergy/data/annual/pdf/sec2_21.pdf, retrieved: 30.09.2016).

Ellis, M., Jollands, N., Harrington, L., Meier, A. (2007): 'Do energy efficient appliances cost more?', Proceedings of the ECEE 2007 Conference, Summer Study, Panel 6: Products and Appliances.

Faberi, S. (2007): LOT14: Domestic dishwashers and washing machines, Task 2: Economic and market analysis, Preparatory Studies for the Eco-Design Requirements of EuPs.

Fine, B. (1999): 'Household appliances and the use of time: The United States and Britain since the 1920s: A comment', *Economic History Review* LII (3), pp. 552–562.

Fox, B. J. (1990): 'Selling the mechanized household: 70 years of ads in *Ladies Home Journal*', *Gender & Society*, 4 (1), pp. 25–40.

Frank, R. H. (1999): *Luxury Fever*, The Free Press, New York.

Giedion, S. (1948) (1969): *Mechanization Takes Command: A Contribution to Anonymous History*, Norton, New York.

Greene, D. L. (1992): 'Vehicle use and fuel-economy: How big is the "rebound" effect?', *Energy Journal*, 13 (1), pp. 117–143.

Greening, L. A., Greene, D. L., Difiglio, C. (2000): 'Energy efficiency and consumption – the rebound effect – a survey', *Energy Policy*, 28 (6–7), pp. 389–401.

Hannuksela, A., Hannuksela, M. (1996): 'Soap and detergents in skin diseases', *Clinics in Dermatology*, 14, pp. 77–80.

Hardyment, C. (1988): *From Mangle to Microwave: The Mechanization of Household Work*, Polity Press, Cambridge, United Kingdom.

Herring, H., Roy, R. (2007): 'Technological innovation, energy efficient design and the rebound effect', *Technovation*, 27 (4), pp. 194–203.

Henkel Survey (1984): 'World soap, detergent growth rate slows', *Journal of the American Oil Chemist's Society*, 61 (8), pp. 1405–1406.

Hewes, A. (1930): 'Electrical appliances in the home', *Social Forces*, 9 (2), pp. 235–242.

Hustvedt, G. (2011): 'Review of laundry energy efficiency studies conducted by the US Department of Energy', *International Journal of Consumer Studies*, 35, pp. 228–236.

Hustvedt, G., Ahn, M., Emmel, J. (2013): 'The adoption of sustainable laundry technologies by US consumers', *International Journal of Consumer Studies*, 37, pp. 291–298.

Jaffe, A. B., Stavins, R. N. (1994): 'The energy-efficiency gap. What does it mean?', *Energy Policy*, 22 (10), pp. 804–810.

Jalas, M. (2002): 'A time use perspective on the materials intensity of consumption', *Ecological Economics*, 41 (1), pp. 109–123.

Khazzoom, D. J. (1980): 'Economic implications of mandated efficiency standards for household appliances', *Energy Journal*, 1, pp. 21–40.

Khazzoom, D. J. (1987): 'Energy saving resulting from the adoption of more efficient appliances: A rejoinder', *Energy Journal*, 10, pp. 157–166.

Klepp, I. G. (2003): 'Clothes and cleanliness', *Ethnologia Scandinavia*, 33, pp. 61–73.

Leibenstein, H. (1950): 'Bandwagon, snob and Veblen effects in the theory of consumers' demand', *Quarterly Journal of Economics*, 64 (2), pp. 183–207.

Madlener, R, Alcott, B (2009): 'Energy rebound and economic growth. A review of the main issues and research needs', *Energy*, 34, pp. 370–376.

Manig, C., Moneta, A. (2014): 'More or better? Measuring quality versus quantity in food consumption', *Journal of Bioeconomics*, 16 (2), pp. 155–178.

Matthies, W. (2003): 'Irritant dermatitis and to detergents in textiles', in: Elsner, P., Hatch, K., Wigger-Alberti, W. (eds.), *Textiles and the Skin*, Karger, Basel, Switzerland.

McCalley, L. T. (2006): 'From motivation and cognition theories to everyday applications and back again: The case of product-integrated information and feedback', *Energy Policy*, 34 (2), pp. 129–137.

Mebane, W. (2007): LOT14: Domestic dishwashers and washing machines, Task 4: Product systems analysis, Preparatory Studies for the Eco-Design Requirements of EuPs.

Mokyr, J., (2000): 'Why "more work for Mother?" Knowledge and household behavior, 1870–1945', *Journal of Economic History*, 60 (1), pp. 1–41.

Morgan, J., Baerwalt, N., Sirageldin, I. (1966): *Productive Americans*, Ann Arbor: Survey Research Center, University of Michigan, MI.

Polimeni, J. M., Polimeni, R. I. (2006): 'Jevons' paradox and the myth of technological liberation', *Ecological Complexity*, 3(4), pp. 344–353.

Postman, N. (1993): *Technopoly: The Surrender of Culture to Technology*, Vintage Books, New York.

Preece, A. G. (1990): *Housework and American Standards of Living, 1920–1980*, Ph.D. Dissertation, University of California, Berkeley.

Rickards, L., Fox, K., Roberts, C., Fletcher, L., Goddard, E. (2004): *Living in Britain: Results from the 2002 General Household Survey*, National Statistics, London.

Robinson, J.P. (1980): 'Housework technology and household work', in: Berk, S.F. (ed.), *Women and Household Labor*, Sage, Beverly Hills, CA.

Robinson, J. P., Milkie, M. A. (1998): 'Back to the basics: Trends in and role determinants of women's attitudes toward housework', *Journal of Marriage and Family*, 60 (1), pp. 205–218.

Roy, J. (2000): 'The rebound effect: Some empirical evidence from India', *Energy Policy*, 28 (6–7), pp. 433–438.

Rudin, A. (2000): 'Let's stop wasting energy on efficiency programs: Energy conservation as a noble goal', *Energy and Environment*, 11 (5), pp. 539–551.

Ruedenauer, I., Griesshammer, R. (2004): *Produkt-Nachhaltigkeitsanalyse von Waschmaschinen und Waschprozessen*, Oeko-Institut e.V., Freiburg, Germany.

Ruprecht, W. (2005): 'The historical development of the consumption of sweeteners: A learning approach', *Journal of Evolutionary Economics*, 15 (3), pp. 247–272.

Salmon, J.D. (1977): 'Politics of scarcity versus technological optimism: A possible reconciliation?', *International Studies Quarterly*, 21 (4), pp. 701–720.

Sammer, K., Wuestenhagen, R. (2006): 'The influence of eco-labelling on consumer behavior: Results of a discrete choice analysis for washing machines', *Business Strategy and the Environment*, 15 (3), pp. 185–199.

Schipper, L., Grubb, M. (2000): 'On the rebound? Feedback between energy intensities andenergy uses in IEA countries', *Energy Policy*, 28 (6–7), pp. 367–388.

Schor, J. (1991): *The Overworked American: The Unexpected Decline of Leisure in America*, Basic Books, New York.

Shove, E. (2003a): 'Converging conventions of comfort, cleanliness and convenience', *Journal of Consumer Policy*, 26, pp. 395–418.

Shove, E. (2003b): *Comfort, Cleanliness and Convenience: The Social Organization of Normality*, Berg, Oxford and New York.

Shove, E. (2003c): 'Users, technologies and expectations of comfort, cleanliness and convenience', *Innovation*, 16 (2), pp. 193–206.

Statens institutt for forbruksforskning [SIFO] (2003). 'An investigation of domestic laundry in Europe – Habits, hygiene and technical performance', National Institute for Consumer Research, Oslo.

Silberzahn-Jandt, G. (1991), *Wasch-Maschine. Zum Wandel von Frauenarbeit im Haushalt*, Jonas Verlag für Kunst und Literatur, Marburg, Germany.

Sorrell, S., Dimitripoulos, J. (2008): 'The rebound effect: Microeconomic definitions, limitations and extensions', *Ecological Economics*, 65, pp. 636–649.

Statistisches Bundesamt, (2007). Wirtschaftsrechnungen, Ausstattung privater Haushalte mit langlebigen Gebrauchsgütern. Fachserie 15 (2), Wiesbaden.

Strasser, S. (2000) [1982]: *Never Done: A History of American Housework*, Henry Holt and Company, New York.

Taylor, P., Funk, C., Clark, A. (2009): 'Luxury or necessity? Things we can't live without: The list has grown in the past decade', Working Paper, Pew Research Center, Washington D.C.

Tomes, N. (1998): *The Gospel of Germs: Men, Women, and the Microbe in American Life*, Harvard University Press, London.

Vanek, J. (1978): 'Household technology and social status: Rising living standards and residence differences in housework', *Technology and Culture*, 19 (3), pp. 361–375.

Vigarello, G. (1998): *Concepts of Cleanliness: Changing Attitudes in France Since the Middle Ages*, Cambridge University Press, Cambridge, MA.

Wilson, M. (1929): *Use of Time by Oregon Farm Homemakers*, Oregon Agricultural Experiment Station Bulletin no. 256.

Witt, U. (2001.): 'Learning to consume: A theory of wants and the growth of demand', *Journal of Evolutionary Economics*, 11, pp. 23–36.

8 Explaining the Patterns of Cleanliness Consumption

This monograph has dealt with the driving forces behind the evolution of cleanliness consumption in the Western world, particularly the United States, from the time of the Industrial Revolution onward. More precisely, we analyzed the driving forces behind changes in the material conditions of clothes washing, particularly the adoption of washing machines and the corresponding growth in laundry quantities. The following research questions have been raised (cf. Chapter 1):

- Which factors have driven the diffusion of washing machines in the twentieth century?
- Why has the proliferation of washing machines throughout the twentieth century coincided with increasing laundry quantities?
- Why do the majority of consumers make use of washing machines for ensuring cleanliness instead of laundry services?
- Why are cleanliness consumption patterns so very similar today?

For conceptual reasons, the analysis has been broken down into several chapters which dealt with distinct phenomena and historical contexts. The most important development in each time period has been highlighted and interpreted in light of the learning approach. In addition, we have shown the compatibility of the learning approach with other relevant strands of literature, and the added value when considering them jointly. Thus, the study was of an interdisciplinary character, containing elements from economic, sociological and psychological theories of consumer behavior. Throughout the analysis, some of the more established views on the subject have been challenged. The recurring theme of the analysis was the 'theory of learning consumers' by Ulrich Witt (2001). This account is based on psychological theories of motivation and learning and relates long-term changes in consumption patterns to the evolved behavioral dispositions and cognitive constraints of modern day humans ('naturalistic approach'). Witt argues that consumers engage in consumption activities for satisfying their innate needs and acquired wants. Changes in consumption behavior come about when consumers learn new associations between consumption goods on one side and basic needs on the other. Vice versa, the diffusion of novel goods is contingent on accompanying learning processes on the part of the consumers and the existence of not yet satiated consumer needs. Such learning processes, in turn, are linked to specific historical circumstances.

For the specific case of clothes washing, we reconstructed the major transitions in consumption patterns as the outcome of consumer learning processes. We examined at which points in time, why and how consumer associations related to cleanliness consumption have been altered and found significant parts of the learning process to have been of a social nature. For the case analyzed here, not only learning capabilities have been paid attention to. Also, consumer motivations behind clothes washing have proven to be an essential element for a profound understanding of long-term shifts in cleanliness consumption patterns. In that regard, we challenged the established economic model for the analysis of housework, i.e. Gary Becker's 'household production function approach' (Becker, 1965; Michael and Becker, 1973). Being a model in the neoclassical tradition, the account focuses on the effect of changes in relative prices on changes in consumer behavior. More precisely, the theory elaborates on the implications of shifts in opportunity costs of time as triggered by rising wages. The motivational side of consumption behavior is explicitly factored out (cf. Stigler and Becker, 1977). Our approach was thus fundamentally different from the neoclassical tradition. We believe to have shown that consumer motivations should be given consideration in the analysis of consumption patterns and household production activities, as they yield a much deeper understanding of the actual historical development.

As to the historical development of the consumption of cleanliness, it can be summarized in a very stylized form as follows. In the nineteenth century, consumers basically fell into two groups, which differed substantially with respect to income, levels of cleanliness and household technology employed. While the well-to-do had the possibility to outsource laundry washing to domestic servants, poorer consumers had to carry out the physically straining procedure themselves. At that point in time, only very simple tools for clothes washing were widely available, namely the washtub, scrubboard and homemade soap (cf. Chapter 4). Doing the laundry under these conditions was a very disagreeable task that earned many complaints from contemporaries. With all the scrubbing of clothes and hauling of water, laundry washing represented a 'backbreaking' as well as a time-consuming chore – an activity which clearly went against the human disposition to avoid heavy physical effort. Given that humans are genetically programmed to avoid physically straining activities, consumers faced a trade-off between wanting clean clothes on one side while seeking to avoid drudgery on the other (in psychology, referred to as the 'approach–avoidance conflict', cf. Chapter 2). Under these conditions, cleanliness was still a mode of social distinction. The poorer consumers showed very low levels of cleanliness and changed their few clothes very rarely; the rich, on the contrary, possessed a much larger and cleaner wardrobe.

This situation began to change during the time of the Hygienic Movement from the middle of the nineteenth century onward, which brought an improved understanding of the causes of disease and the role of hygienic living in public health. In this historical context, the emergence of a social norm of cleanliness was triggered – a process which probably spanned the period from the end of the nineteenth century to the first half of the twentieth century. In simple terms, consumers started to expect one another to be clean, according to a shared definition of cleanliness. This meant that, particularly, the not so well-to-do consumers had to be cleaner than before. The more consumers changed their consumption patterns (with growing income), the more did the exclusiveness of cleanliness vanish. As a result, upper- and middle-class households could no longer signal their superior social status by being cleaner than the rest of society. Interestingly, a group of upper-class consumers applying scientific principles to the domain of housework – referred to as 'home economics' – helped to manage the process of norm emergence instead of opposing it. Apparently, health concerns have superseded status considerations. The common conjecture of the 'trickle-down' of lifestyles and social emulation on the part of the poorer consumers, therefore, does not entirely capture the process that took place here. At the end of this process stood an assimilation of consumption patterns in terms of the level of cleanliness produced, reflected in the social standard of cleanliness. Thus, the emergence of the social norm of cleanliness was the origin of the mass market for cleaning products such as soap, and later, washing machines, by substantially increasing the consumption level and the number of consumers.

The homogenization of consumption patterns did not only concern standards of cleanliness but also applied to the household production technology employed, i.e. the tools with which clean clothes were achieved. With the beginning of the twentieth century, two central conditions changed. First, consumer income was expanding during times of industrial development. Second, large, stepwise advances in laundry technology took place, covering the phases of mechanization, electrification and automation. Technological progress resulted in the electric, automated washing machine, which is widely in use today. These technical advances were accompanied by further complementary developments in the wider technological system in terms of the wiring and plumbing of urban and rural homes. In the course of these technical advances, the proliferation of washing machines took place, resulting in the present situation of a saturated market – a condition holding not only for the United States and the United Kingdom, but for practically all Western countries alike.

With the widespread diffusion of modern washing machines throughout the twentieth century, the drudgery that had formerly been involved in doing the laundry was practically eliminated. Hence, once a household could afford the improved technology, the trade-off between cleanliness and drudgery was eliminated. This argument holds specifically for lower-class consumers. An additional condition was necessary to make upper-class consumers appreciate these products, namely the decline of domestic servants. When domestic servants declined in availability, upper-class consumers also had an incentive to buy washing machines as a substitute for domestic help. As the emerging ideology of housework also urged women to 'home-produce' such desired commodities as clean clothes themselves, the adoption of washing machines was preferred over the alternative, the use of commercial laundries.

Technological progress in laundry technology and the diffusion of washing machines in the twentieth century is thus the story of how consumers have eventually overcome the approach-avoidance conflict in the consumption of cleanliness. The prospect of achieving time savings in doing the laundry might also have contributed to the diffusion of washing machines from the 1940s onward, when these devices became automatic. In addition, one cannot easily rule out a possible impact from increased female labor force participation on the demand for these appliances, although empirical analyses do not detect this relationship (cf. Chapter 6). In other words, women entering the labor market might indeed have adopted washing machines as a strategy to cope with the reduced availability of time for household chores (time substitution). However, full-time homemakers also had a strong incentive to acquire washing machines – namely to reduce the drudgery of laundry washing. In view of the emerging social norm of cleanliness and the absence of domestic servants, in particular, all households alike were in need of a technology which allowed for physical labor savings. That is why, nowadays, households that differ in terms of the employment status of the wife do not differ in terms of the ownership of clothes washers. Hence, not only is there no difference between richer and poorer consumers in terms of the household technology used to ensure cleanliness, there is also no systematic difference in household technology between single- versus dual-earner households.

At the same time that these appliances diffused more strongly, consumers increased the levels of cleanliness produced (cf. Chapter 7). Although arguments could be advanced that point to decreasing shadow prices of cleaning clothes (the neoclassical argument), the Cowan paradox of rising household standards probably has to be attributed to the emerging social norm of cleanliness. The social norm has its origin in the context of the Hygienic Movement, but unfolded its strong impact on consumption patterns only when technological progress in washing machines made this feasible. Two historical processes are thus intimately linked: on the one hand, technical advances in clothes washers eliminated the tendency of households to avoid the task of laundry washing. On the other hand, consumers also had an incentive to make use of this improved technology when the social norm of cleanliness came into being.

The present residential patterns of laundry washing thus reflect consumers' past learning processes in terms of linking clean clothes to health and social recognition and associating washing machines with a decline in drudgery. Although further improvements in washing machines, in terms of energy efficiency, do imply a reduction in the utilization costs of washing machines (i.e. shadow prices of clean clothes), consumers' reaction to technological progress will depend on the satiation properties of the underlying needs. As the social norm of cleanliness has been identified as crucial to the rising laundry quantities in the past, the satiation properties of that exact need are largely decisive for future cleanliness consumption patterns. Social recognition is a need that is hard to satiate (Witt, 2001); consumption activities related to that need thus have an immanent tendency to rise. However, an upward tendency in consumption is only to be expected, as long as further increases in cleanliness consumption can be demonstrated to the social environment ('boundary of visibility'). We found that the boundary of visibility has already been met. Thus, from the perspective of the basic needs involved and their properties of satiation, rebound effects of technological progress are not to be expected in the future.

With respect to the background of these historical developments, our argumentation aiming at explaining the main features of the evolution of cleanliness consumption has been laid out as follows. The first chapter introduced the research questions which this book sought to address, defined the central terms of the analysis, introduced the theoretical and conceptual basis of the study and laid out the structure of the book. By consumption of cleanliness, we understood any consumer activity undertaken in order to clean consumer clothes, covering the purchase of products, particularly washing machines, and the utilization of these products in the activity of laundry washing itself. Cleanliness, in the form of clean clothes, was defined as the outcome of a household production activity. Clean clothes were assumed to have instrumental value for more fundamental consumer preferences, namely basic needs in the sense of Witt (2001). In Chapter 1, we explained that the evolution of cleanliness consumption over the past two centuries would be studied through the lens of consumer learning processes, which we defined as behavioral actions that establish new associations between the satisfaction of consumer needs on one side and consumption activities on the other ('means–ends-relationships'). We argued that the development of cleanliness consumption patterns over time would be looked at as the complex interplay between consumer motivations for cleanliness consumption, technical advances in laundry washing and consumer learning processes.

The theoretical and conceptual basis of our analysis was presented in more detail in Chapter 2. A great part of the exposition has been devoted to a presentation and critical assessment of Gary Becker's 'household production function approach'. We found this detailed examination of Becker's theory to be necessary in view of the fact that it is a very well-established account for analyzing the technical change in nonmarket production and the demand for household appliances. In addition, it offers a plausible hypothesis to start from – the time substitution hypothesis. Chapter 2 provided an extensive critique of Becker's treatment of preferences. Although Becker acknowledges that consumer motivations exist independent of goods by introducing the concept of household commodities, he does not intend to elaborate on the role of preferences for household production processes: the commodity concept is underspecified, and Becker explicitly factors out preferences for the use of time. The substitution process of capital goods for time, as triggered by rising wages, is thus predicted independently of the arguments of the utility function. Our discussion of Becker's treatment of preferences revealed that changes in household production processes can only sufficiently be explained, however, when explicit assumptions about consumer motivations are integrated into the analysis – specifically in the form of preferences for the use of time. In order to substantiate our claim, we turned to psychological theories of motivation as well as behavioral psychology, and reviewed established findings on the basic principles of human behavior. On the grounds of these insights, the 'theory of learning consumers' by Ulrich Witt (2001) was introduced as an alternative to Becker's account. With the theory of learning consumers, a systematic analysis of the role of consumer motivations for changing consumption behavior is feasible. Moreover, Witt's account is compatible with the findings from the behavioral sciences reviewed here. In Chapter 2, we set up a behavioral account for analyzing changes in household production processes by highlighting some basic principles driving the adoption and utilization patterns of household technology. We have referred to it as 'the learning approach'. The central contribution of Chapter 2 is to have shown that the concept of preferences for the use of time can be given a behavioral interpretation: when human behavior, in general, is guided by the striving for rewarding experiences and the avoidance of pain, then household production activities might also follow this principle. The household's production objectives correspond to the goals, which the consumer seeks to attain, but the consumer might forgo goal achievement when it calls for a form of behavior that goes against his or her basic behavioral dispositions. Alternatively, consumers might seek to master the avoidance tendency. The invention of tools and the adoption of advanced household technology have thus been interpreted as a strategy to overcome the conflict between ultimate goals on one side and actions for achieving these goals on the other.

Chapter 3 studied the process by which the social norm of cleanliness came into being. We developed a model of norm emergence that built on common conjectures from the respective literature, namely that norms might emerge as a reaction to consumption externalities, that the emergence of norms is fostered by social feedback and that central agents diffusing new knowledge in society play a central role for norm emergence. To these common conjectures, additional hypotheses were added. We hypothesized that individuals share certain basic preferences and derive utility from the same actions due to commonalities in the human genetic basis, thus making them jointly recognize certain situations as problems. Moreover, the emergence of social norms as commonalities in consumer behavior is more likely to occur the more strongly a problem affects consumers' basic needs, and the more difficult it is to solve the problem on an individual basis, thus making consumers turn to expert consumers for advice. By linking externality problems to the concept of basic consumer needs, we opened up a psychologically informed perspective on norm emergence that could shed some light on what affects the consumer's willingness to cooperate in situations of social dilemma, despite the possibility of free riders. When externalities jeopardize consumers' needs, the learning of strategies for externality internalization corresponds to forming associations between consumption activities and the satisfaction of consumer needs. To depict norm emergence as a learning process means to reject the assumption that actors know ex ante which kind of strategy or behavior will bring about the internalization of a newly occurring externality. The framework has then been applied to trace back the emergence of the cleanliness norm in the United States and the United Kingdom during times of industrial development to consumer basic needs and learning processes. Chapter 3 has thus demonstrated that the assumption of some commonalities in consumer preferences enhances our understanding of the emergence of social norms. More in general, we have proven the compatibility of the body of literature on norm emergence and the psychologically substantiated learning approach. Beyond that, we introduced a new case study into the literature on social norms. Finally, Chapter 3 demonstrated that the social significance of a consumption activity need not be an arbitrary property of that exact activity.

Chapters 4–6 dealt with changes in the domestic production of cleanliness in the United States during the twentieth century. These chapters addressed the widespread diffusion of washing machines as the key household technology for ensuring cleanliness. We scrutinized the explicative potential of two alternative hypotheses regarding the driving forces behind washing machine ownership, i.e. the time substitution hypothesis and the drudgery avoidance hypothesis. The time substitution hypothesis is a central element of the household production function approach. It relates the purchase of household appliances to rising opportunity costs of time as a result of rising wages. According to this hypothesis, differences between households in terms of the employment status of the wife (i.e. dual- versus single-earner households) should be reflected in differences in the ownership of time saving goods and the consumption of laundry services. By the same token, the increase in female labor force participation over time was a sufficient condition for the more widespread proliferation of washing machines. The drudgery avoidance hypothesis figures prominently in the sociological literature on the mechanization of the household, albeit without a connection to behavioral psychology. Our hypothesis links the demand for washing machines to an innate human disposition to avoid heavy physical effort – a disposition shared by all consumers through their common genetic inheritance. This hypothesis is plausible when bringing to mind the conditions of laundry washing in the nineteenth century and linking this observation with the psychological insights on human behavior reviewed earlier (cf. Chapter 2). More precisely, with the drudgery avoidance hypothesis, we analyze the role of preferences for the use of time for changes in household production processes.

Three different approaches have been taken in order to assess the explicative potential of the alternative hypotheses. We began, in Chapter 4, by taking a look at the phases of technological progress in laundry technology from the middle of the nineteenth century onward, arguing that the adoption of washing machines for reasons of time and/or physical labor savings is contingent upon technical progress making such achievements feasible. We found that technical change in washing machines did indeed allow for savings of time and physical labor in clothes washing, but that reductions in drudgery were achieved earlier than time savings. This observation brought us to conclude that the time substitution hypothesis cannot explain the early diffusion of washing machines. In the fourth chapter, we also took a closer look at changes in the material situation of different consumer classes from the nineteenth to the twentieth century. For the specific case of cleanliness consumption, the Becker hypothesis appears not to grasp the actual processes that have taken place. From a historical perspective, the first adopters of washing machines were middle-class women who did not want to enter the labor force, but replaced domestic servants who had formerly done the laundry. By substituting washing machines for servants, the households actually 'insourced' work and increased the time they spent doing the laundry. Paradoxically, these consumers did not make use of commercial laundries, an alternative option which would have demanded smaller inputs of time.

Also in Chapter 5, where we carried out a study of washing machine advertisements appearing in the U.S. women's magazine *Ladies' Home Journal* between 1888 and 1989 (altogether, 70 years), we reached the conclusion that the time substitution hypothesis cannot explain the early diffusion of washing machines. We assumed shifts in advertisement content over time to reflect changes in the motivations for adopting clothes washers and examined the advertisements with regard to the reasons given for purchasing washing machines. We found both motives of time savings and physical labor savings to have been of central importance as they appeared in the washer ads for roughly seven consecutive decades. But again, the labor saving motive dominated the washer ads at the beginning, i.e. until 1919, while time savings were referred to in the ads more often from 1940 to 1960.

In a third step, the time substitution hypothesis has been examined in Chapter 6 by means of a literature survey on empirical studies. The cross-sectional studies reviewed do not support Becker's hypothesis, as households with employed wives were not more likely to own washing machines or to resort to laundry services than were families with nonworking wives. The household's income, on the contrary, was almost always found to have had a positive impact on the demand for these products. On a longitudinal perspective, the widening gap between rates of ownership of washing machines and rates of female labor force participation also puts into question whether changing opportunity costs of time were the core driving force behind the diffusion process. Instead, the shared human motivation to avoid heavy physical effort might have led every household to purchase an electric, automatic washing machine as soon as this was affordable. That substantial time savings in laundry washing have indeed been achieved in the course of the twentieth century is consistent with Becker's account, but need not be taken as evidence in favor of the opportunity cost argument in a more narrow sense.

Based on the empirical material gathered in Chapters 4–6, we concluded that both motives of time savings and physical labor savings have triggered the diffusion of washing machines in the twentieth century, albeit at different points in time. But as household income and not the value of time was decisive for making the switch to the technically advanced products, the drudgery avoidance motive alone might have been sufficient for the proliferation of washing machines. We hence assert that washing machines would have diffused 'anyway' during the past century, in the sense that this process was independent of women entering the labor force in increasing numbers. Chapters 4–6 made the following contributions. First, we demonstrated that preferences for the use of time were an important explanatory factor behind changes in the consumption of cleanliness. Consumers did not only care about the output of the household production process, i.e, clean clothes, but also about how the objectives were achieved, i.e. the absence of drudgery. Second, the analysis revealed that the learning approach can fruitfully be connected with the body of literature on technical change. Third, with the advertisement study, we gathered some quantitative information and original historical data ourselves.

The major limitation of the analysis covering Chapters 4–6 was the comparatively large interpretative element in deciding on the explanatory power of the alternative hypotheses. In contrast with an econometric study, the information gathered here does not yield test statistics which indicate if two variables are related, if they are positively or negatively related and what the magnitude of the relationship is. This problem was particularly pronounced for our analysis in that different approaches (i.e. technology study, advertisement analysis, review of econometric studies) had to be consolidated. However, for assessing the time substitution hypothesis, we could at least take into account the findings of previous econometric studies, which more or less reveal the same message. For the drudgery avoidance hypothesis, on the contrary, no such econometric studies existed. Hence, in econometric analyses, the rejection of the Becker hypothesis was taken as indirect evidence in support of the alternative drudgery avoidance hypothesis.

Chapter 7 turned to the current situation of cleanliness consumption and analyzed the rebound effect of energy-efficiency progress with regard to washing machines. We sought to evaluate whether the diffusion of more energy-efficient devices is likely to be accompanied by take-back effects in that washing machines are being used more intensively than before, thus partly offsetting achievable energy savings. Washing machines are an example of technological progress throughout the twentieth century having coincided with a growth in laundry amounts – a phenomenon referred to in the sociological literature as the 'Cowan paradox' of rising household standards. Hence, the occurrence of rebound effects as a consequence of further efficiency improvements in clothes washers is a plausible scenario. We addressed the research question from a theoretical perspective and pointed to the added value of integrating, in the body of literature, the concepts of consumer needs and their satiation properties. Drawing upon the learning approach, we formulated the hypothesis that direct rebound effects – as a reaction to technological progress in a consumption activity – will only occur when the consumer needs appealed to by this consumption activity are not yet satiated. We attributed the major impact of the past increase in laundry quantities to a decline in drudgery and the emerging social norm of cleanliness. With regard to the satiation properties of these needs, we argued that a more intensive use of washing machines is not to be expected in the future; the need for social recognition should not lead to further upward spirals in consumption as the satiation level of that need – with respect to cleanliness consumption – has already been met (the boundary of visibility). In terms of its contribution, our analysis is one of few studies addressing the rebound effect from a theoretical perspective while taking a point of departure beyond neoclassical consumer theory. We have shown how the concepts of consumer needs and their satiation levels can be integrated into the analysis of rebound effects. By analyzing the rebound effect in context with the consumption of cleanliness, we addressed a case study that has hardly been tackled in the respective literature yet.

The case study chosen here, the evolution of cleanliness consumption over the past 200 years, has proven to be an extremely rich case to analyze. Naturally, this book did not manage – and by no means tried – to give a full account of all the different aspects of this particular case study, which has so many different facets. Quite the opposite: we embarked on the endeavor to elaborate on the insights that a heterodox, psychologically informed consumption approach had to offer, when starting from a material specification of preferences and from hypotheses on consumer learning processes.

References

Becker, G. S. (1965): 'A theory of the allocation of time', *The Economic Journal*, 75 (299), pp. 49–517.

Michael, R. T., Becker G. S. (1973): 'On the new theory of consumer behavior', *Swedish Journal of Economics*, 75 (4), pp. 378–396.

Stigler, G. J., Becker, G. S. (1977): 'De gustibus non est disputandum', *American Economic Review*, 67 (2), pp. 76–90.

Witt, U. (2001): 'Learning to consume – A theory of wants and the growth of demand', *Journal of Evolutionary Economics*, 11, pp. 23–36.

Index

For Product Safety Concerns and Information please contact our EU representative GPSR@taylorandfrancis.com Taylor & Francis Verlag GmbH, Kaufingerstraße 24, 80331 München, Germany

Printed and bound by CPI Group (UK) Ltd, Croydon, CR0 4YY

01/05/2025

01858355-0005